IMAGES
of America

AURORA
A DIVERSE PEOPLE BUILD THEIR CITY

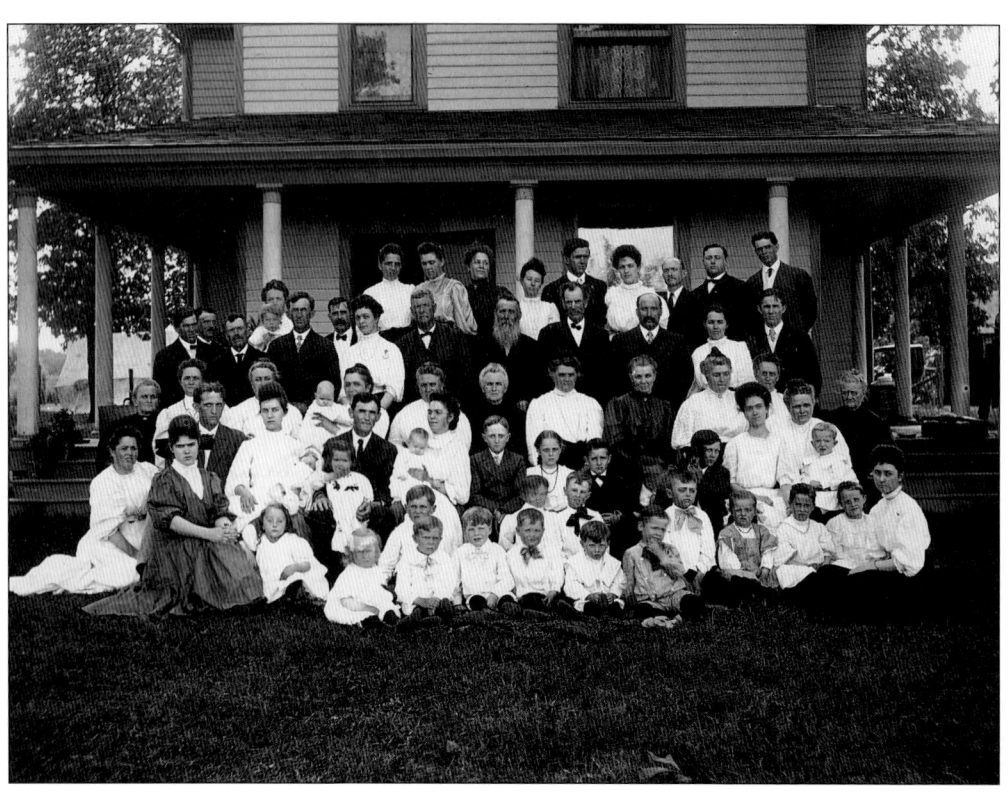

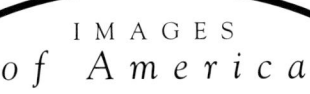

IMAGES of America

AURORA
A DIVERSE PEOPLE BUILD THEIR CITY

Jim and Wynette Edwards

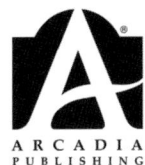

ARCADIA
PUBLISHING

Copyright © 1998 by Jim and Wynette Edwards
ISBN 978-0-7385-6374-9

Published by Arcadia Publishing
Charleston SC, Chicago IL, Portsmouth NH, San Francisco CA

Printed in the United States of America

Library of Congress Catalog Card Number: 98-87142

For all general information contact Arcadia Publishing at:
Telephone 843-853-2070
Fax 843-853-0044
E-mail sales@arcadiapublishing.com
For customer service and orders:
Toll-Free 1-888-313-2665

Visit us on the Internet at www.arcadiapublishing.com

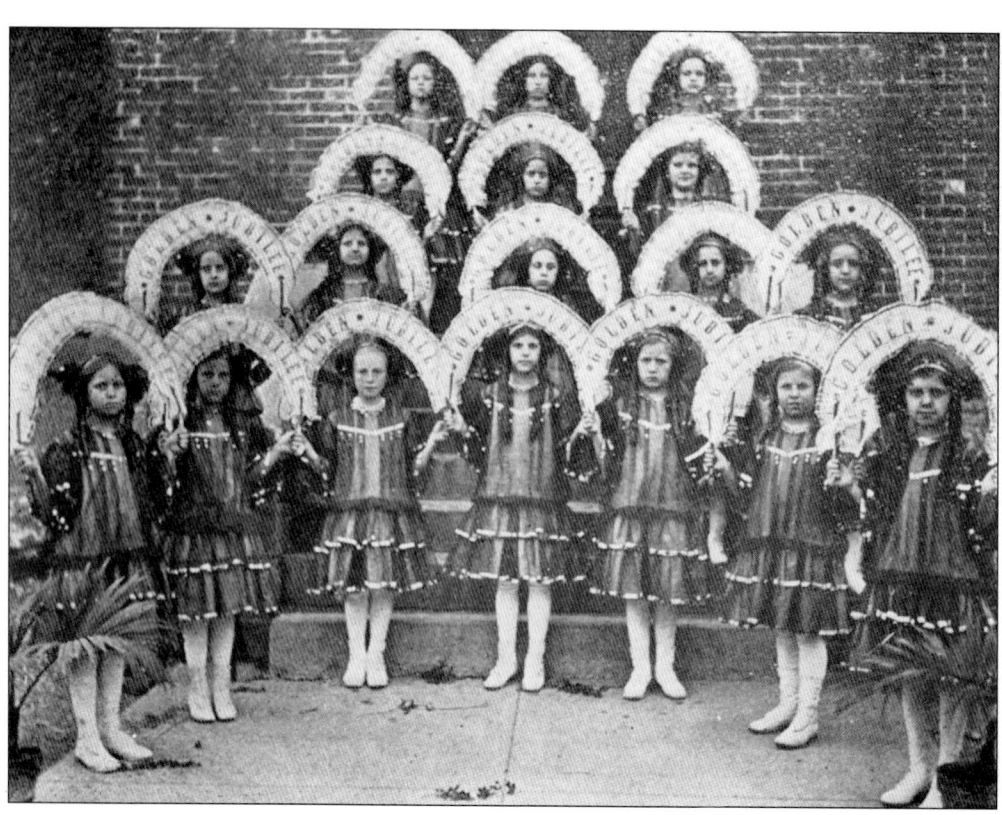

Contents

Acknowledgments		6
Introduction		7
1.	Settling In, Building a City	9
2.	Railroading Comes to Town	25
3.	Lottie Describes Her City	37
4.	Wagons, Corsets, and Heavy Machinery	49
5.	Picnics, Violins, and Front Porches	67
6.	Out and About: Elephants, Parks, and Schools	87
7.	The Image Makers and Their "Dream Factories"	103
8.	Those Who Served at Home and Abroad	117

ACKNOWLEDGMENTS

Aurora is fortunate to have an historical society with a large archive of images to research. Thanks to the Aurora Historical Society for collecting resources and for making them available. Several other community sources were also valuable: Blackberry Farm-Pioneer Village, the Regional Fire Museum, GAR Museum, the Aurora Public Library, Aurora Public School Districts 129 and 131, and Aurora University.

Churches are a wealth of information about early ethnic groups because the church was usually the first place that immigrants met with those who spoke their language. Many thanks go to the staff and volunteers who led us to the history:
First Congregational Church, New England Congregational Church, First Baptist Church, First Presbyterian Church, Main Street Baptist Church, First United Methodist Church, Wesley Methodist Church, St. John's African Methodist Episcopal Church, Trinity Episcopal Church, St. Paul's Lutheran Church and School, Temple B'nai Israel, St. Mary's Catholic Church, St. Nicholas Catholic Church, Holy Angels Catholic Church, and St. Michael's Romanian Greek Catholic Church.

Institutions give us the facts but people give us the stories and family pictures. Many thanks to all of the following for their wonderful tales of beginnings or helpful direction in finding those with the tales: Marcy Armstrong, Alfreda Lewis, John Lies, Guy Prisco, Sam Alschuler, Don Nylin, Marie Wilkinson, Fred Rogers, Mark Ruby, Edith Katz, Dick Haussmann, Al Cinto, Ray Torres, and Susan Palmer. Special recognition goes to all the photographers of Aurora who recorded images that made this book possible.

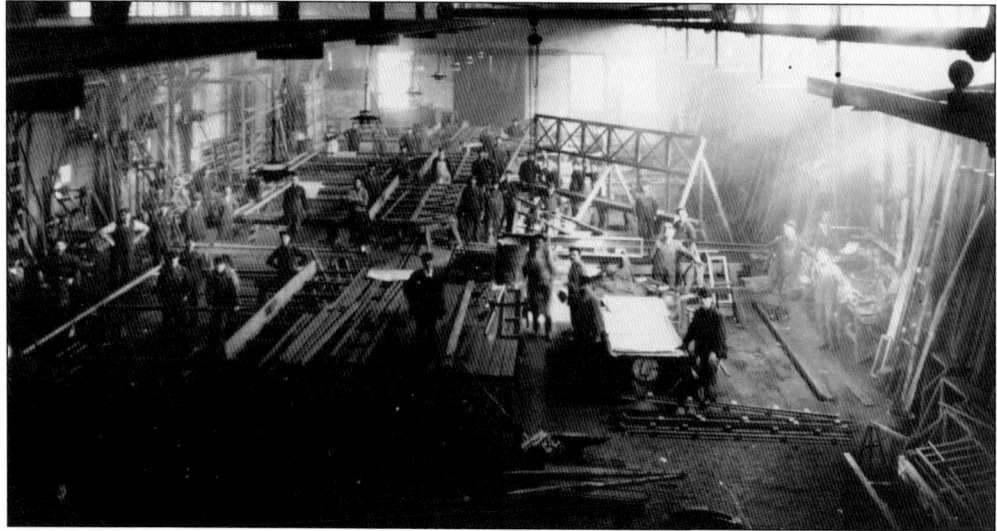

INTRODUCTION

Aurora is a typical American city. For the last century and a half it witnessed a dynamic population growth and was a leading shaper of America's golden industrial age following the Civil War. Thus growth and influx of new people, with their different cultures, at first rattled "old" Aurorans but eventually added a rich ethnic color to the quality of life in the "City of Lights."

We have talked to people from each of these ethnic groups and collected pictures of their first years in Aurora. Some had many images to choose from, some had none. Industry was the reason almost all of the immigrants chose to settle in Aurora. Only the descendants of the earlier wave of Luxemburgers gave farming as their reason. Therefore, it seemed reasonable to weave the growth of Aurora's industry with the growth of population in researching this book.

When people have a sense of their community's distant past, this knowledge gives them the basis for looking at the forces at work in the present. Such understanding also helps all of us cope with the future as we say goodbye to the 20th century and welcome a new millennium.

Chief Waubonsie, a Native American who lived in Aurora before it was settled, learned how to coexist with the new Europeans in his valley. He especially respected Joseph McCarty because McCarty could provide Waubonsie with ground cornmeal. Waubonsie and McCarty needed each other to make life economically and socially better in Aurora. Over the years English, Luxemburgers, Germans, Irish, French, Scots, Swedes, African Americans, Italians, Jews, and many others have also learned this basic truth. They have all blended into the mainstream life of a great city that is constantly re-inventing itself and its industries.

One
SETTLING IN, BUILDING A CITY

Migration into the Fox River area began slightly before the time settlers migrated into California and the western plains. As Chicago began to take on the characteristics of an eastern seaboard city, people began to travel west into the Native American lands. The Fox Valley, with its mighty river, was perfect for settlement. At first, Native Americans seemed to be able to coexist side-by-side with the settlers, but soon the Native Americans were removed to their own territory west of the Mississippi. Settlers not only farmed but also located mills and other factories along the riverbanks using waterpower to drive their machinery.

Although in the 1840s and 1850s immigrants came to the valley from Canada, Luxemburg, and Ireland, the real growth of the City of Aurora coincided with the nation's great thrust for railroads and low-priced manufactured goods. After the Civil War, more and more agrarian immigrants came to America and to Aurora from southern and eastern Europe. They found themselves not working their own farmland but in factories as unskilled or semiskilled workers. The success of the factories depended on this cheap influx of labor to keep prices down.

The early settlers from New York brought their Protestant faiths, and it was in the mid- and late century that various Catholic faiths were introduced to Aurora. The new waves of immigrants tended to congregate together and to cling to the old ways. They melted slowly into the general cultural scene in Aurora. These new people established large neighborhoods around factories, built churches, and rejoiced in their ethnicity.

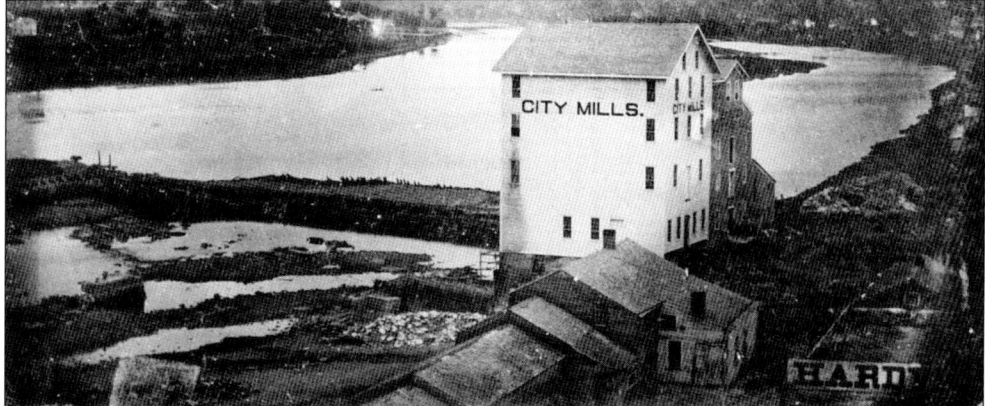

City Mills was owned by Charles Gill who purchased the property from the McCarty brothers. In 1835, the McCartys opened the first saw- and gristmills in what was to become Aurora. By 1838, one gristmill, two sawmills, a bridge across the river, a hotel, a post office, and several stores were on the banks of the Fox.

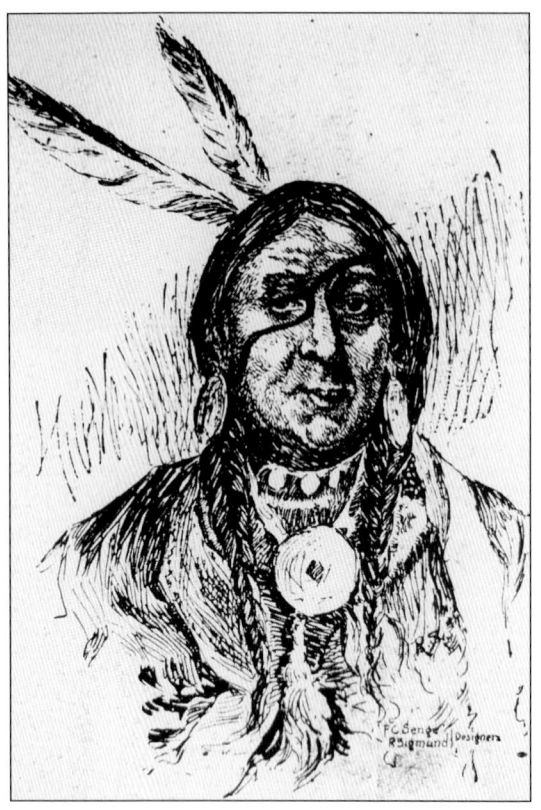

Chief Waubonsie's village of Pottawattomies was a little north of where the McCartys staked their claim. During the building of the dam and sawmill, Waubonsie helped the brothers by bartering with them. There was quite a bit of friendly interaction and very little friction between the Native Americans and the few settlers around the McCarty's mill.

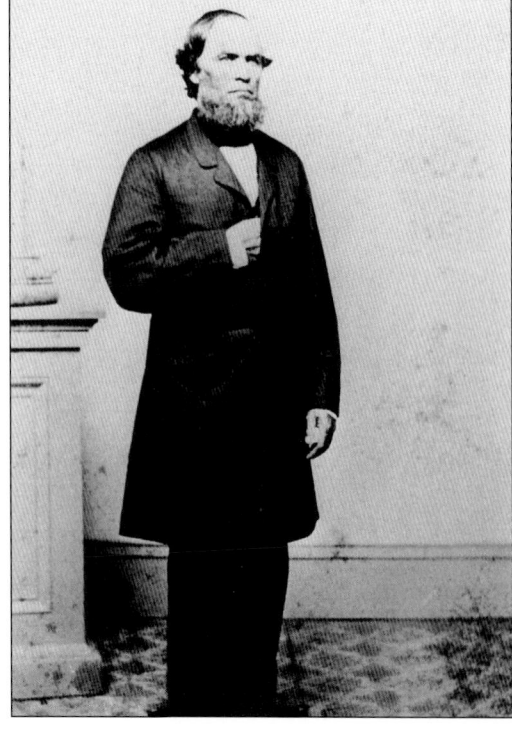

Zaphna Lake reached the Fox Valley a few months after the McCarty brothers, Joseph and Samuel, and purchased the McCarty's west bank claim. He returned to Ohio to bring back his brother Theodore, pictured to the right. The Lake brothers set up the their first store on the west side. Theodore settled in the Fox Valley permanently and helped develop the Village of West Aurora in 1842.

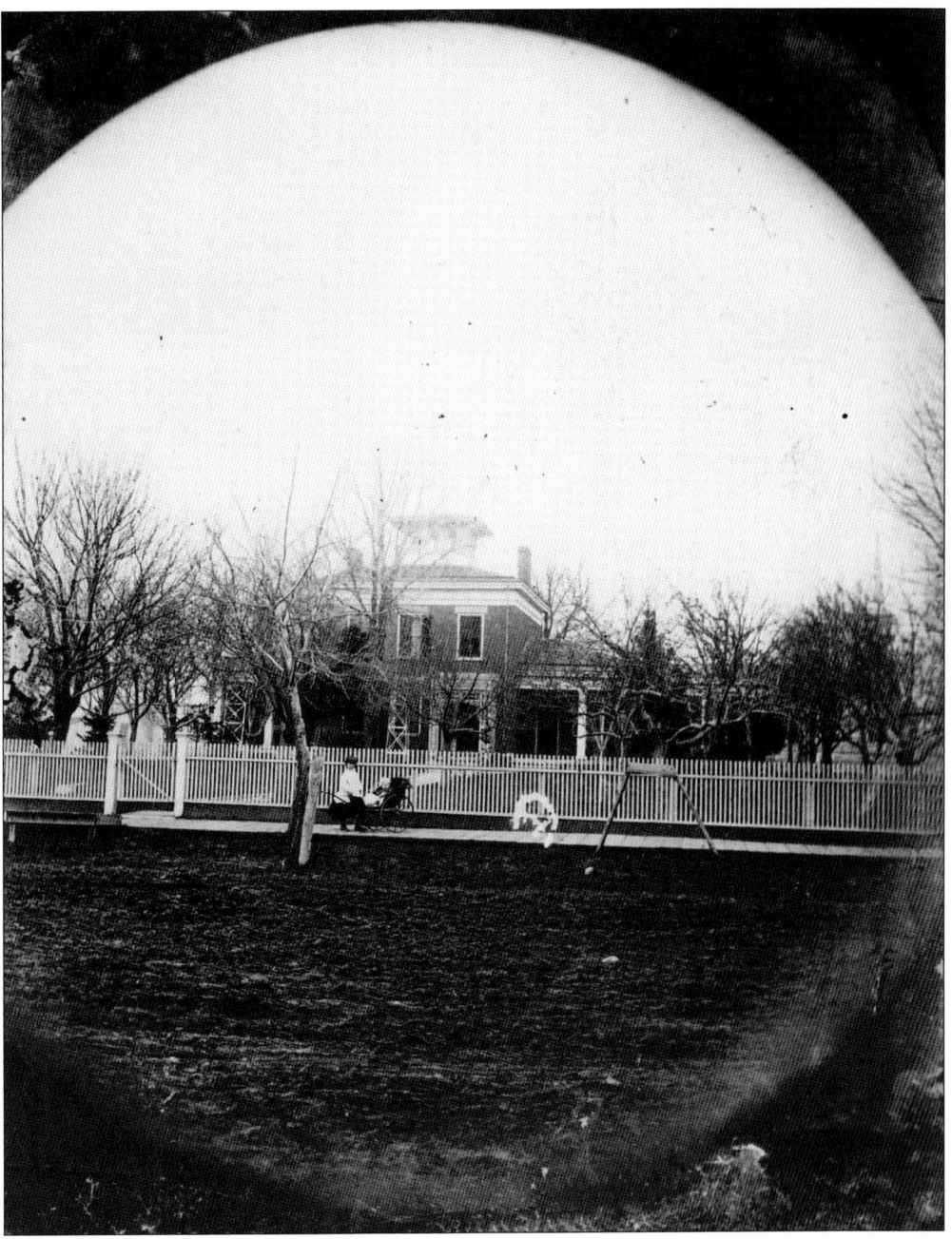

The McCarty brothers came to the Fox Valley in 1834, dammed the river, and built mills and a couple of cabins. The area was called McCarty's mill until the first post office, named Aurora, opened on this site in 1837. The Village of Aurora was incorporated in 1845. The population was just over one hundred at this point, mostly settlers from New York. In 1857, the present City of Aurora was incorporated taking in both the villages of Aurora and West Aurora.

In these early days, before the building of permanent structures for prayer, people gathered in homes to worship. The first meetings of the First Methodist Episcopal Church were held in McCarty's home (pictured above) beginning in the fall of 1837.

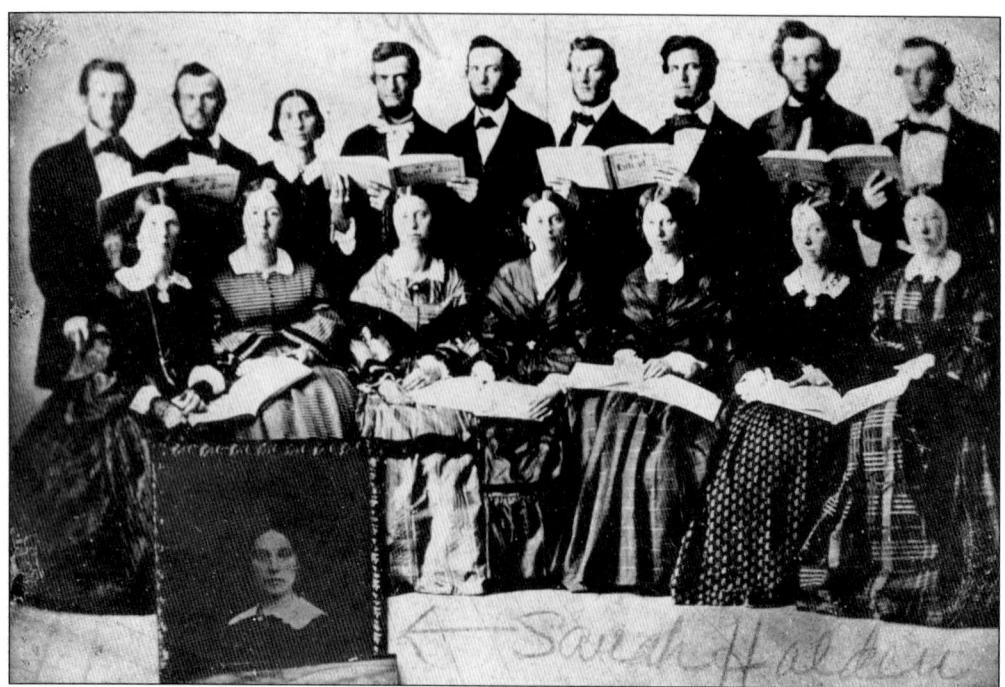

Aurora the City of Bridges lists these members of the First Congregational choir in 1859, from left to right, as follows: (front row) Mrs. M. Tabor, Helen Burroughs, Kate Fuller, Mrs. H.C. Paddock, Mrs. C. Wilson, Mrs. A. Annis, and Mrs. Ella Huntington; (back row) T.N. Holden, Chas. Strong, Mrs. Chauncey Lee, Levi Isbell, J.L. Holden, H.C. Paddock, Kinney Isbell, and Dr. C. Wilson. Inset, Mrs. J.L. Holden. This group sang at the first Republican Party convention.

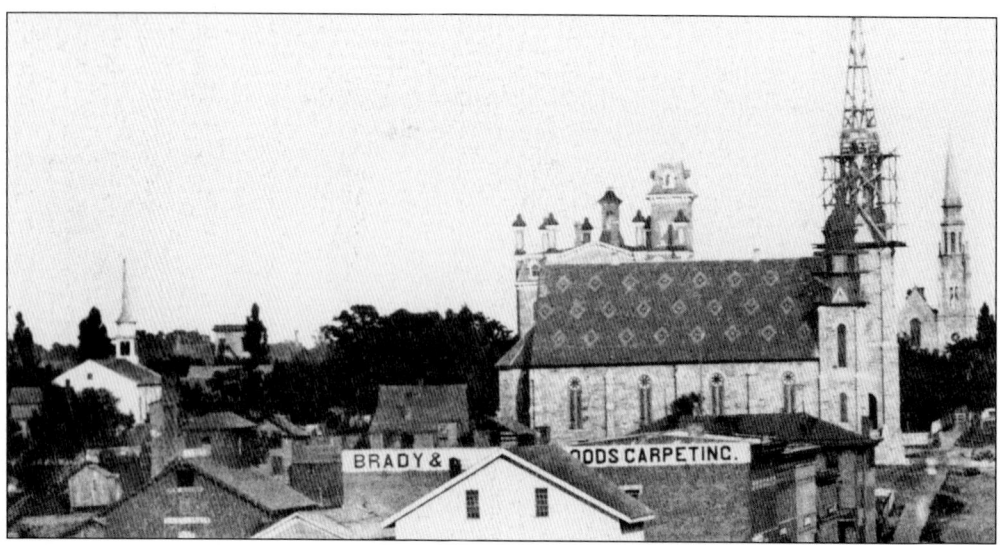

Pictured are the original (to the left) and second (background to the right) structures that housed the First Congregational Church. The steeple on the original church was 115 feet high. This congregation began as a Presbyterian church in 1838, but changed their form of governing in 1848. In 1858, 13 families petitioned to organize another Congregational church in the West Division of the city. This is the present New England Congregational Church.

St. Paul's Church, organized in 1853, was the first German Lutheran church in Aurora. In 1855, the congregation built a church on the east side, and a school was started in 1865. The second wave of Germans, immigrating from 1890 to 1900, helped expand the size of this congregation.

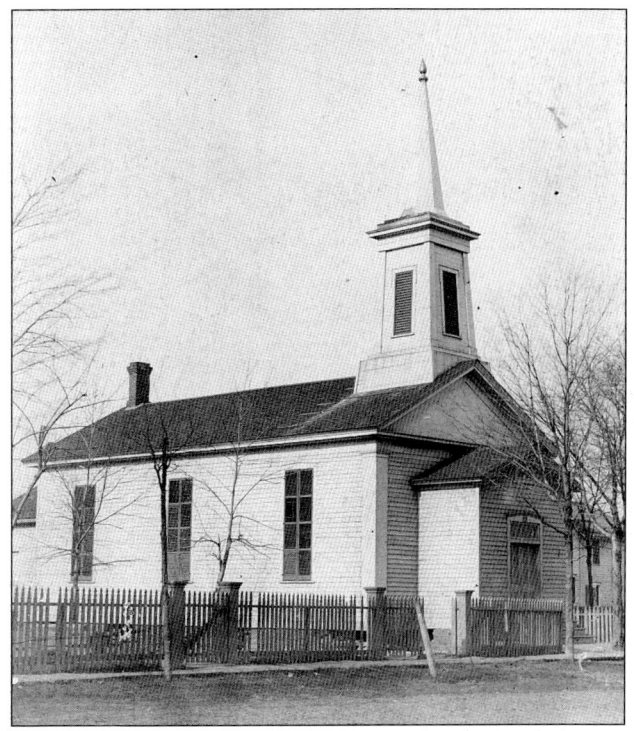

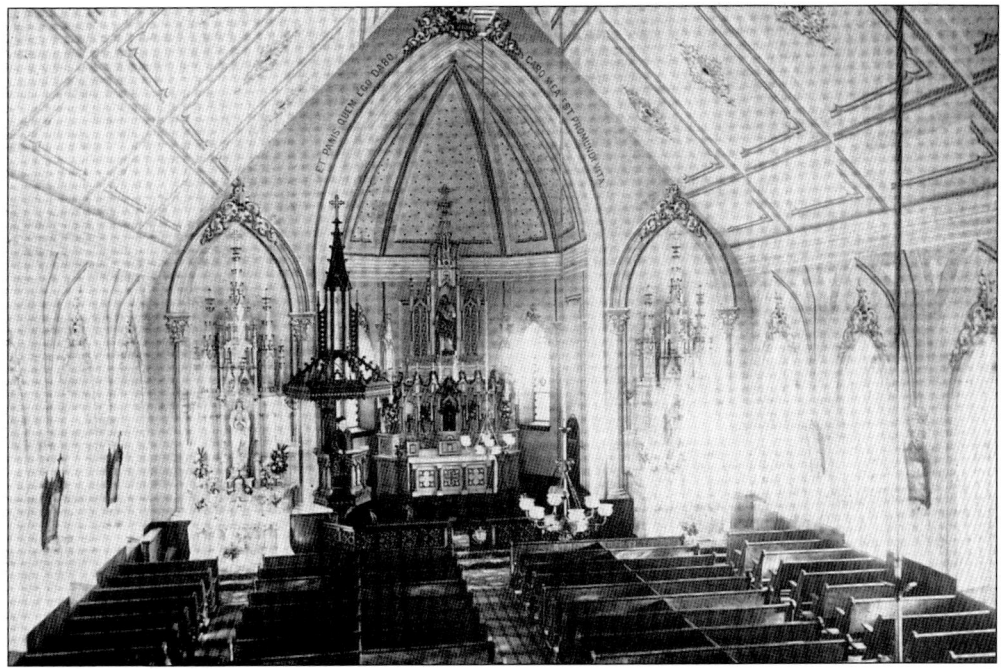

St. Mary's Catholic Church sanctuary is also in its second church building. The original church was organized in 1850 to serve the mostly French Canadian Catholics in the area. These immigrants were soon joined by Catholics from Luxemburg and Ireland. After the Luxemburgers built St. Nicholas Church in 1859 and the French built Sacred Heart Church in 1866, the Irish built St. Mary's Church in 1875.

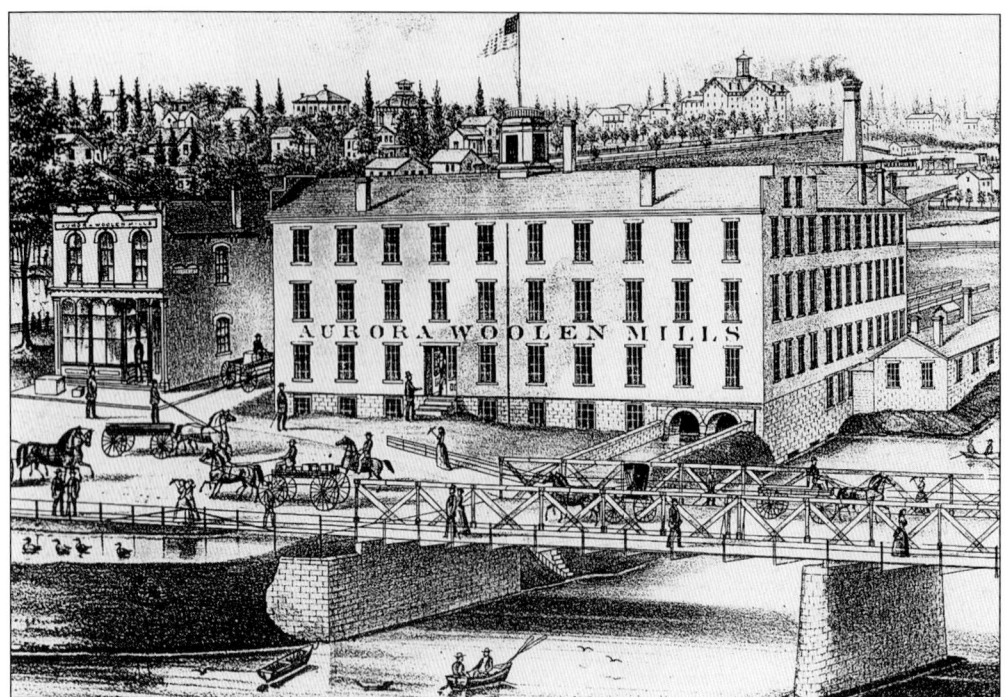

The industrial birth of Aurora may be said to have taken place when Joseph G. Stolp arrived from the east on June 12, 1837. Stolp noted, "When I came there were perhaps a dozen families on the east side of the river and three on the west." On the third day after his arrival, young Stolp began cutting timber for the erection of a carding mill at the north end of his island. This was Aurora's first true factory. The earlier saw- and gristmills could only meet the settlers' daily needs.

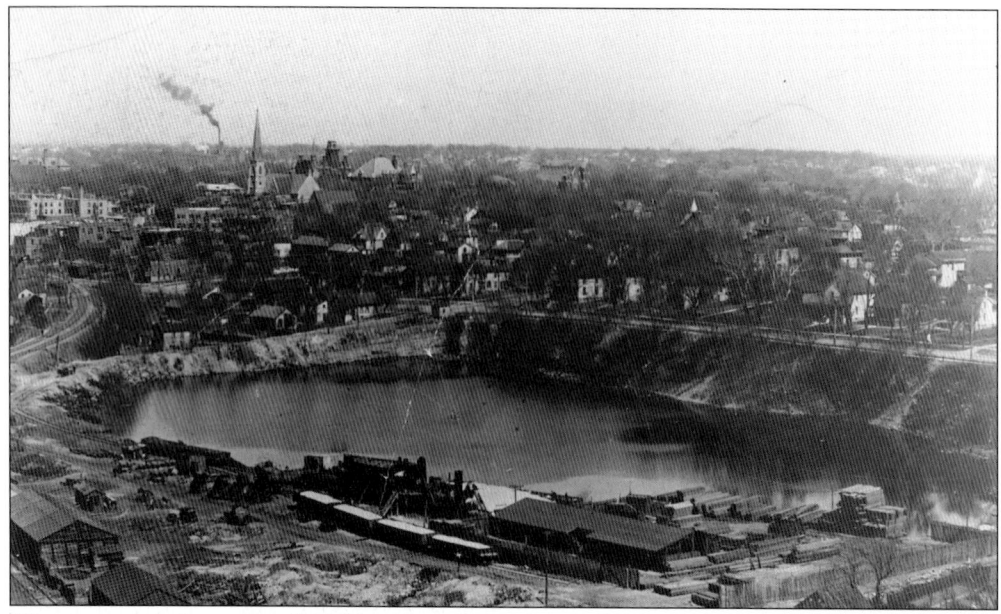

The quarry on the west side of Broadway was just north of North Avenue. Stone from this quarry was used for building many structures in Aurora.

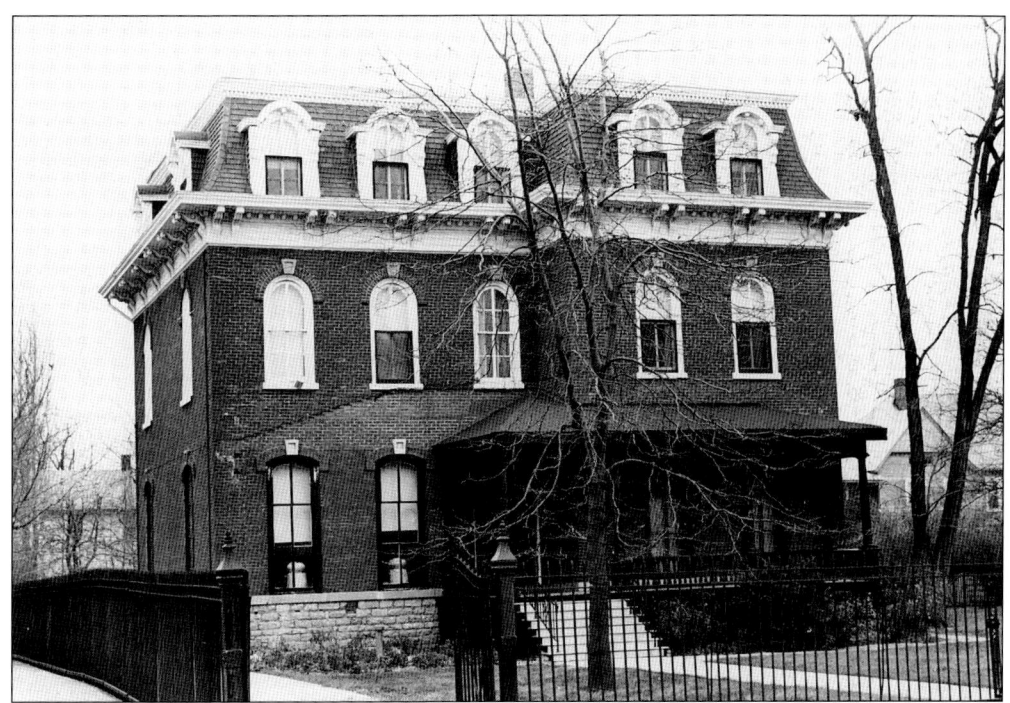

David Hurd's house, built in 1850 and located at 429 W. Downer, was an impressive structure. It was reported that Hurd lived in this house with ten other people: four boys and men and seven women. The fence was added in 1925.

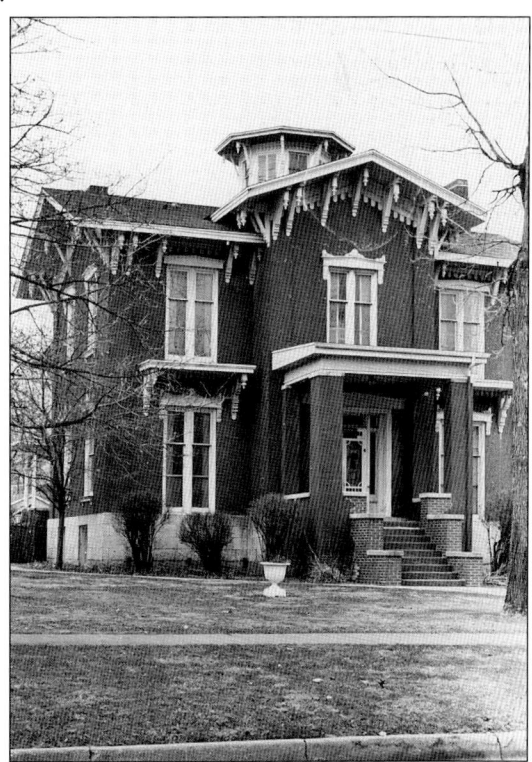

William A. Tanner moved to Aurora in 1852. In 1856, he built this house at 305 Cedar. The house was the first Aurora home to have gaslights and carpeting. It featured an Italian marble fireplace, 13-foot ceilings, and 30 rooms.

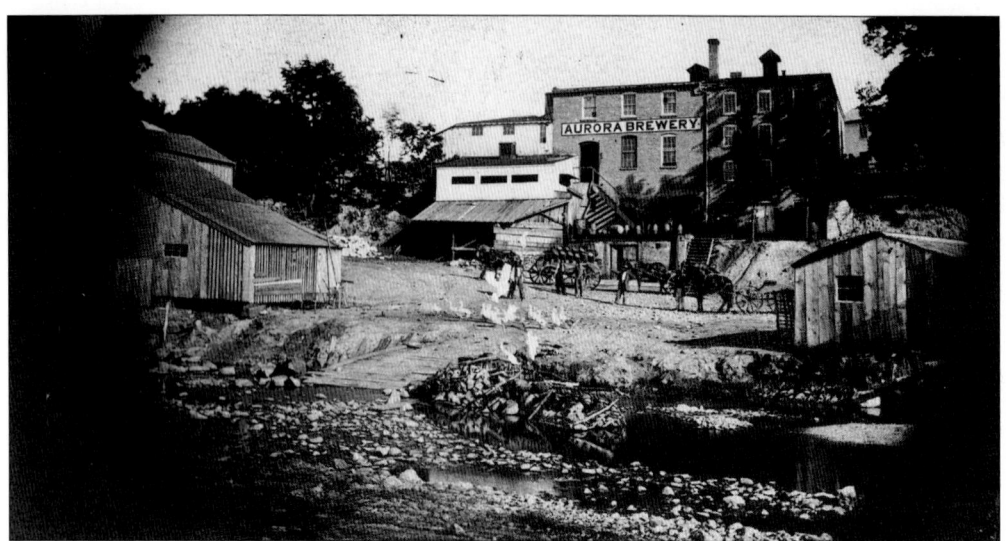

"In July 1855, two Germans, Charles Blasey and Gottfried Egger, came to Aurora from Switzerland. 'Not finding profitable employment elsewhere, they put up a small building shanty fashion, at a cost of not over $100 and commenced the manufacture of beer, a business they had learned in Germany.' Here they continued until 1858, hard at work, and keeping a 'Bachelor's Hall.' " (From the 1868 Aurora City Directory.) In 1858 Blasey purchased Egger's interest, and kept on the business.

Brewing beer was an art form that included the brew master carefully recording ingredients and the final test results of each batch. This 1910 record sheet is from the Aurora Brewery brew master's logbook.

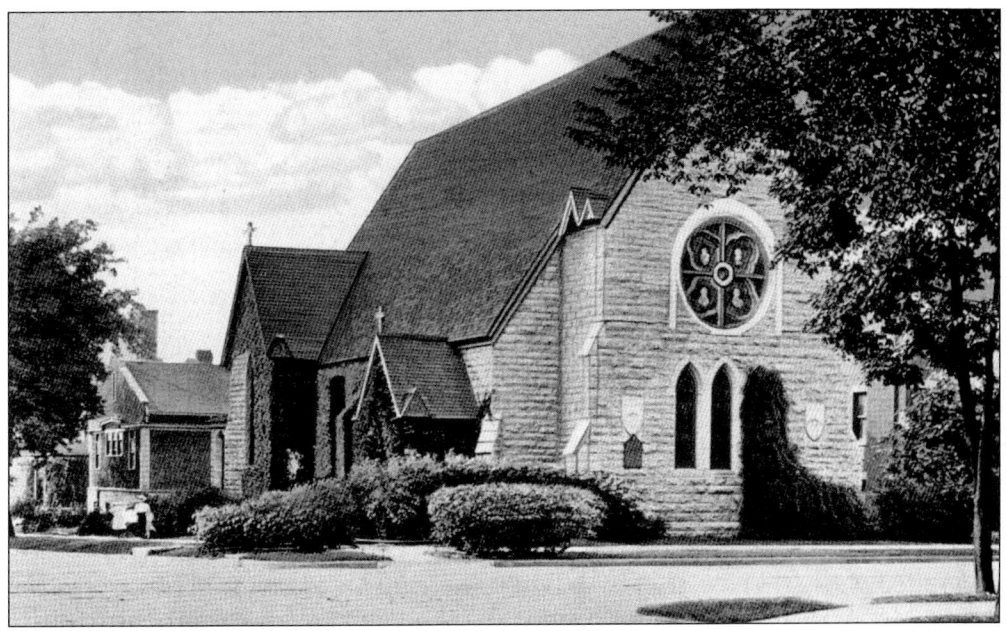

Trinity Episcopal Church was organized in May 1849. The first wardens were P.K. Rockwell and Myron V. Hall, editor of the *Aurora Beacon*. Vestrymen were P.A. Allaire, M.D.; Wm. Golding; L.A. Hoyt; and L.P. Hoyt. This postcard pictures their second house of worship. The first service was held here in 1871.

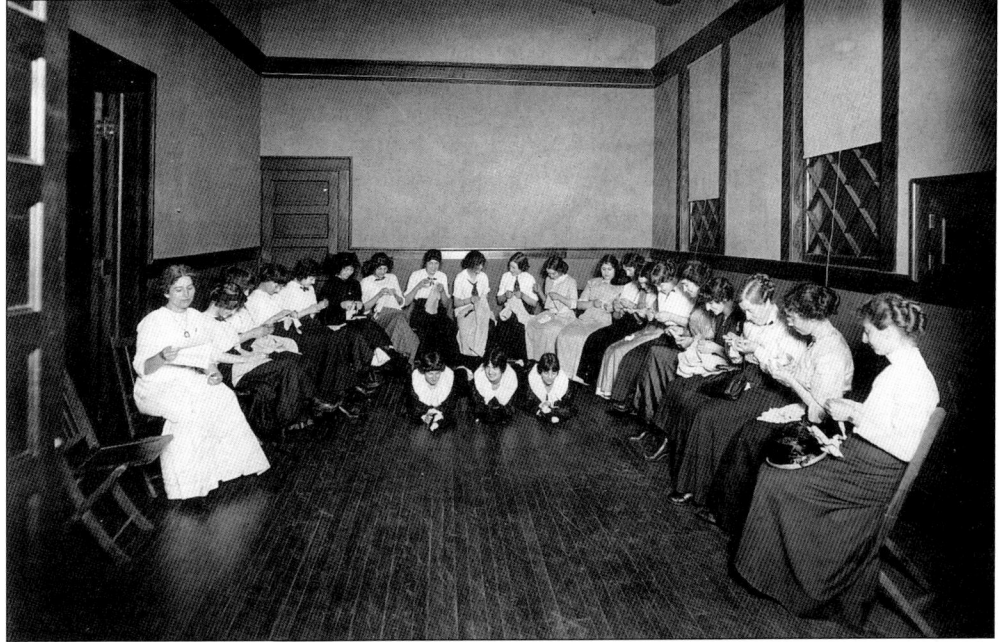

Within the early churches, the men and women each had their own clubs or groups. A sewing circle was a typical activity for women. Each of these women of Trinity Episcopal Church appears busy. Some are designing hats, others are repairing men's jackets, and one lady is not sewing but reading from a document. The three girls on the floor have just finished practicing for a play and have wandered in to be put into the circle for the picture.

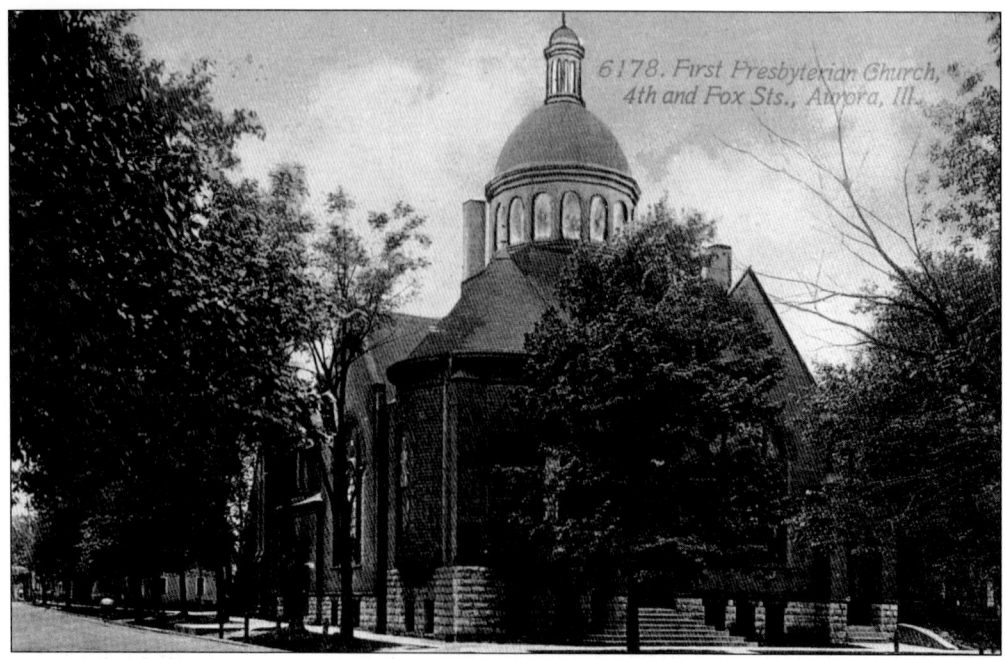
First Presbyterian Church was organized in 1858 and the members hired their first pastor in 1859. This was one of the two early Swedish churches in Aurora.

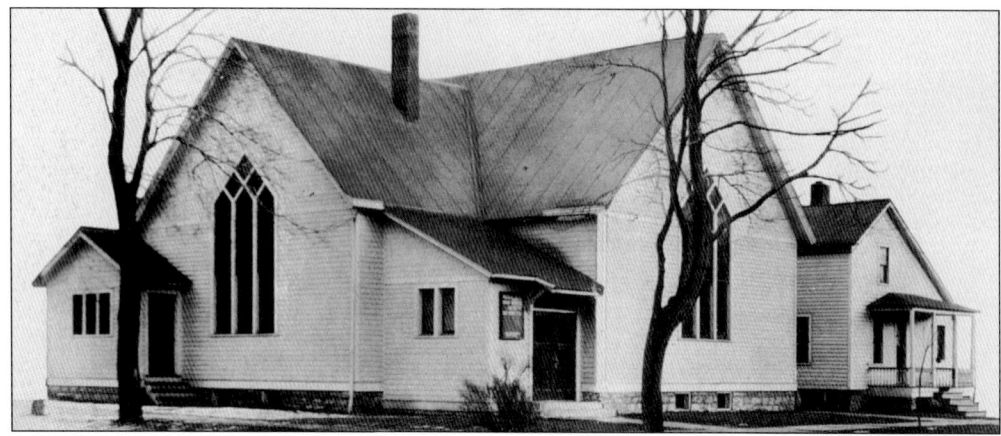
Locust Street Methodist Episcopal Church was a Swedish congregation organized in the summer of 1884. At first, the congregation met in rented halls. This is their second building. For many years, the language of the church was entirely Swedish. This congregation merged with the Wesley Methodist Church in 1948.

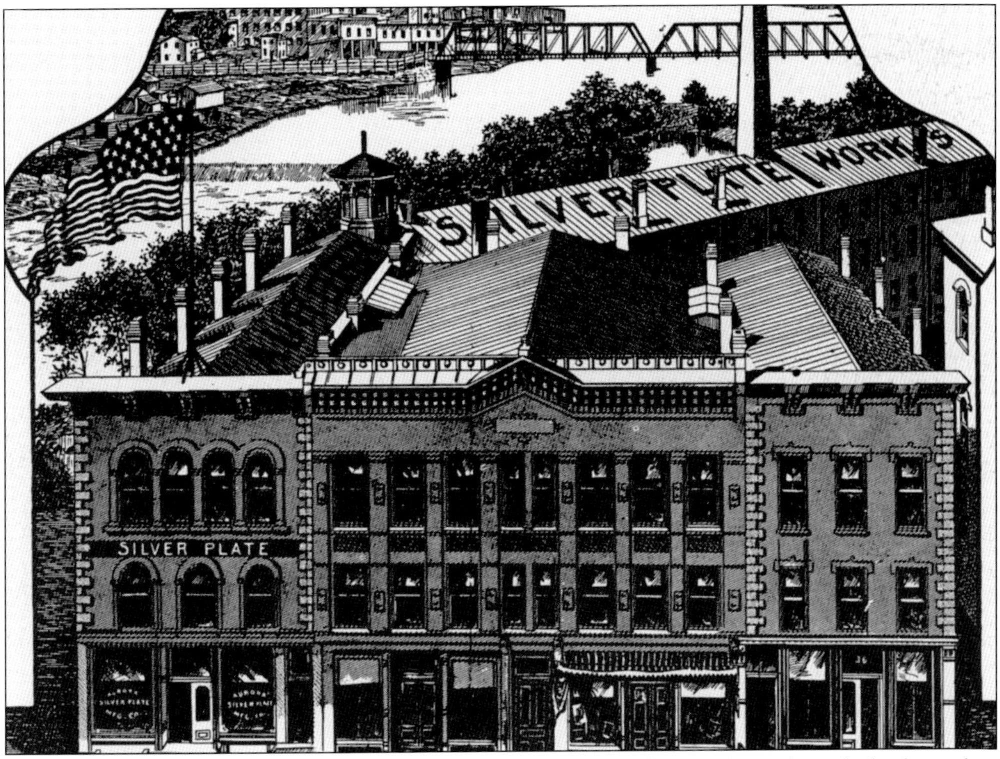

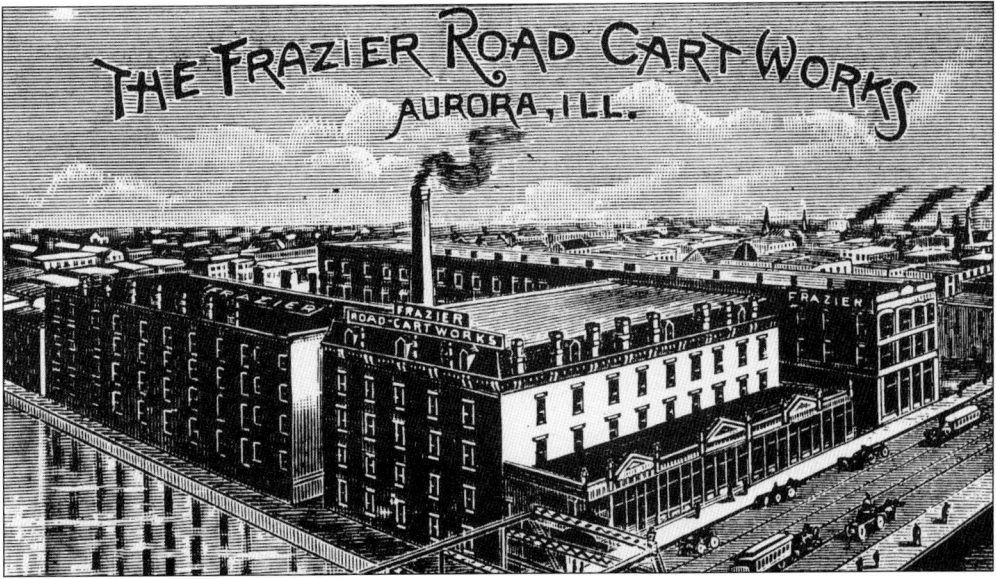

Aurora Silver Plate Manufacturing Company was organized in 1869 and made high-quality silver plate items. Soon their silverware began to appear on the tables of Americans from coast to coast.

The Frazier Road Cart works established a small factory in 1881 to produce Frazier's improved training cart. Very quickly it became necessary to lease larger manufacturing facilities. At one time, Frazier manufactured 20 styles of these carts and track sulkies, employing two hundred workers.

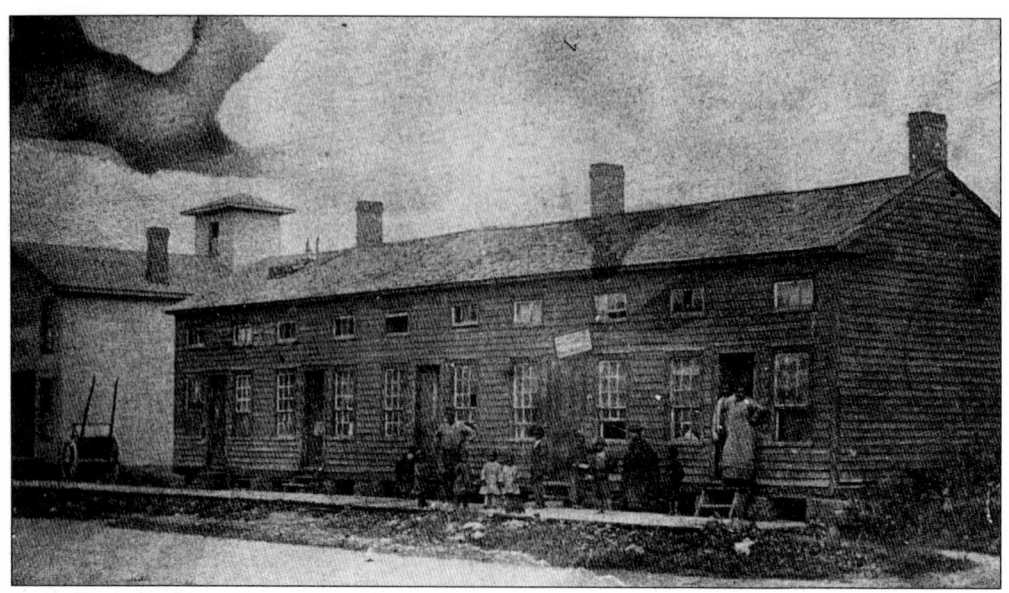

According to Olive Beaupre Miller, author of *Engines and Brass Bands*, African-American settlers were situated north of the railroad tracks on north Lincoln Avenue between Smith and Spring Streets near the railroad works. She also noted that African-American cabins were built on the south side of north Lincoln Avenue. This was one of the many immigrant groups that lived on north Broadway and Lincoln.

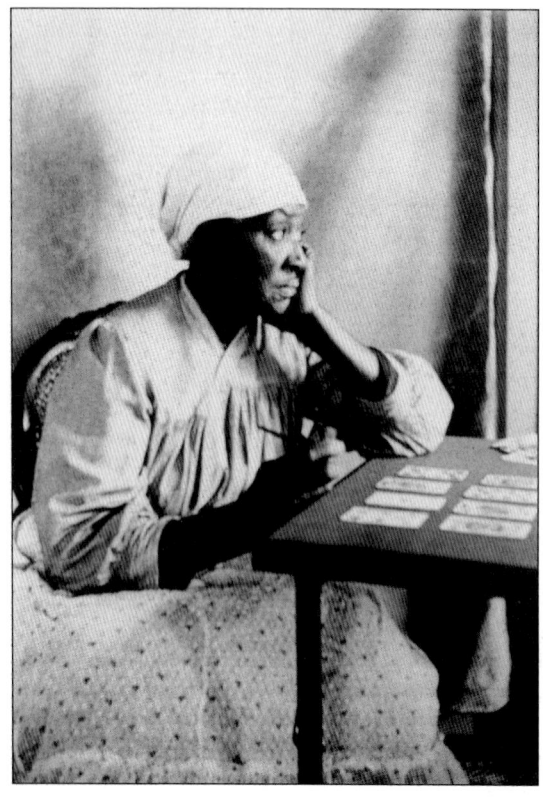

This is a reflective picture of "Anty" Jackson. Ms. Jackson worked as a domestic for Carrie Potter around 1915 at Potter's fine boardinghouse at 59 S. Fourth Street.

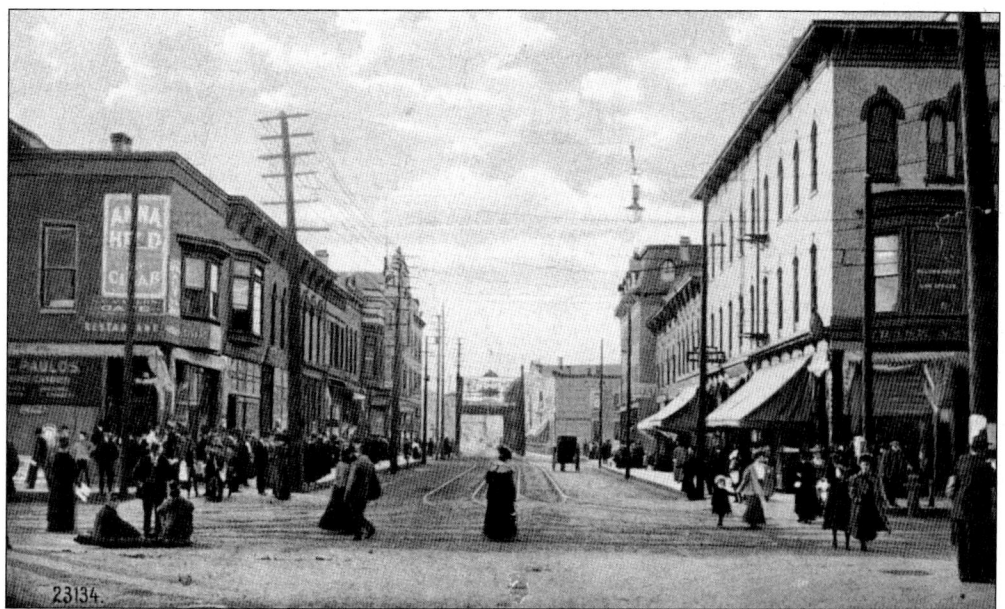

This picture shows a busy street scene in downtown Aurora at the turn of the century. Note the bridge over the Fox River in the distance, the overhead telephone and electric cable car lines, and the cable car tracks down the center of the street. This scene is from Broadway looking down Fox Street facing west.

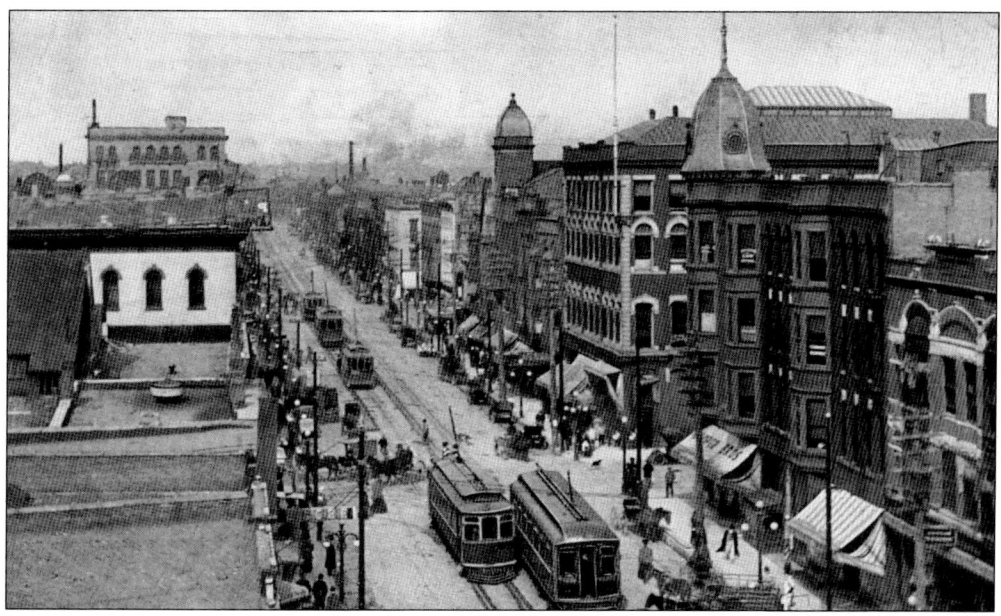

Cable cars are also featured prominently in this photograph taken on Broadway looking north from Benton Street. Notice the famous Aurora streetlights. The postcard features what came to be the moniker for Aurora, "The City of Lights." Along this avenue were the latest tall buildings of this period, which were the "skyscrapers" of their day.

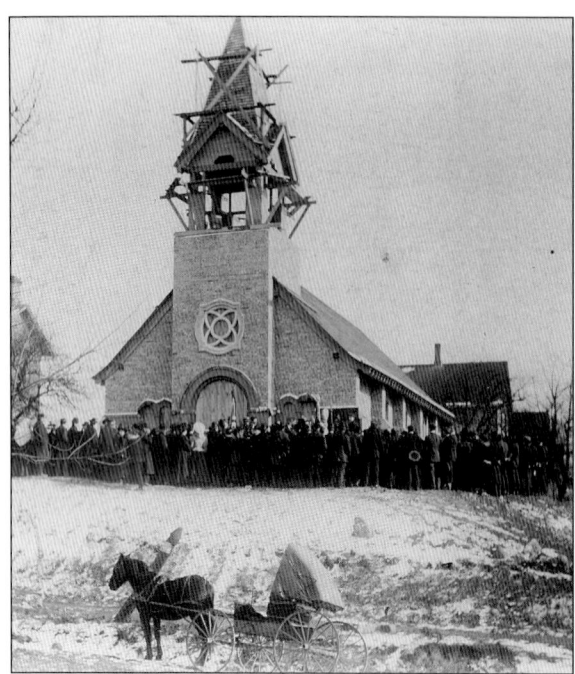

This winter scene was shot in 1909 when the first St. Michael's Romanian Greek Catholic Church was under construction. Mass was celebrated in the parishioners' native language in this church as it was in many other churches. Note the scaffolding around the tower and the gathered congregation in front. The buggy in the foreground probably belonged to the photographer.

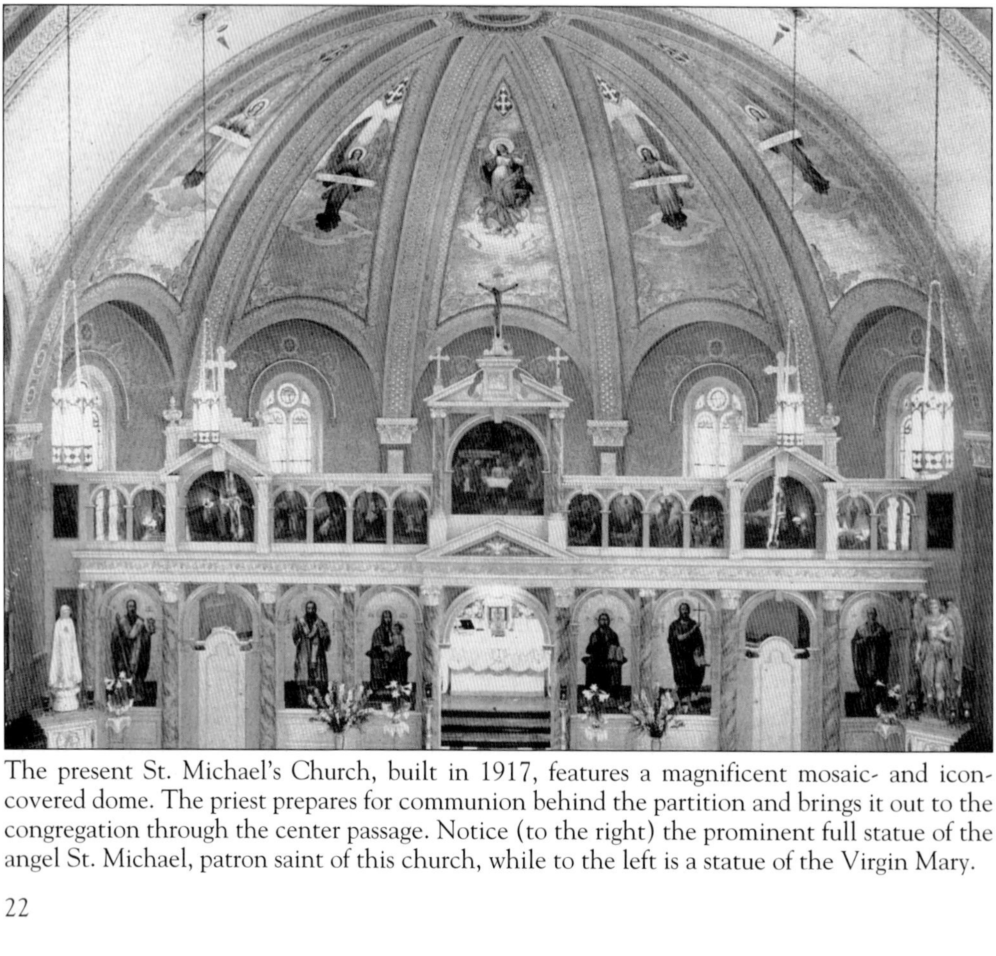

The present St. Michael's Church, built in 1917, features a magnificent mosaic- and icon-covered dome. The priest prepares for communion behind the partition and brings it out to the congregation through the center passage. Notice (to the right) the prominent full statue of the angel St. Michael, patron saint of this church, while to the left is a statue of the Virgin Mary.

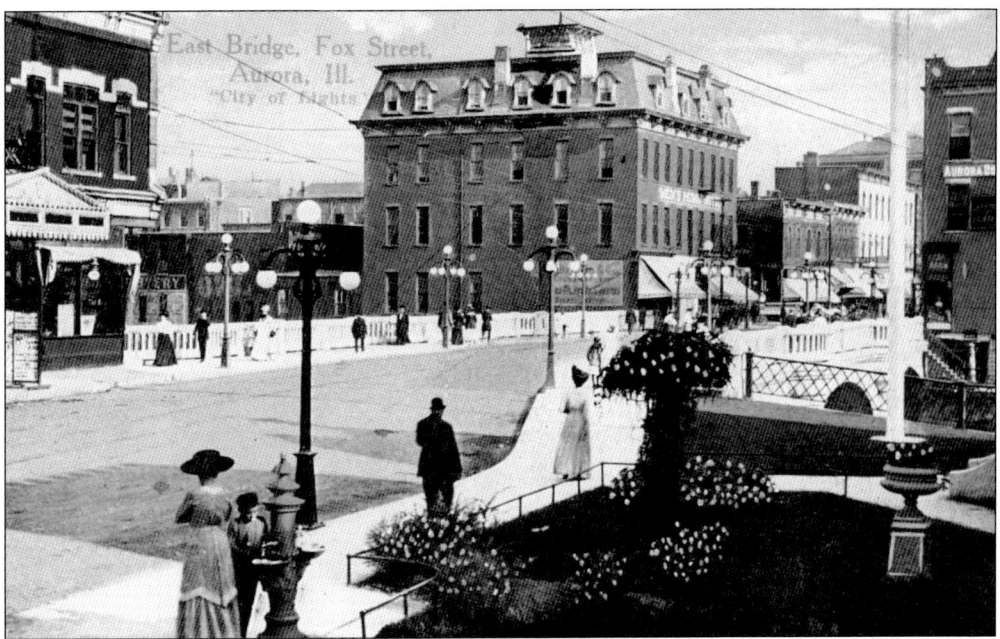

This postcard pictures a new east bridge on Fox Street (now Downer) that replaced the metal bridge shown on a previous card. In the upper left-hand corner is the Fox Theatre that would have been showing silent movies at this time. The large structure in the center is a hotel and across the street is the Aurora Business College.

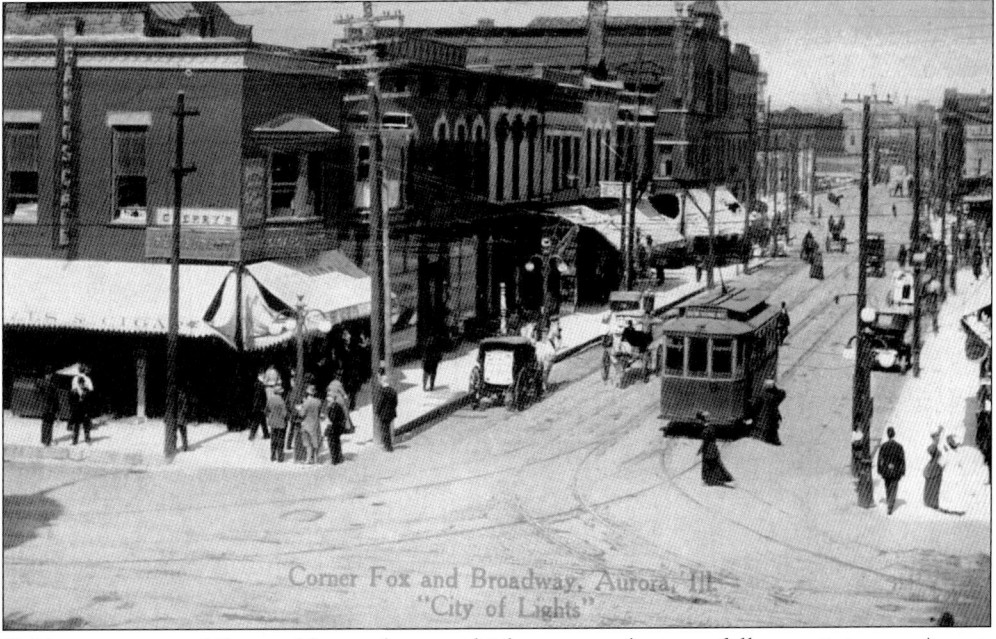

Cable cars, automobiles, and horse-drawn vehicles seem to be peacefully coexisting on Aurora streets. Major downtown streets in Aurora were double-tracked and, in some cases, triple-tracked to handle the cable car traffic. The sewer cap in the photograph was probably made at the Love Brothers Foundry. Under these streets of Aurora were steam pipes that heated the first floors of many downtown buildings.

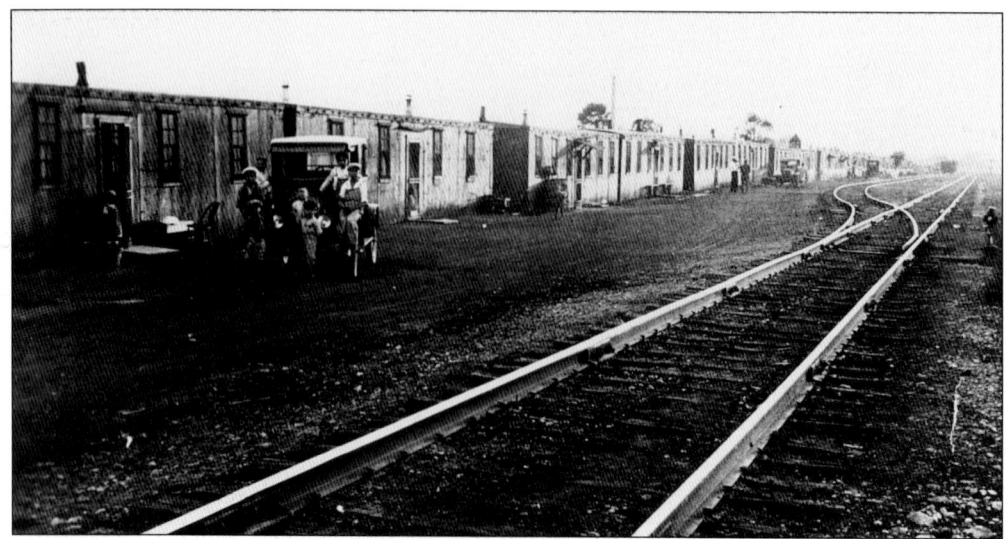

Mexicans came to work in the railroad yards in the boom days of the 1920s just as many immigrant groups before them. Because they came from a closer country, they usually brought their families with them from the beginning. There were two areas where this newest immigrant population lived, near the Broadway Chicago, Burlington & Quincy car shops and in the "boxcar" community (shown above) on the eastern edge of the city.

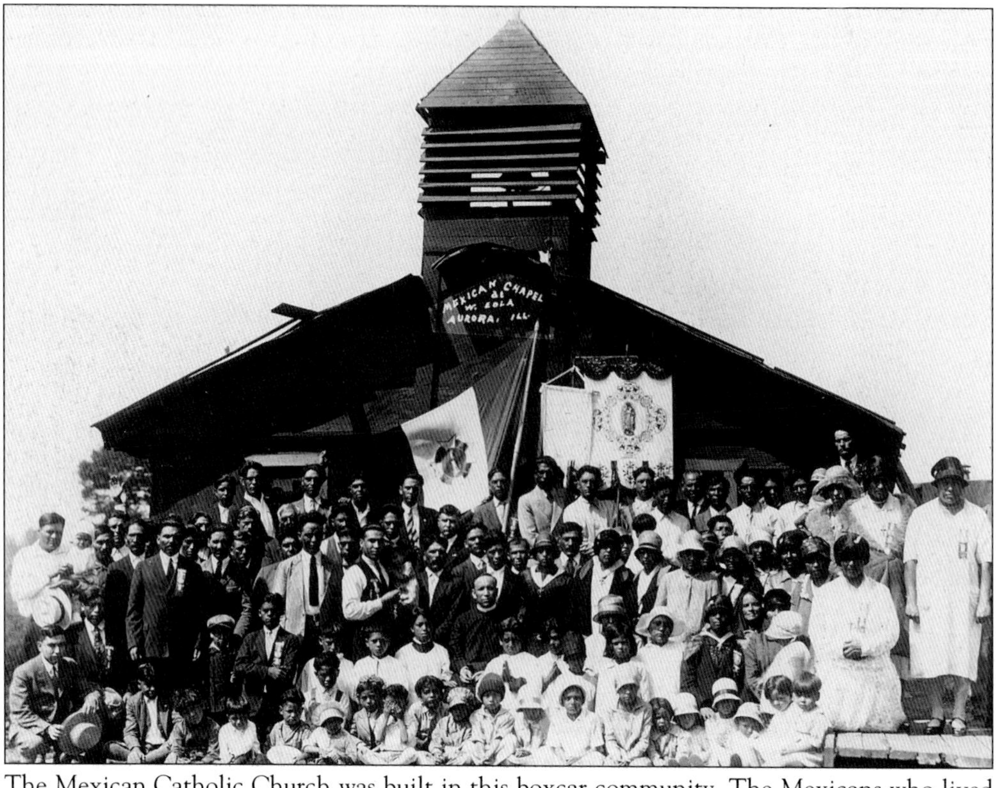

The Mexican Catholic Church was built in this boxcar community. The Mexicans who lived in town would go to a Catholic church near their home but would also, from time to time, walk out to this church to worship with this Mexican community.

Two

Railroading Comes to Town

The railroad industry was the backbone of America's mighty industrial growth. The railroad came to the Fox Valley many years before the boom days at the end of the century. It all began with a meeting of businessmen from Aurora and Batavia in late 1848 that led to the issuing of a state charter for the Aurora Branch Rail Road on February 12, 1849. Twelve miles of track from Aurora to the Galena and Chicago Railroad junction soon became consolidated with Quincy & Chicago and the Peoria & Burlington, putting into place the main Illinois line of the CB&Q system in 1864. Such growth demanded appropriate repair shops and terminal facilities.

Throughout the years the complex was expanded and improved upon, using Fox River limestone from Batavia and a local quarry for building material. The three sections of the existing roundhouse were constructed in 1855, 1859, and 1861.

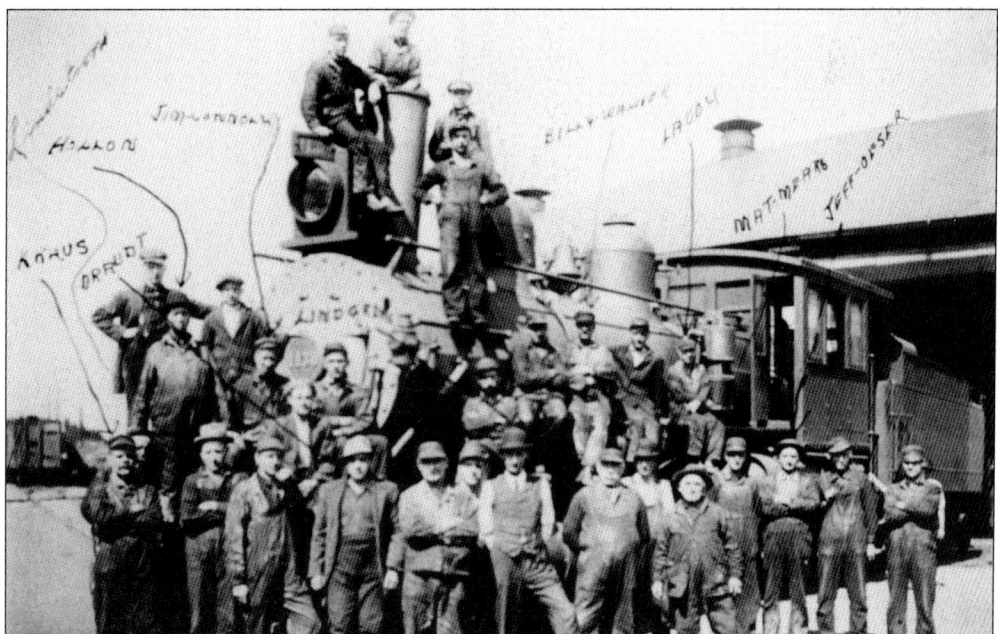

The locomotive works were subdivided into six different departments: machine shop, boiler works, blacksmith shop, brass foundry, tin shop, and erecting shop. In these various departments, the work of building the locomotive was carried along until the new "iron monster" was perfected and ready for the track.

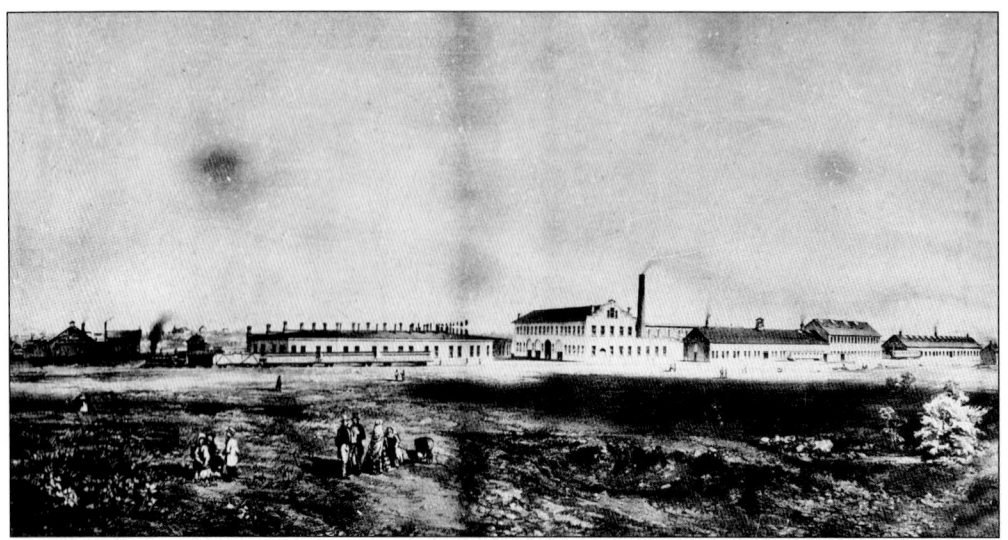

Chicago, Burlington & Quincy Railroad began building their car works in the fall of 1855 and completed them in the fall of 1856 under the supervision of C.J. Allen, architect, and J.R. Coulter, master mason. The works consisted of a roundhouse and various specialty shops, such as car shop, carpenter's shop, paint shop, and lumber kiln. The buildings and yards extended for nearly a mile on Broadway at the height of activity.

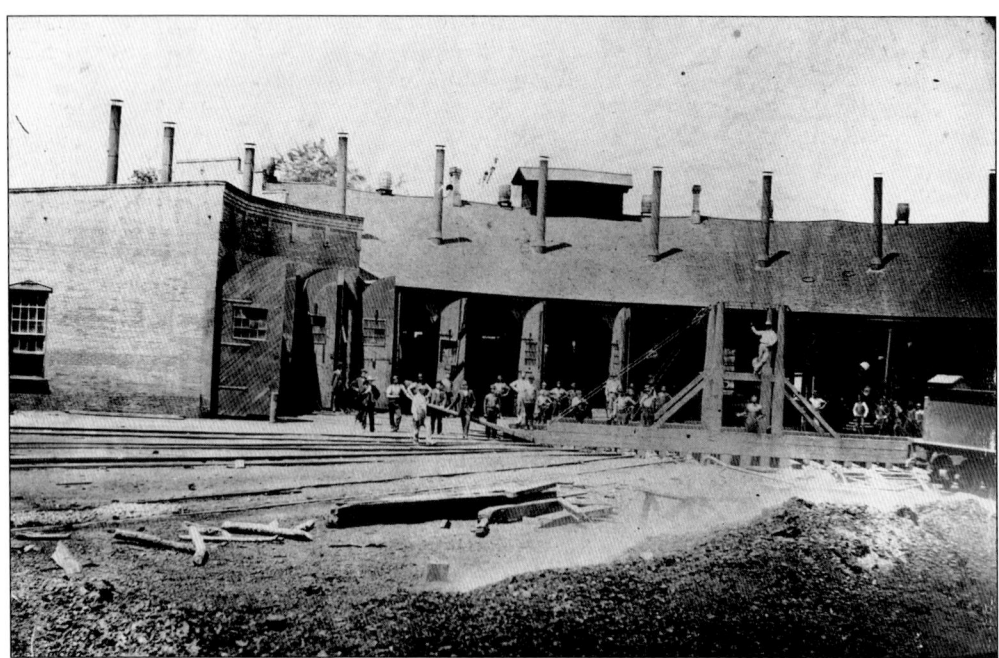

Three sections were built in semicircular fashion to form a complete roundhouse. This was done to accommodate the turntable, situated in the center. Locomotives entered and exited from the large portal at the south end of the roundhouse onto a manually operated turntable. In this manner they could be "steered" into the appropriate stall for inspection or repairs.

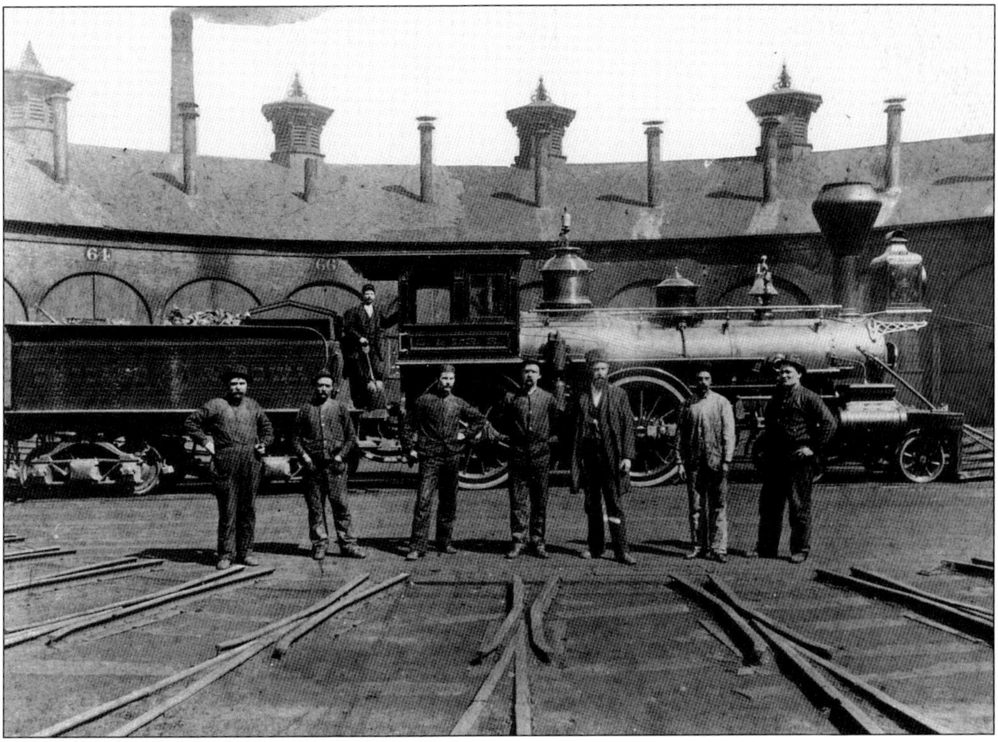

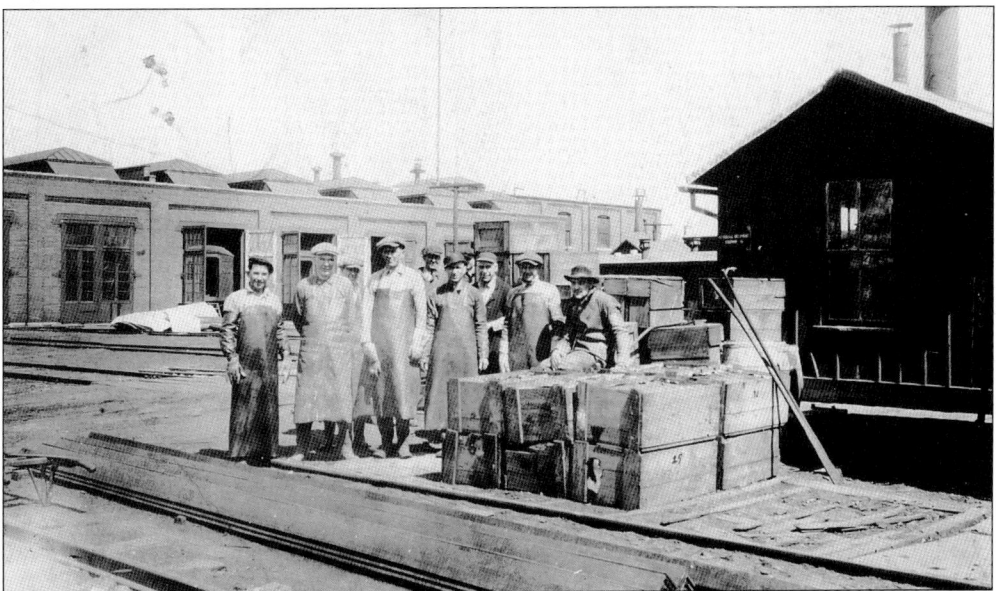

The roundhouse was built of hewn stone and was 264 feet 4 inches in diameter through the center of the turntable. In the beginning it contained tracks and stalls for 22 engines. In 1859 and 1861, eight, and later ten, stalls were added. This complex became the erecting shops where engines were built and repaired from the late 1860s to the 1920s.

Machine shop A was where the major repairs and construction activities took place during the first decades of operation. Erected in 1856 as a two-story building, the Machine Shop A experienced a fire in 1863 that destroyed the second-story walls.

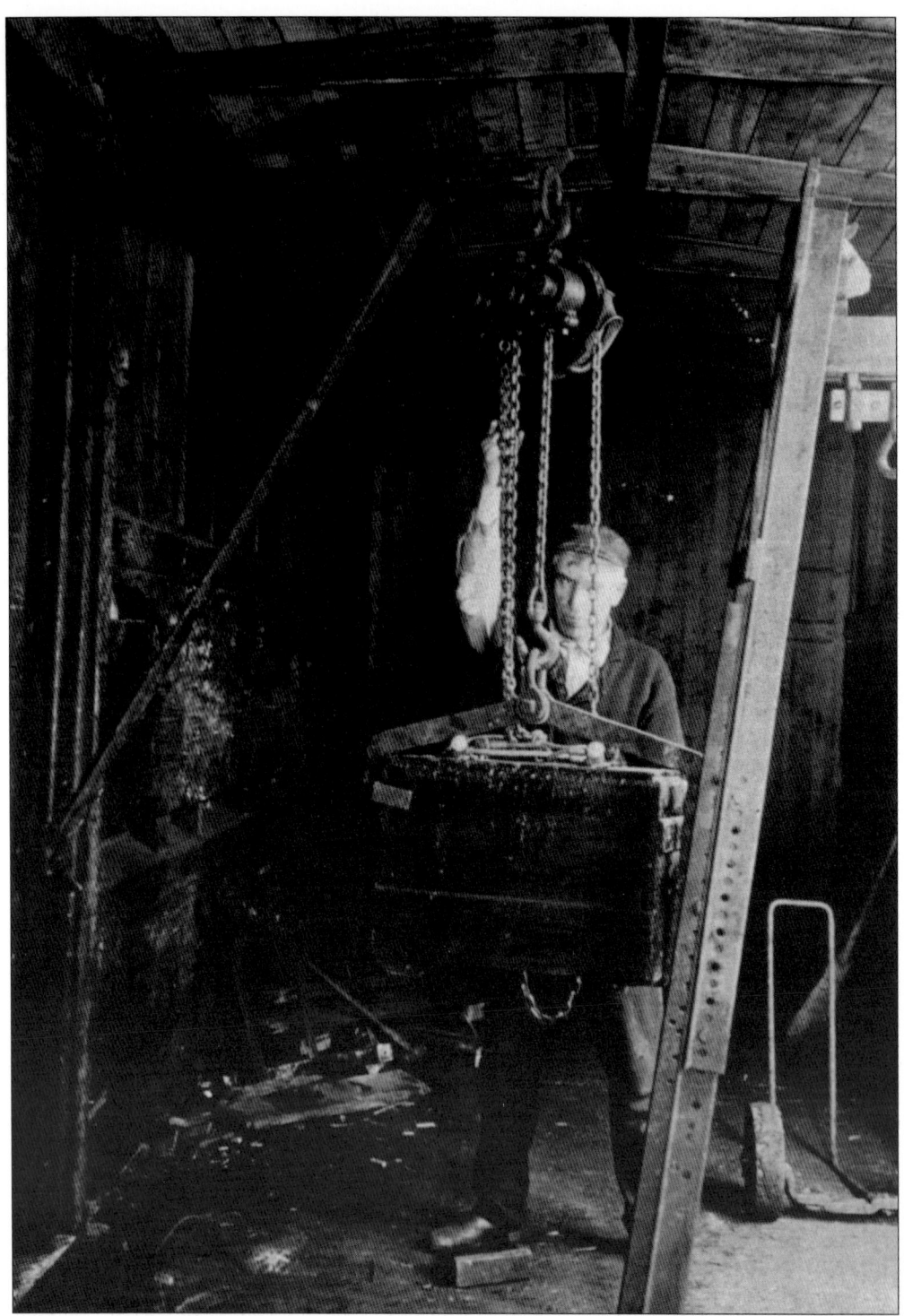
In the early days, the entire assembly process took place in individual stalls with little movement until the engine was completed. This was due to the absence of mechanical lifting equipment.

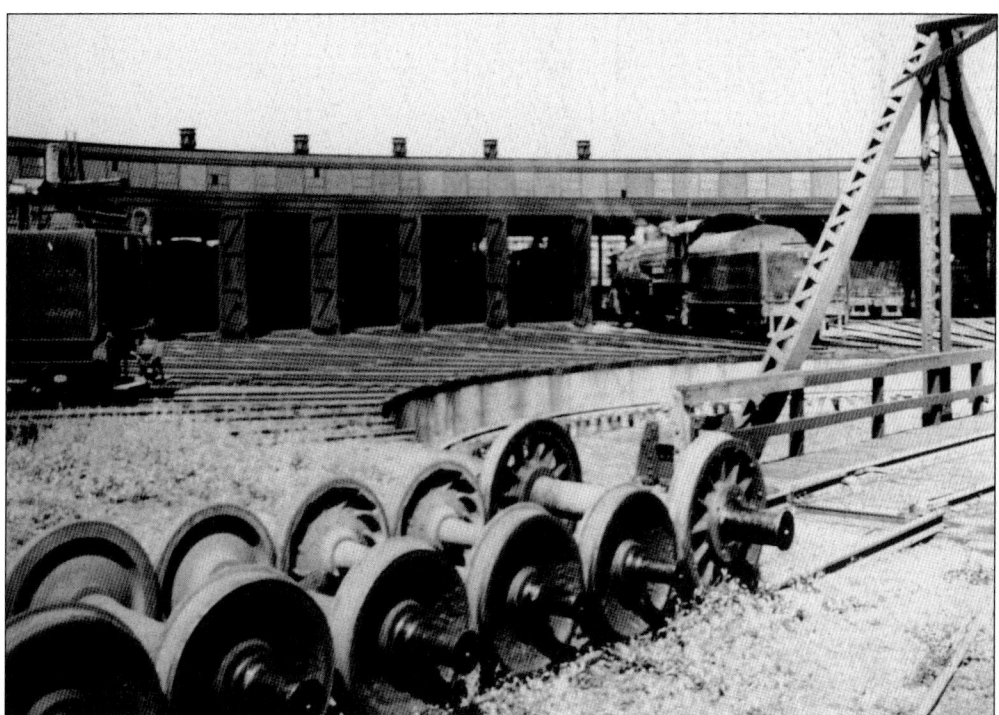

The shops were able to build two freight cars daily, and by 1872, 50 car wheels were being cast every day. By then, more than 50 Pullman Palace cars had been manufactured. All passenger coaches were run into these shops once each year for general repair and refitting. By 1909 the annual output in Aurora was five locomotives, 30 mail and baggage cars, and the repairing of 250 locomotives, 350 passenger cars, and thousands of freight cars.

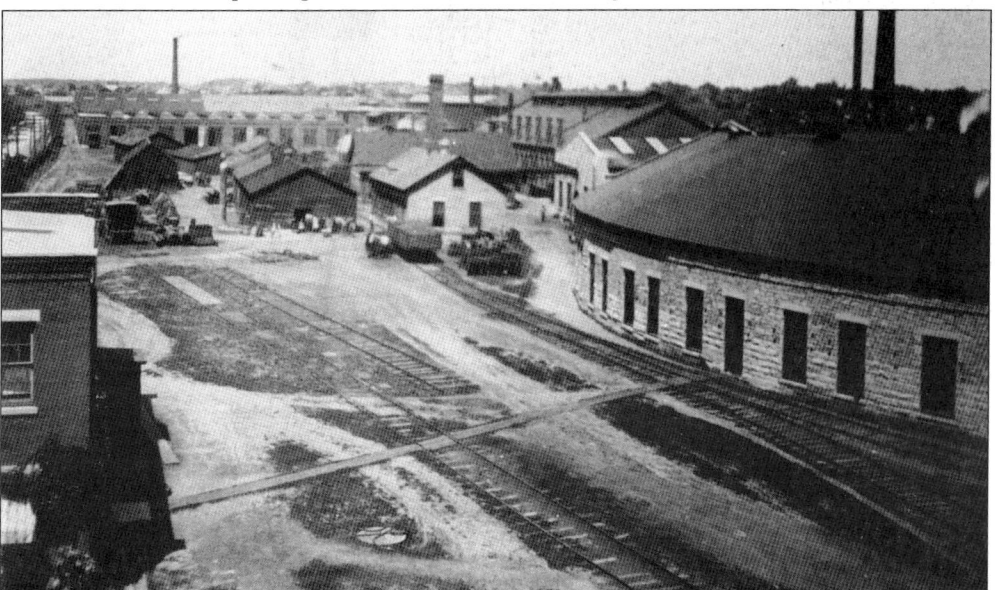

Machine Shop B was constructed in 1863 as a connecting building between the roundhouse and Machine Shop A. It became the principal erections shop until activities moved into the roundhouse.

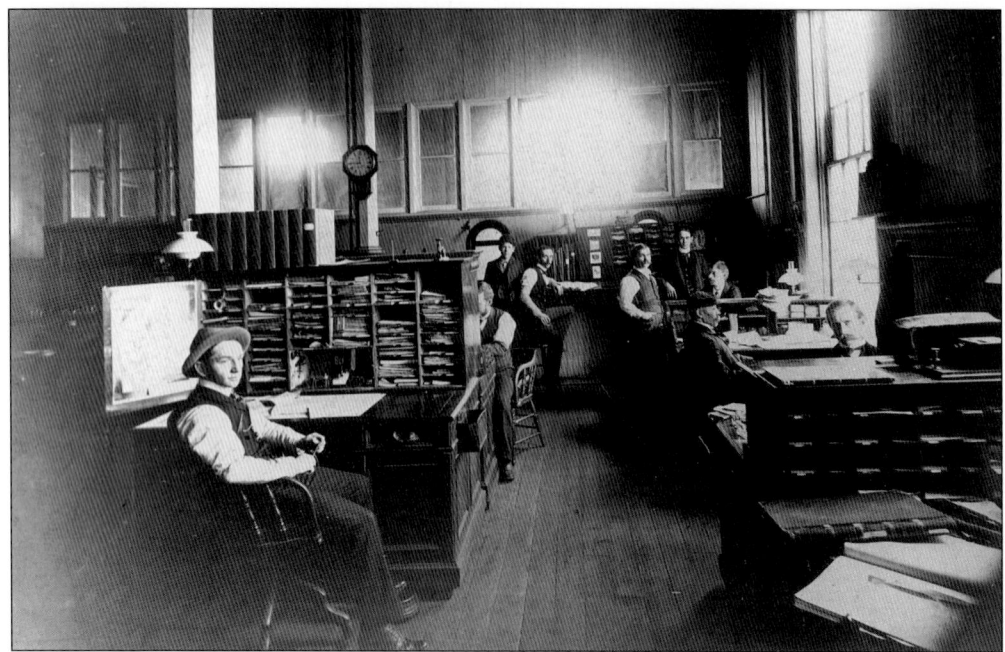

The "Q" shops employed about 350 at first, but by 1872, some 2,000 were employed to build freight cars, passenger coaches, and several steam locomotives, besides maintaining repair and machine shops. Pictured above are 1890 storehouse office workers. H.G. Goodale is shown fifth from the left.

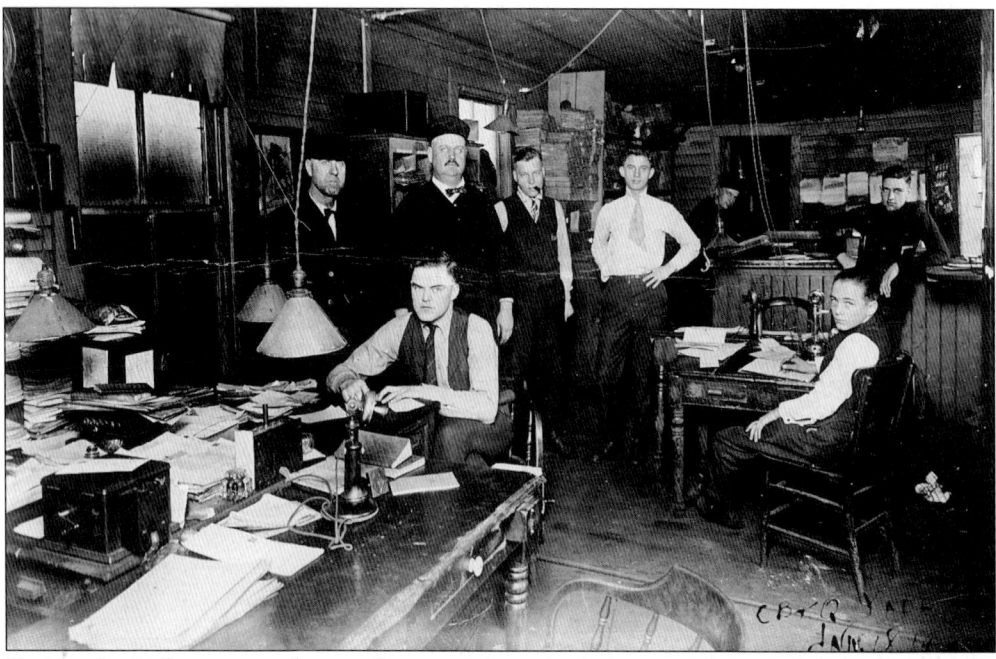

During the 20th century, changes from construction and repair of steam locomotives to the construction of streamlined passenger cars paralleled developments throughout the general railroad industry. This scene shows the yard office in 1917. Aurora shop operations were discontinued in 1974.

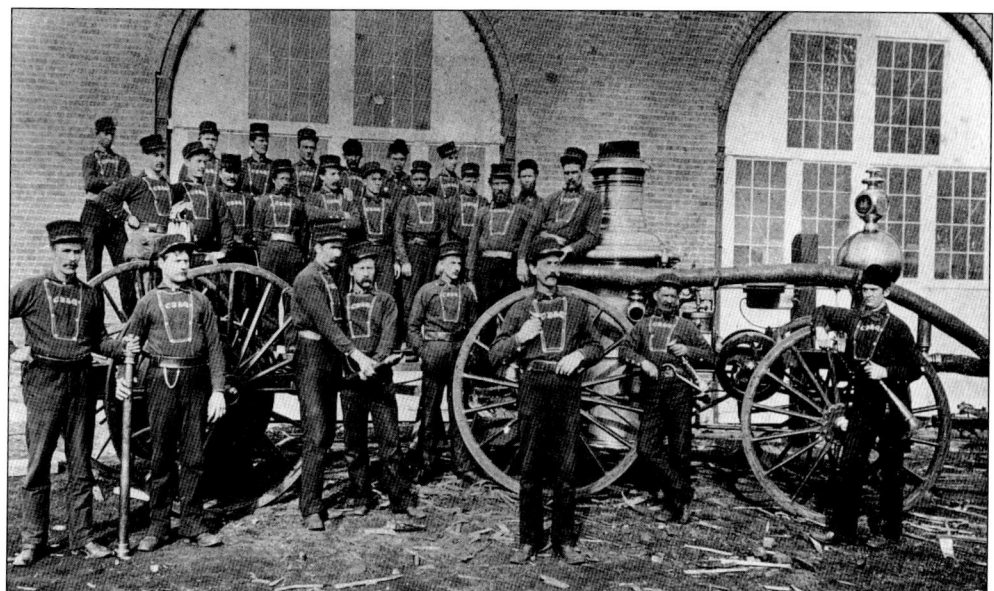

At first, the Burlington supported its own fire department, but it later merged with the Aurora Fire Department. Many firemen served in both firefighting units. The 1886 firemen are pictured as follows: (first row) Frank Flannigan, Bill Muschler, Stafford, Eberly, Carney, Thompson, Hollis, and James; (second row) Tiffany, Race, Holt, Hanson, Coughlin, Rees, Kelley, Clince, Scaegg, Breese, and Reynolds; (third row) Holland, Miller, Abel, Randall, Mileham, A. Plummer, and Geo. Plummer.

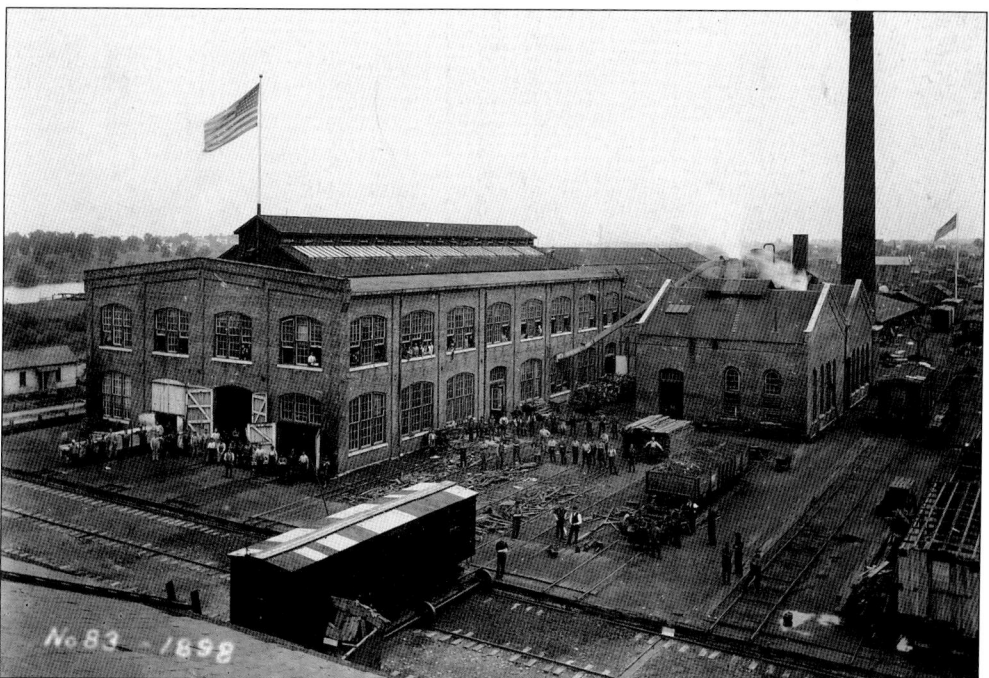

The 45-star flag dates this picture c. 1896–1907. The large building housed the woodworking mill on the first floor and the cabinet, pattern, and telegraph shops on the second floor. The power plant was located in the small building.

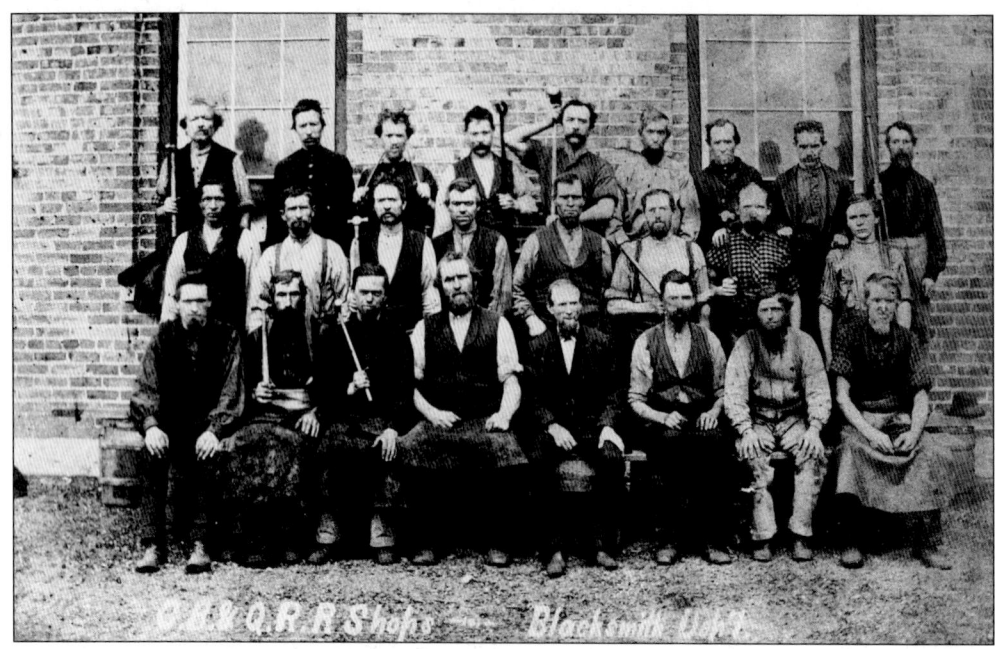

Pictured above is the 1890 blacksmith department. The car shops include blacksmith, woodworking and carpenter shop, upholstery department, pattern, and inside finish shops and paint shops. Freight cars and passenger coaches were also made here.

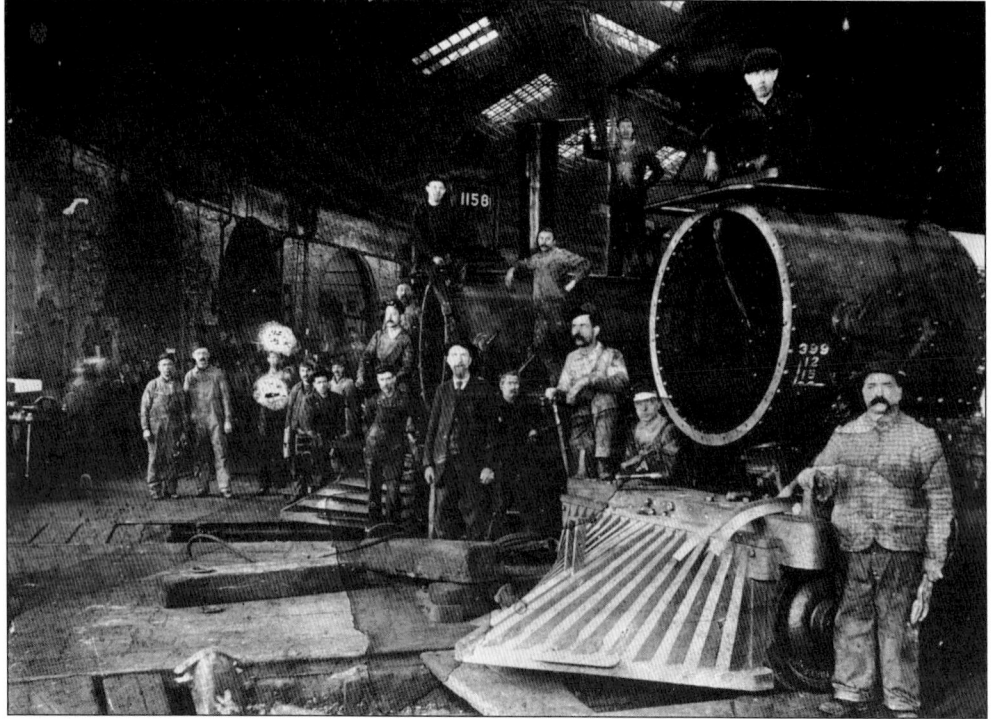

The men here are hard at work building a locomotive in the "Q" shops. Notice the stalls in the background, the overhead skylights that let in much needed light, and a cowcatcher that is mounted on the front of the locomotive. The man at the right is Mat Schamer.

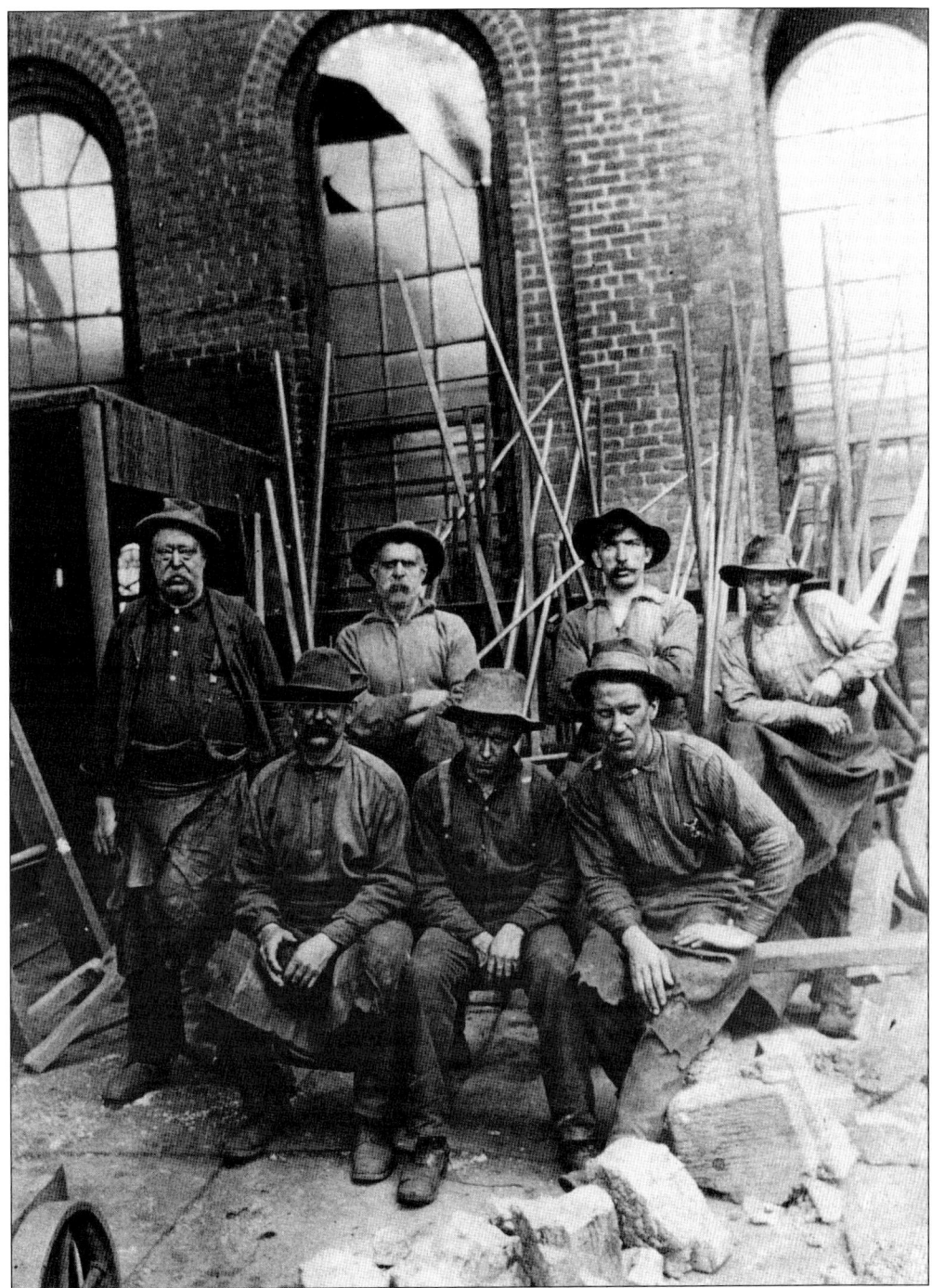

This 1903 picture features the day furnace gang as follows: (front) Matt Loser, James McGowan, and Fred Miller; (second row) Les Lindholm, Mike Peiffer, Peter Stearn, and Ed Millen. The long poles are thongs that were used to handle the hot metal. Gloves and hats were worn to protect the blacksmiths from flying sparks.

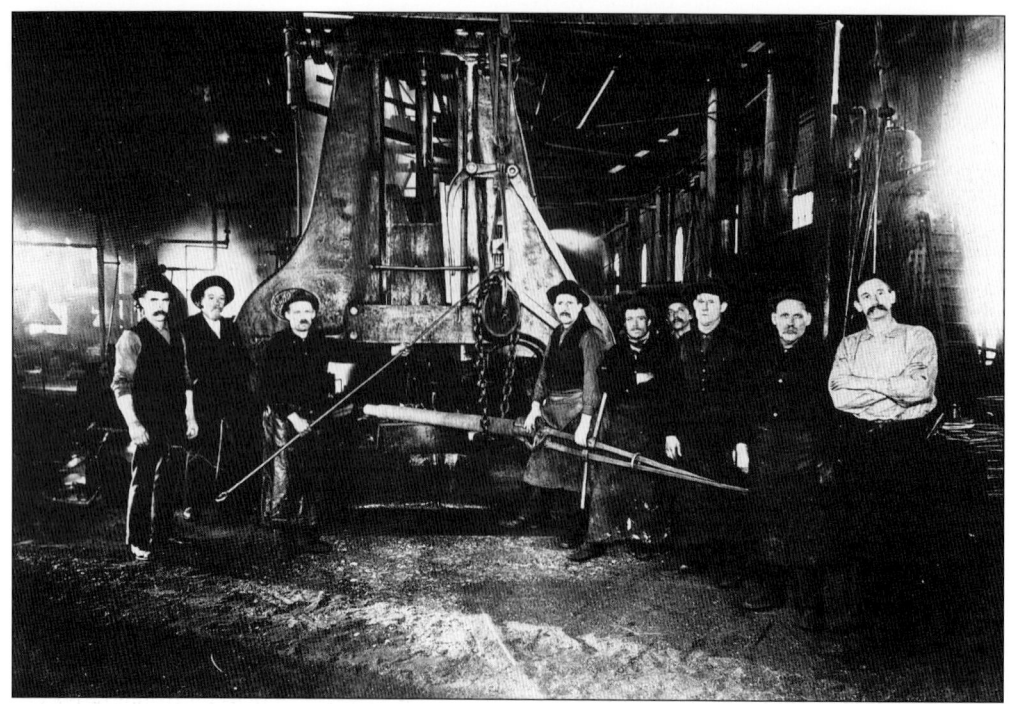

Pictured from left to right are Jack Hill, James Walker, Gus Kodler, John Altinger, Henry Stadler, Joe Kifowit, Ed Sweeney, Phil Heath, and William Mathews, all of whom were blacksmiths in the 1903 CB&Q blacksmith shops.

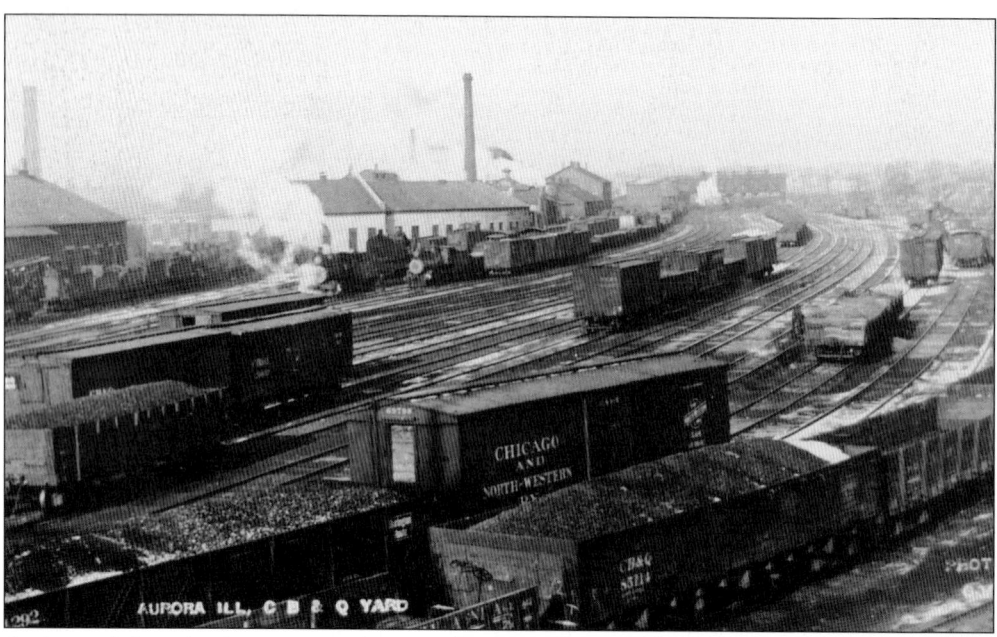

At its peak later in the century, the complete roundhouse complex covered 70 acres of land servicing more than 13,000 miles of track.

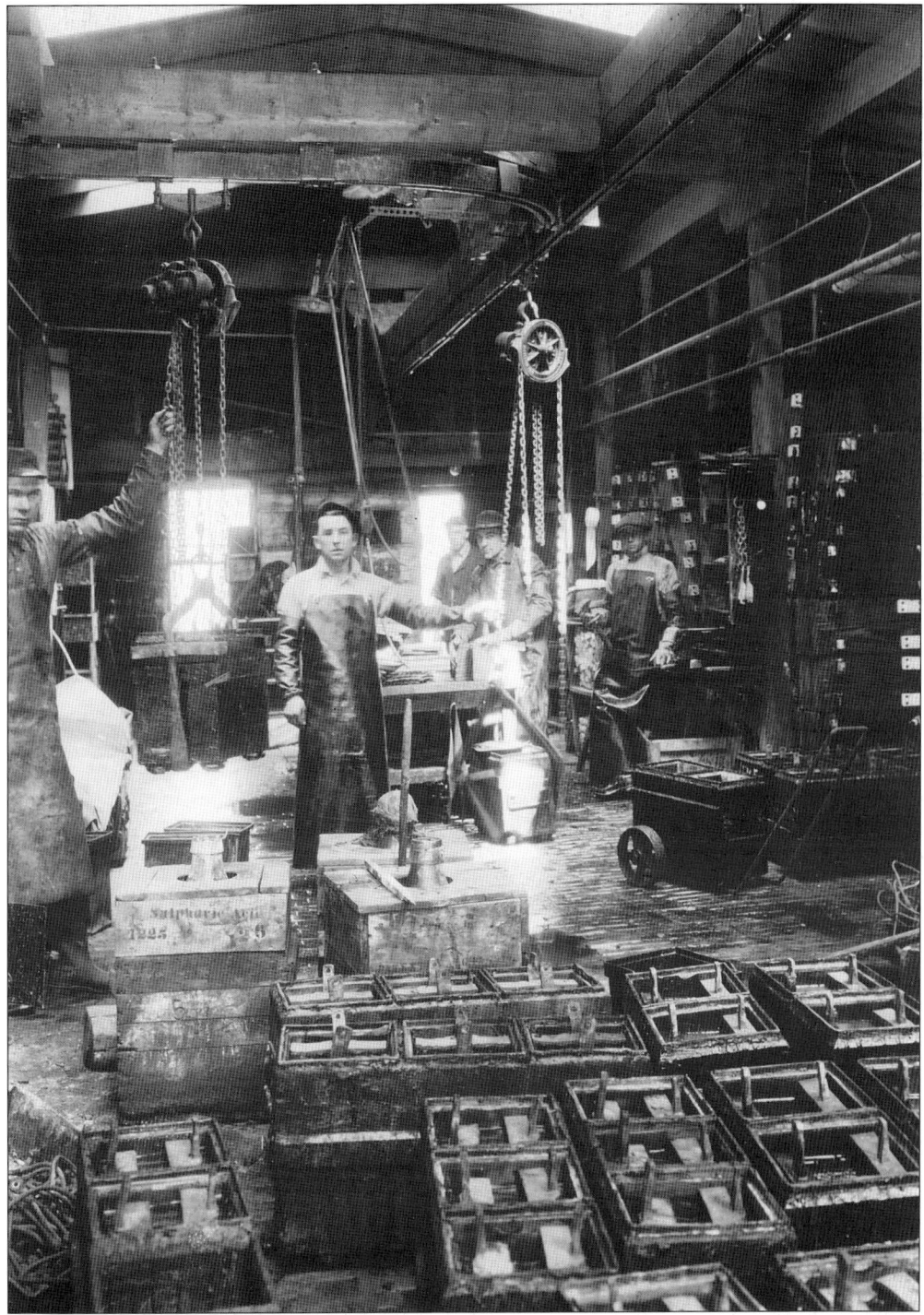

CB&Q was a major employer of mid- and late century immigrant craftsmen and laborers, first being the German, Irish, and French Canadians, and later the second wave of Luxemburgers, along with Swedes, Blacks, Romanians, and Mexicans. Early immigrants often lived on Broadway and Lincoln, near the shops.

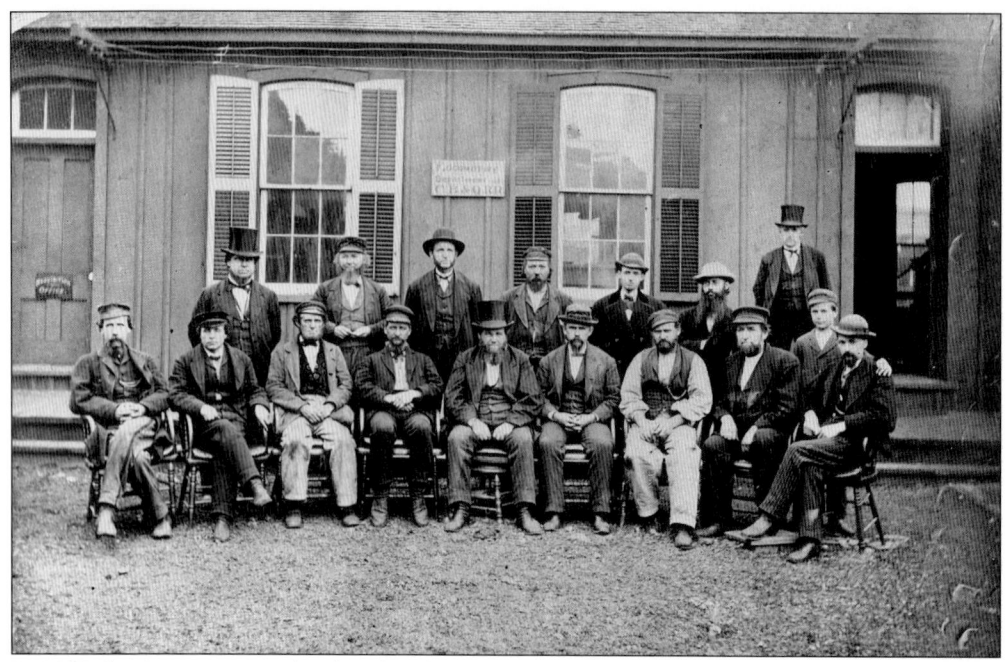

In 1877 there was a national railroad strike, although the railroad employees in Aurora remained on the job. During another national strike in 1888, the local trainmen joined the strike while the shop men remained on the job.

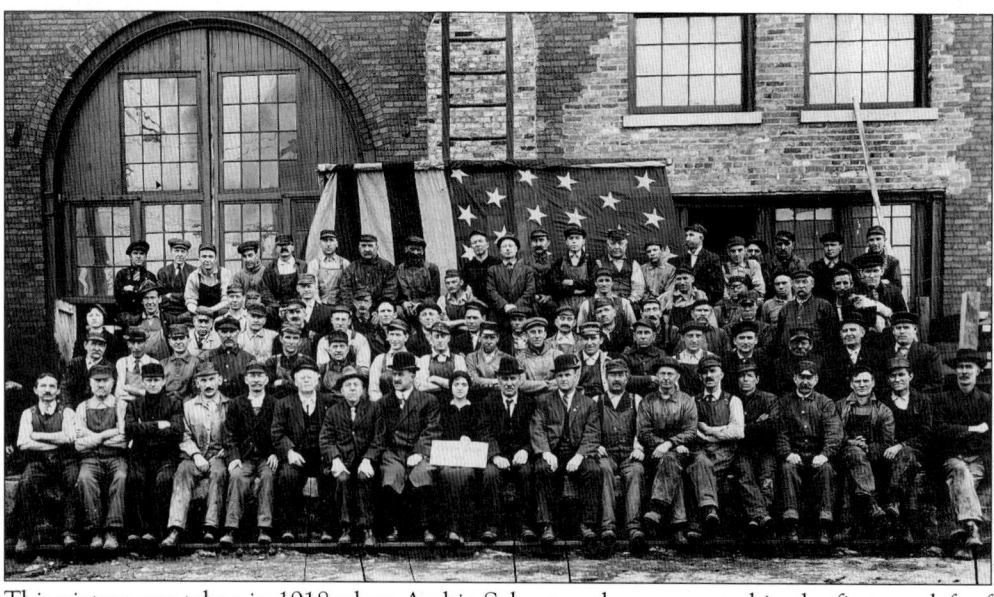

This picture was taken in 1918 when Archie Sylvester, the man seated in the first row left of the woman with a sign, quit the shops and moved to California. She is one of two women in the picture. The Aurora Historical Society has this picture with all except one person identified.

Three

LOTTIE DESCRIBES HER CITY

The following description of the city of Aurora in 1887 was written by Lottie Kellogg, a young Aurora Oak Street school girl who lived on the west side of Aurora. This account is a collector's treasure because such student accounts are rarely saved. Not many student papers today survive to the end of the semester, nor is it likely that they would still be around after 112 years.

This essay was written as a class project and placed in a leather bound volume, part of a continuing series, entitled in gold, *Aurora, Illinois, West Side Language, 1887*. There were 12 other accounts equally fascinating. The book also held descriptions of New York City, all carefully researched, as well as students' original short stories.

At some time in the past, the school district, probably in an effort to clean house or save space, discarded all the old volumes of students' works. This volume, picked up at a flea market, is all that remains to give us a very personal glimpse of the early days of West Aurora schools.

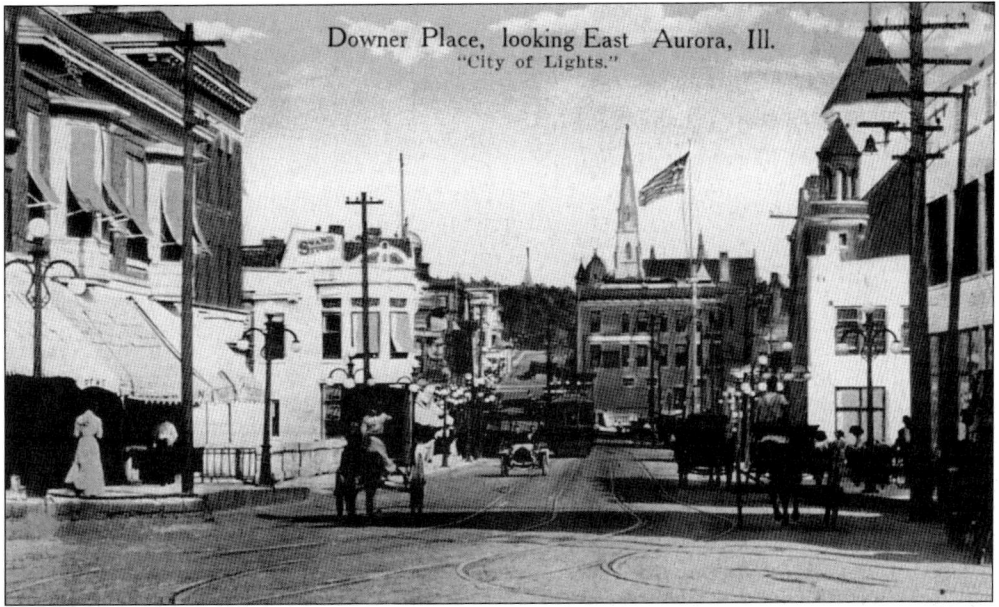

"Aurora is a flourishing city with a population of 20,000. Aurora is what we might term a manufacturing (sic) town. The largest of these manufactories are the C.B. and Q. car shops covering about 100 acres of land, and employing about 2,500 men. It is situated in the northeast part of the city."

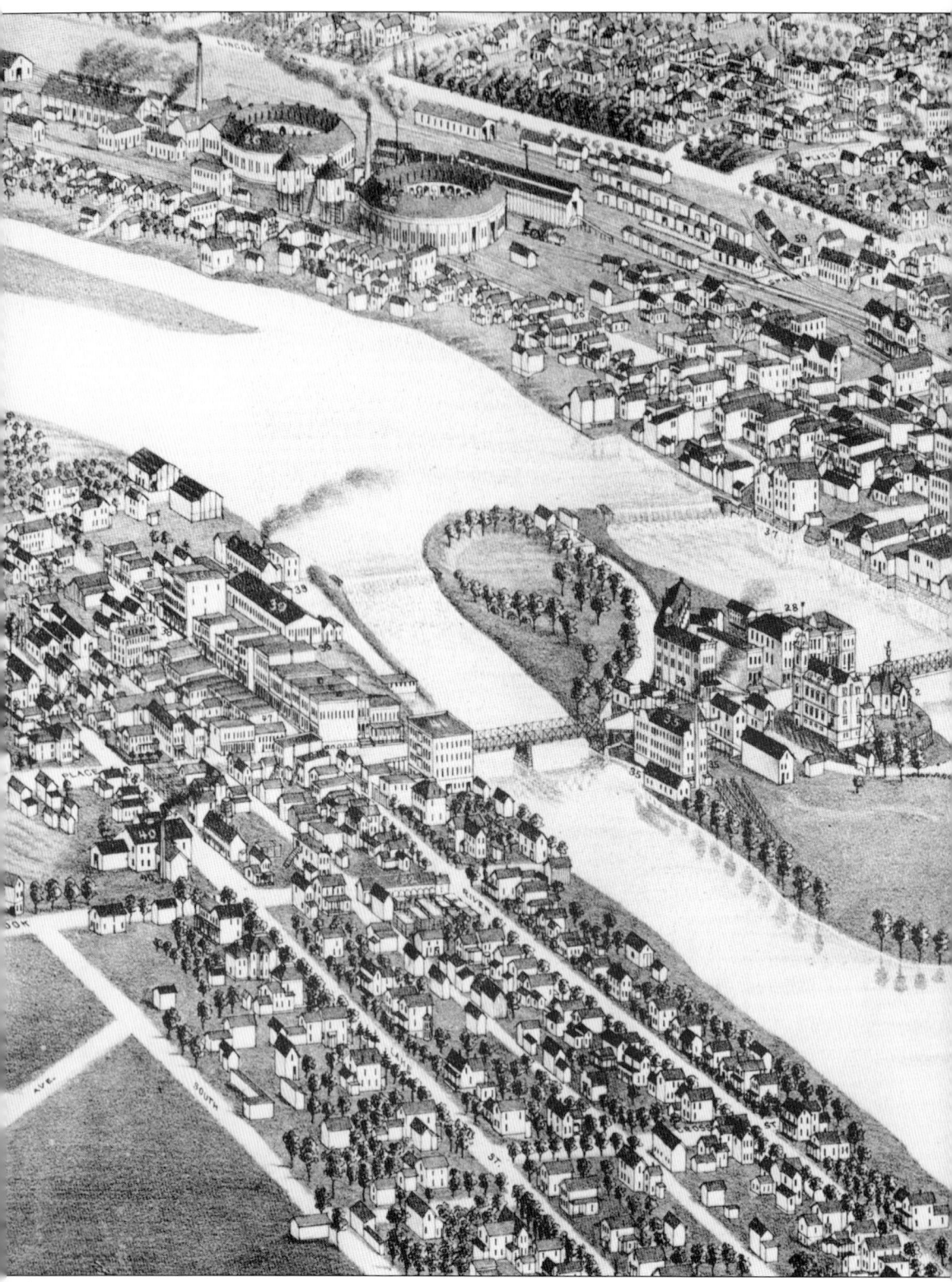

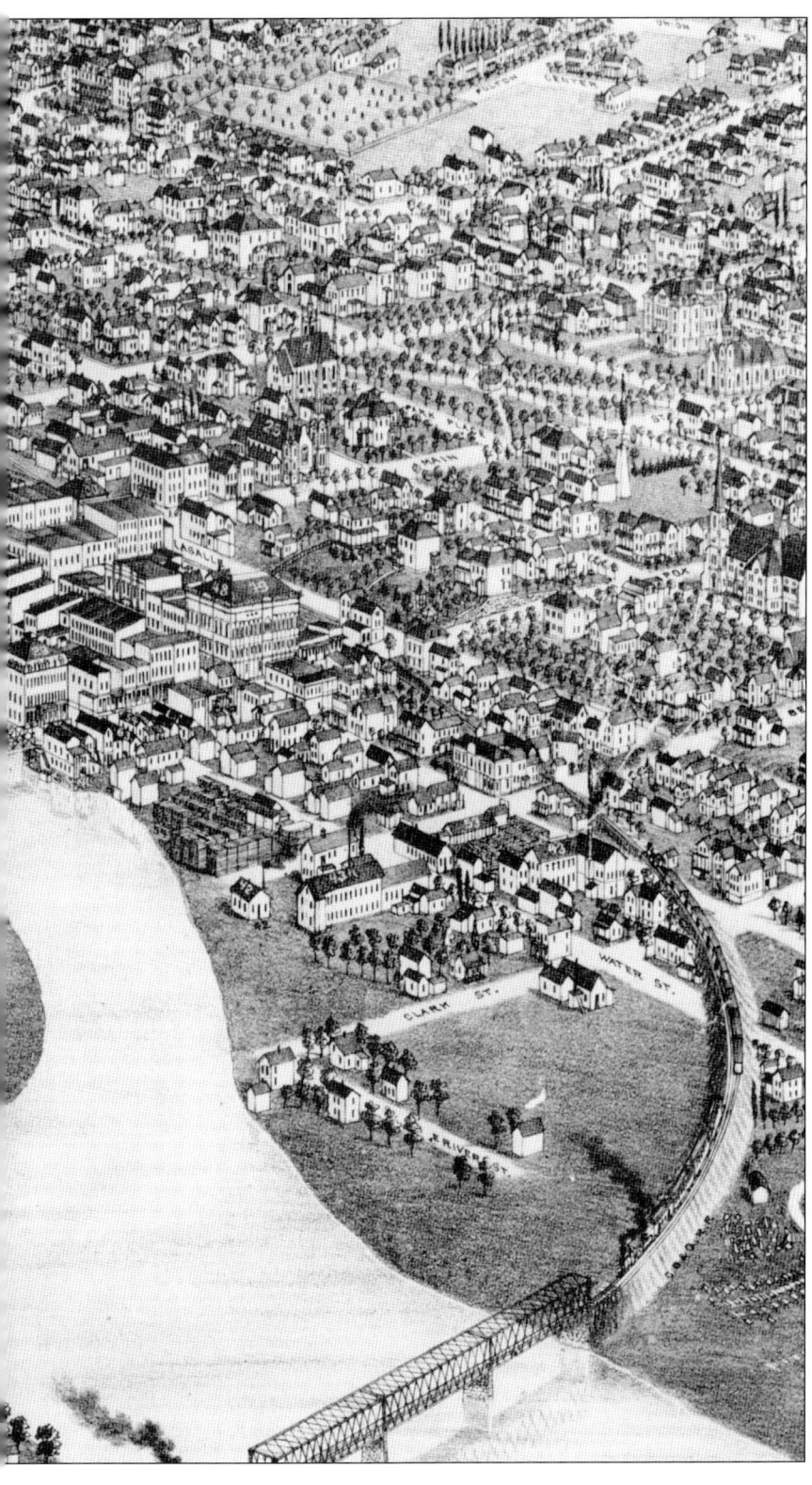

This drawing shows the city of Aurora at the approximate time of Lottie's essay.

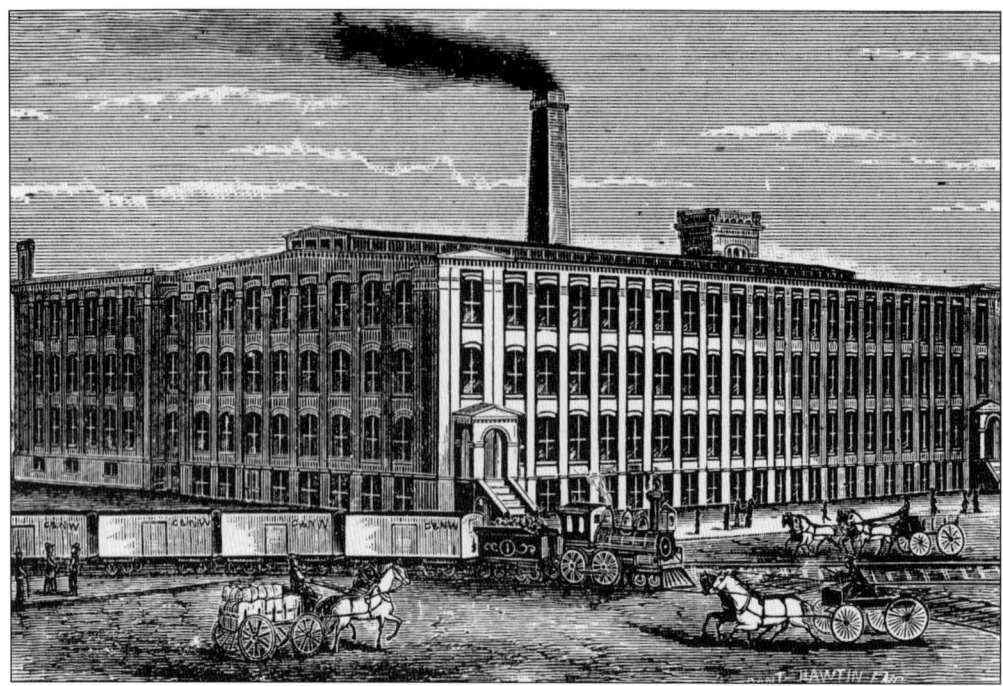

"The second of these manufactories is the large brick cotton mill near the west end of New York street bridge. It gives employment to about seven hundred men and women."

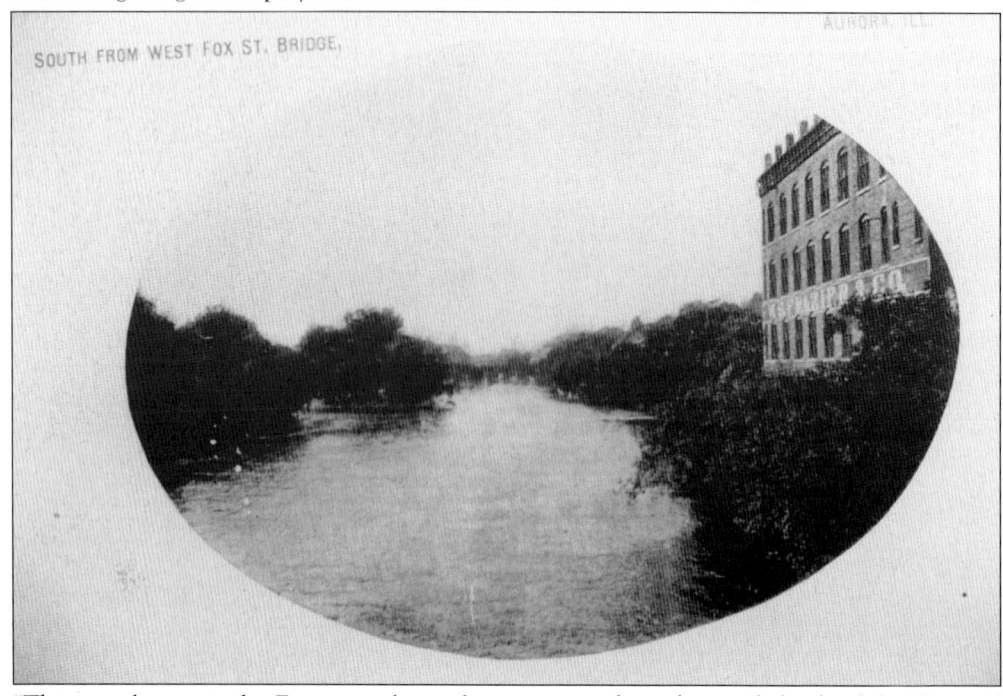

"The next largest is the Frazier road cart factory situated on the south bank of the Fox and at the west end of the Downer Place bridge. The next of importance is the Chicago Corset factory situated at the corner of Claim and Union Streets. It gives employment to about eight hundred girls."

"The next two of importance are the Silver Plate factory and the Watch factory. Both are doing a very large business. There are many smaller manufactories too numerous to mention."

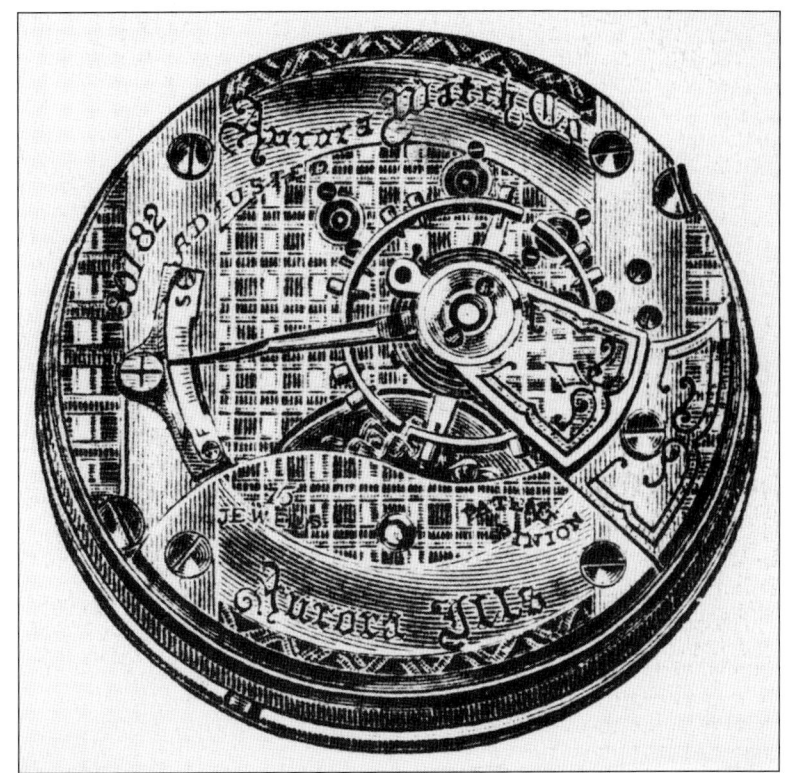

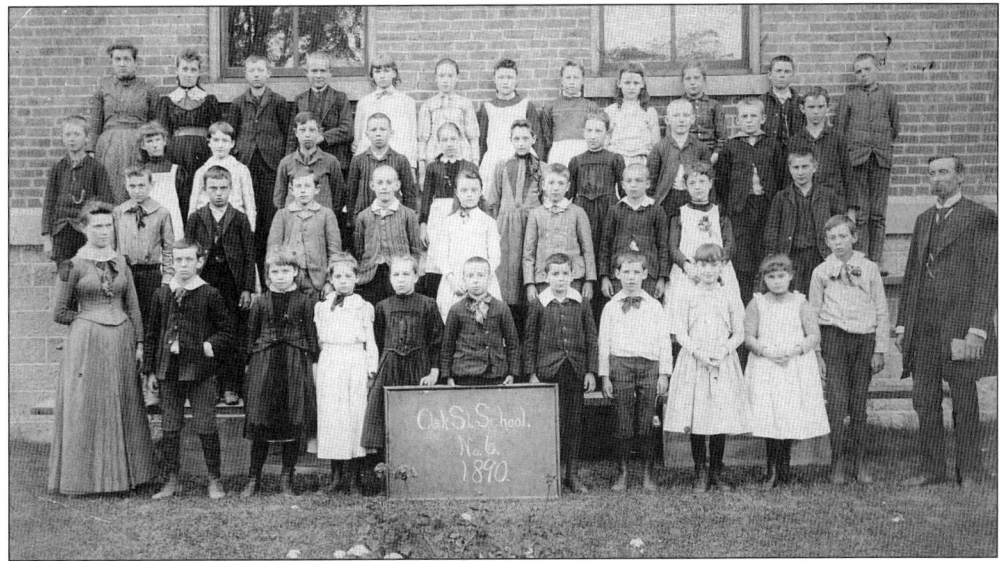

"Aurora is noted for its good schools. The largest is Jenning's Seminary a Methodist school. It is situated at the corner of Broadway and North Avenue. Mr. Robinson is the principal of the institution. The next largest is the Centre school situated at the corner of Main and Root Streets. There are two smaller public schools on the east side the Brady and the Young. The prettiest and the most expensive of the public schools is the Oak Street on the west side. About six hundred pupils are now attending school here. Mr. Chas. Riley is the principal. A smaller branch of the Oak Street will be found on South Lake Street."

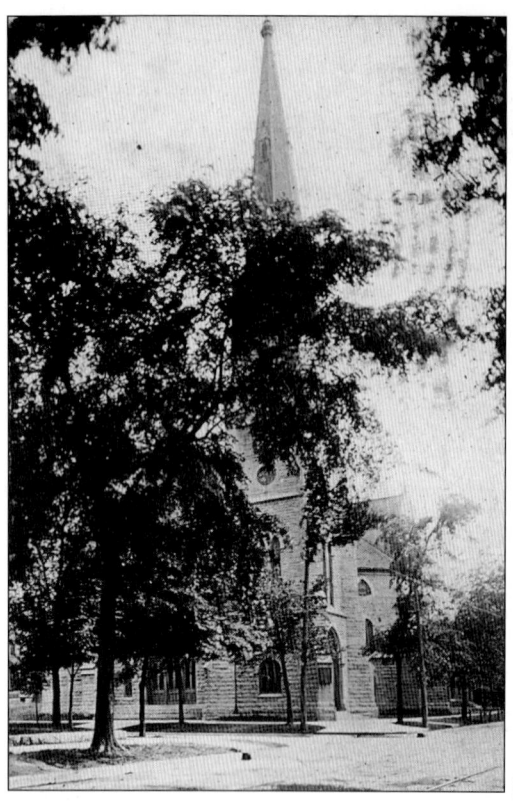

"Aurora has many fine churches, among the largest are the German Catholic, St. Mary's, the Methodist Episcopal and Park Place Baptist on the east side, the Methodist Episcopal and First Baptist are the largest on the west side." (Pictured is the Methodist Episcopal Church.)

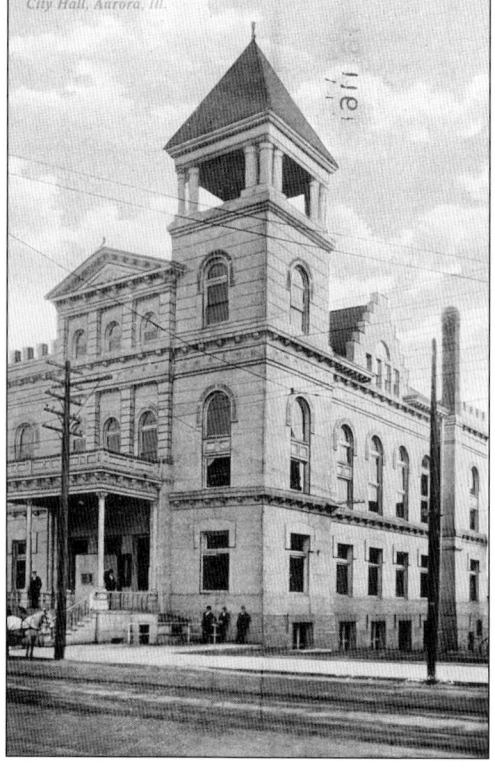

"The largest of the Public Buildings is the stone Court House situated on the Island. In this building you will find the City Hall, post office, Jail and City Clerks office. Music Hall is the small building situated on Broadway."

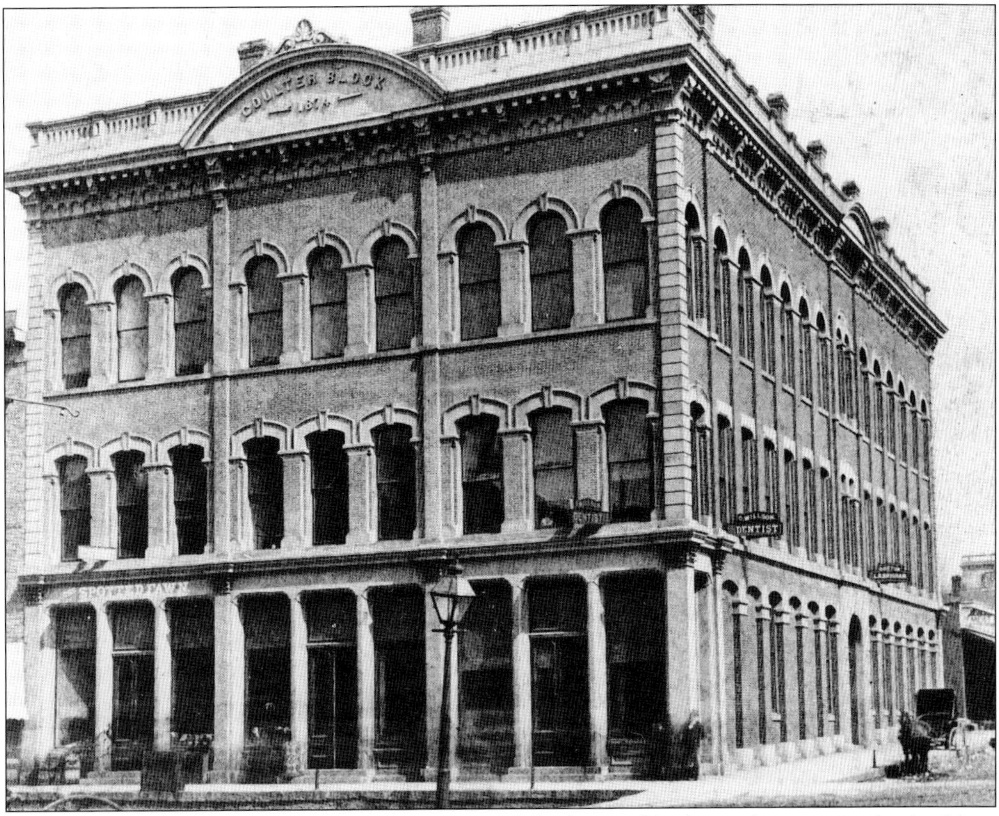

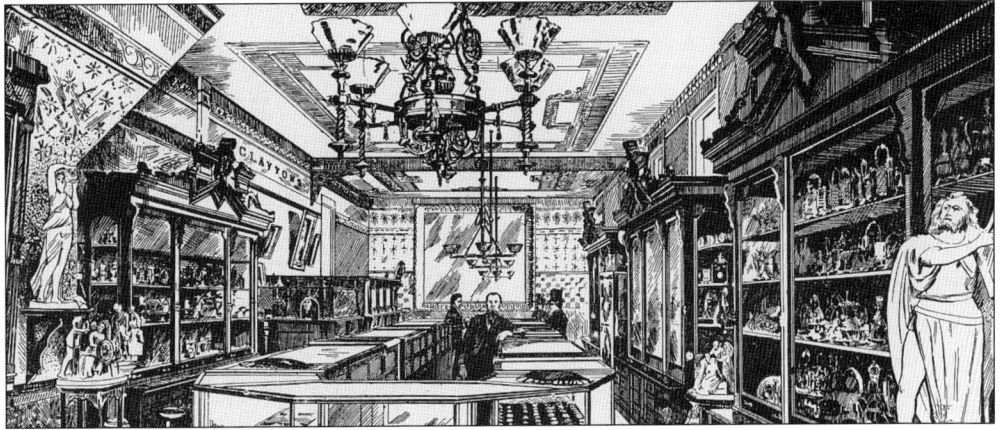

"Coulter block, owned by Mrs. Coulter, is one of the largest blocks in the city. In this building we will find the opera, 2nd National Bank and many small offices."

"Among the largest dry goods houses we will find Geo. Wilcoxes, McMillian, Scott and Pease, and E.W. Gilbert's on the west side. S.S. Sencenbaugh's, Sawyer's, A.K. Perry's and Ira J Wilcox of the east side. Among the grocery stores of the east side Roystin Bros. are carrying on the largest trade. Titus and Marshall are also carrying on a large business on the east side. E.W. Trask and O.S. Clayton both have large jewelry stores. O.S. Clayton also deals in wall paper. Mr. T.O. Fiske is a dealer in granite and marble monuments. There are two express offices here, the American and the United States. The former is the largest." (Pictured is an interior view of O.S. Cayton & Sons, Jewelers and Decorative Arts.)

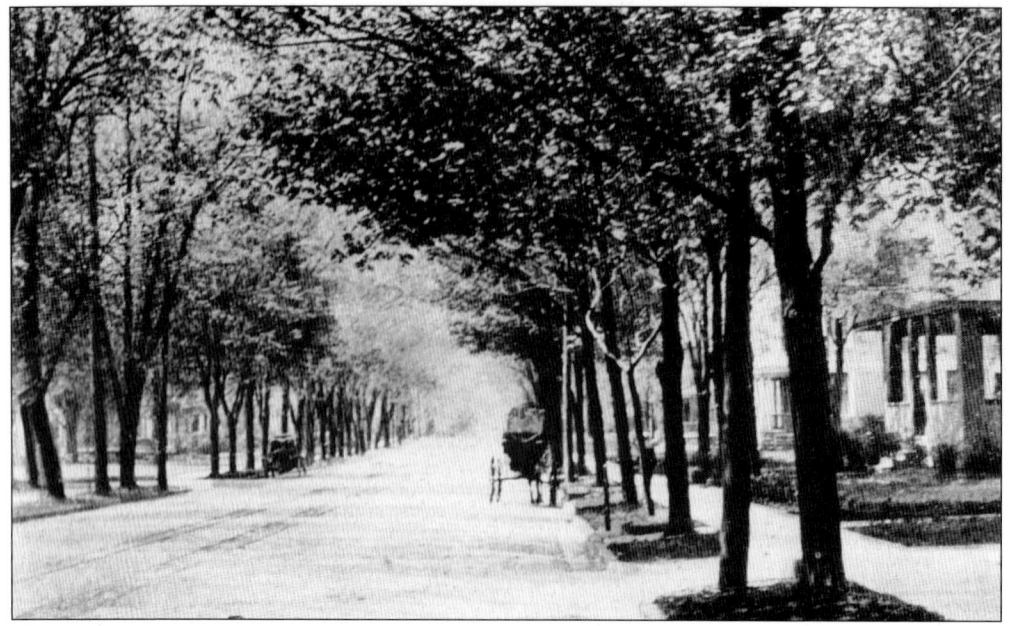

"Aurora has many pretty cemeteries. Spring Lake is the largest and is on the southern part of the city. The west side cemetery is the next in size. It is situated in the northern part of the city. Olivet, German Catholic are small cemeteries. There is a potters field on the east side. Aurora has very many pleasant streets. Among the prettiest are Downer Place, Lake, Lincoln Ave. and Galena." (Downer Place is pictured.)

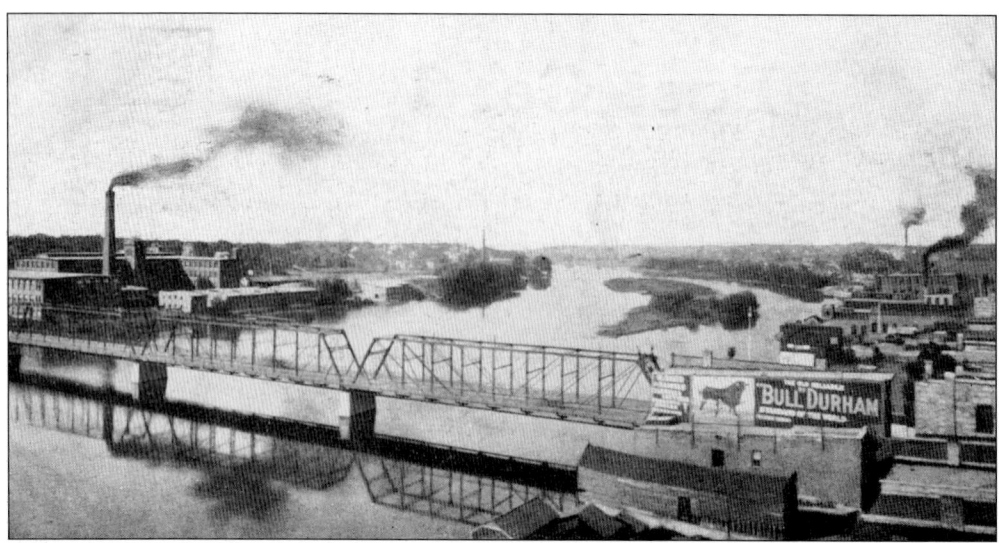

"The business streets are Fox, Broadway, Main and part of River St. There are four bridges crossing the river besides the railroad bridges. There is quite a large stone quarry on South Water Street, furnishing stone for city purposes, and also the adjoining city's."

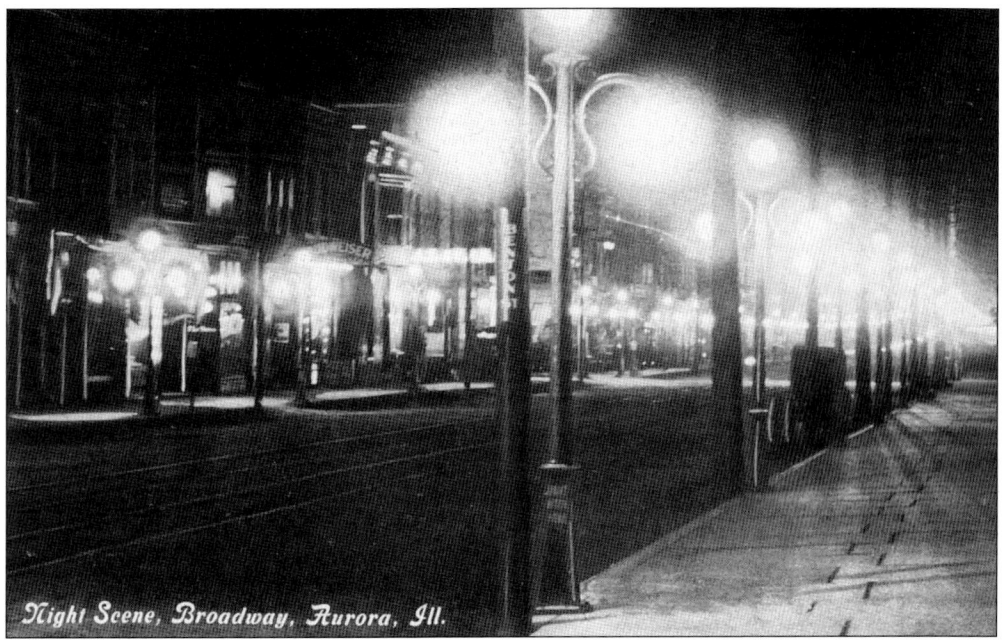

"Aurora is well lighted on dark evenings by seventy electric lights."

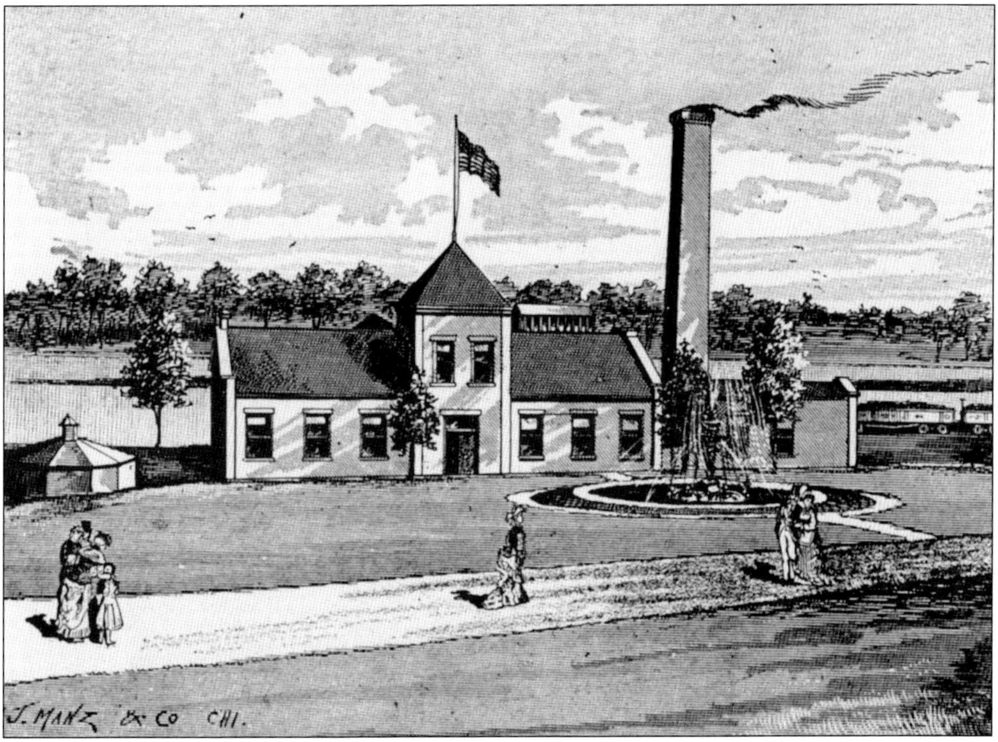

"The city is also furnished with water from the water works, situated about a mile north of the Court House on Lincoln Avenue."

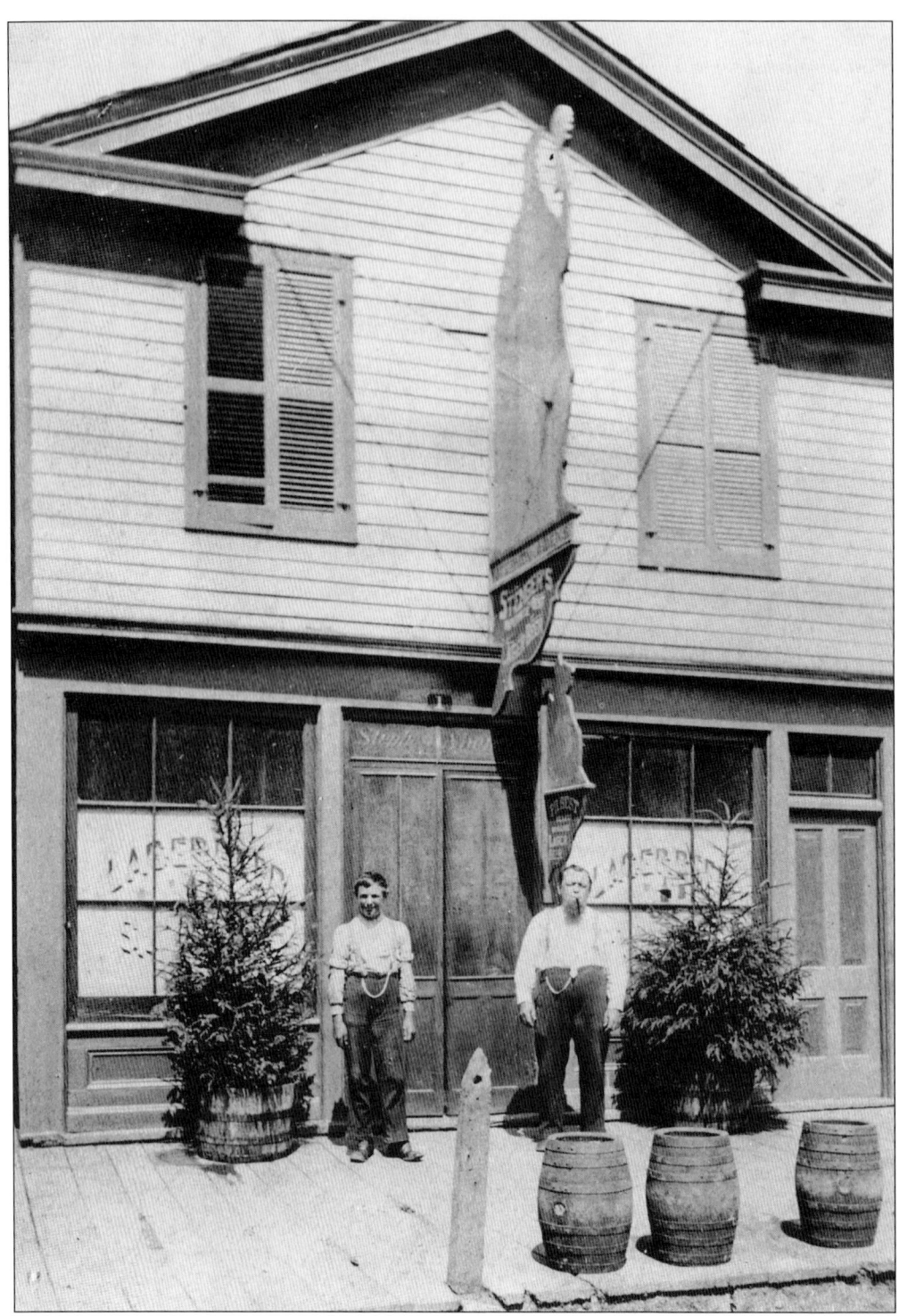

"The city also boasts of a fine patrol wagon and with the thirty saloons doing their terrible work it is kept quite busy. Aurora has just had a new fire alarm system put up but it hasn't learned to control it yet."

"Among the prominent citizens and most wealthiest we will find Mr. Fridley (pictured), Mr. Stolp, and Mrs. Coulter, also many others too numerous to mention."

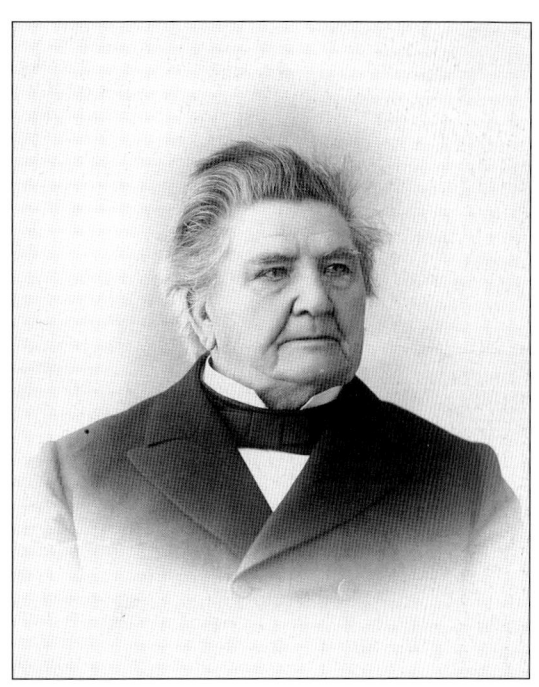

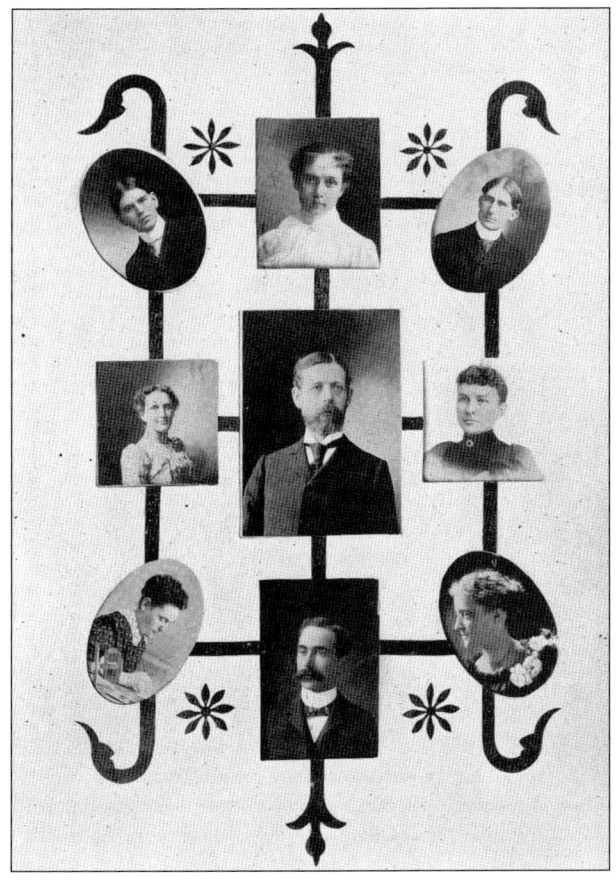

Katherine H. Reynolds was the teacher who assigned this essay to her class. In the next school year, 1887–1888 she was made principal of West Aurora High School where she was also an instructor in Latin. Miss Reynolds is pictured to the left of the gentleman in the center.

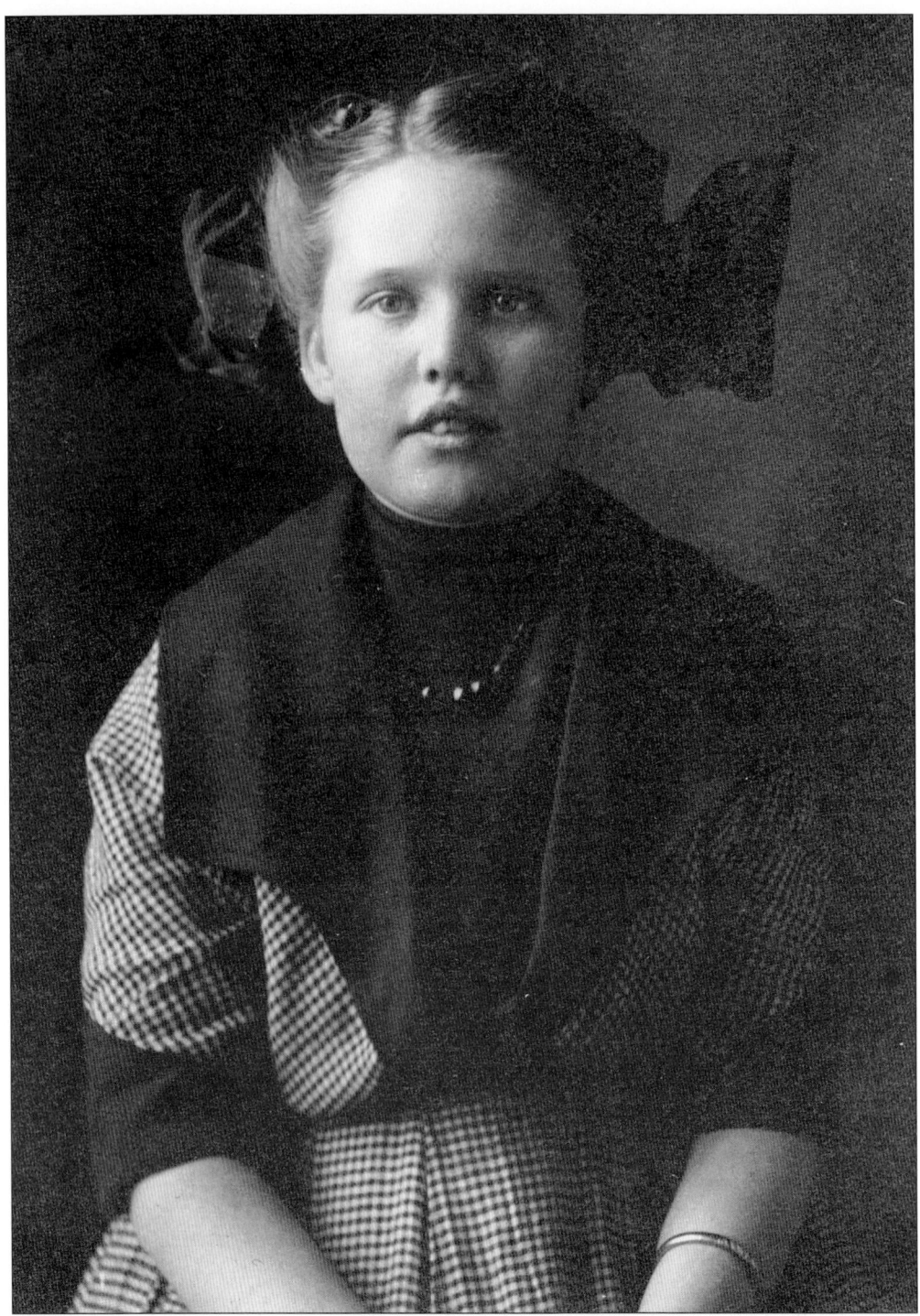

Lottie Kellogg was one of 13 students in Miss Kittie Reynolds's class. Students ranged in age from 12 years and 9 months to 17 years and 3 months. Eleven were girls. This photograph is not Lottie but it is as close as one can get. This is a picture of a young girl, of the approximate age and time of Lottie, from Aurora.

Four
WAGONS, CORSETS, AND HEAVY MACHINERY

While the nation celebrated and entered its second century with a stupendous, scientifically focused centennial exposition in Philadelphia, the sounds of industry were ringing loud in Aurora, Illinois. One of Aurora's largest industries, Love Brothers Foundry, was born, and immigrants were pouring into the city in ever-greater numbers to man new and expanding factories. The factories of the new century became assembly lines of endless products with a work force that required less time to train to do their part of the job. The products of many manufacturers were capital goods, machines used to make other products or do other services. In any case, whether an Aurora factory was cranking out road equipment or making a watch, each product or service contributed to the new age that ushered the United States into the forefront of world economic greatness.

On the national scene, as America expanded and got Teddy's canal built in Panama, Aurora was there supplying essential conveyor machines to move the mountains of rock and soil. As women around the world dressed in the latest gowns, Aurora was there with mountains of corsets to make the fashion possible.

Companies owed their success to the wheeler-dealer spirit of the companies' founders such as Love, Chapman, and Barber and their hard-working employees.

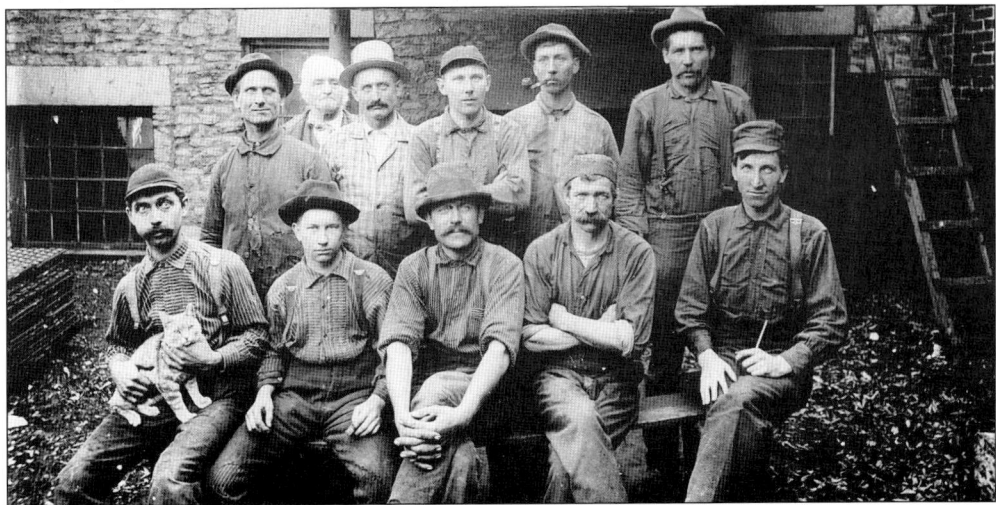

Workers at Hoyt's American Woodworking Machine Company in 1897 are listed from left to right as follows: (front row) Ed Adair, unidentified, Emil Borg, Frank Voght, and Ben Skeen; (back row) Anton Burg, two unidentified, Carl Peterson, and two unidentified.

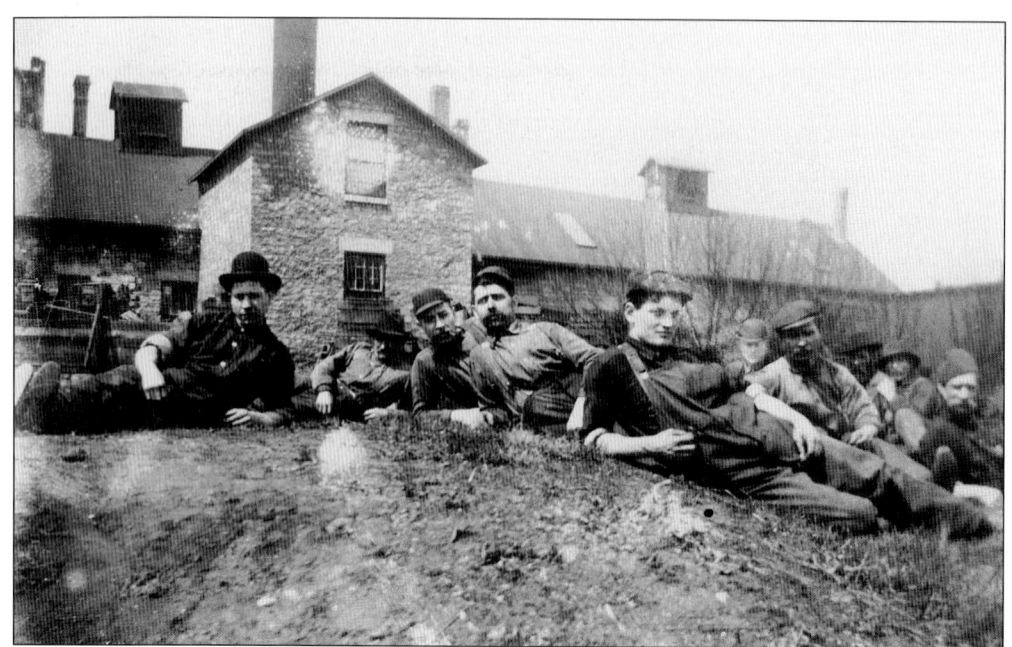

The Hoyt family began business in Aurora in 1842 with a flouring mill, continued with a planing mill, and later established the American Woodworking Machine Company. Here workers from the American Woodworking Machine Company enjoy a break in their work day.

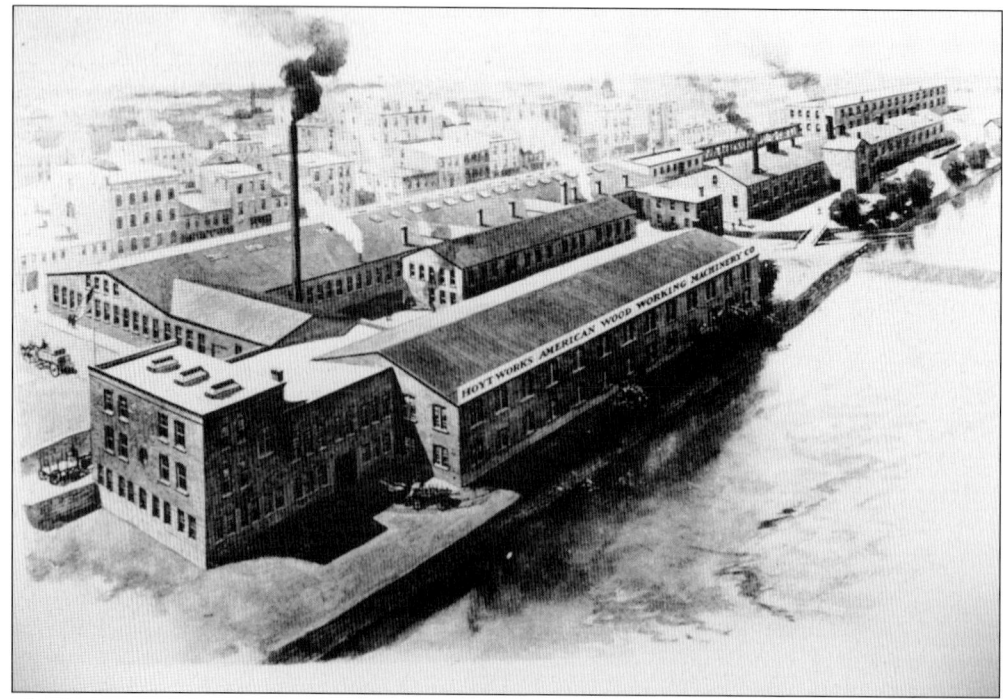

The Hoyt Works/American Woodworking Machine foundry was located on the banks of the Fox River between Downer and New York Streets. The Galena Bridge had not yet been built. River water was the main source of power for many years.

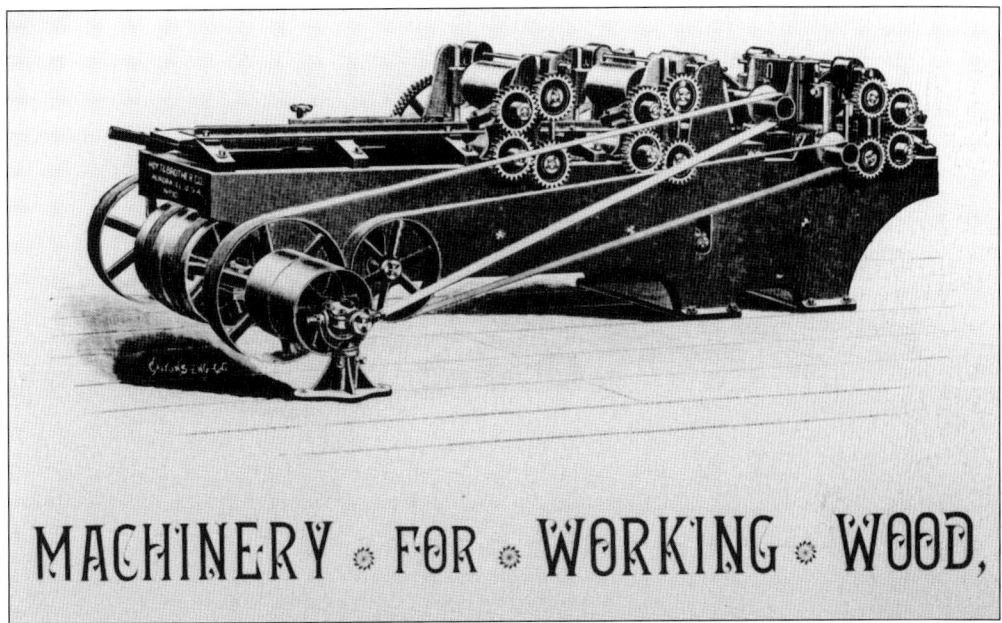

This drawing is of one of the machines produced for either a furniture maker, an agricultural implement producer, or another type of woodworking factory.

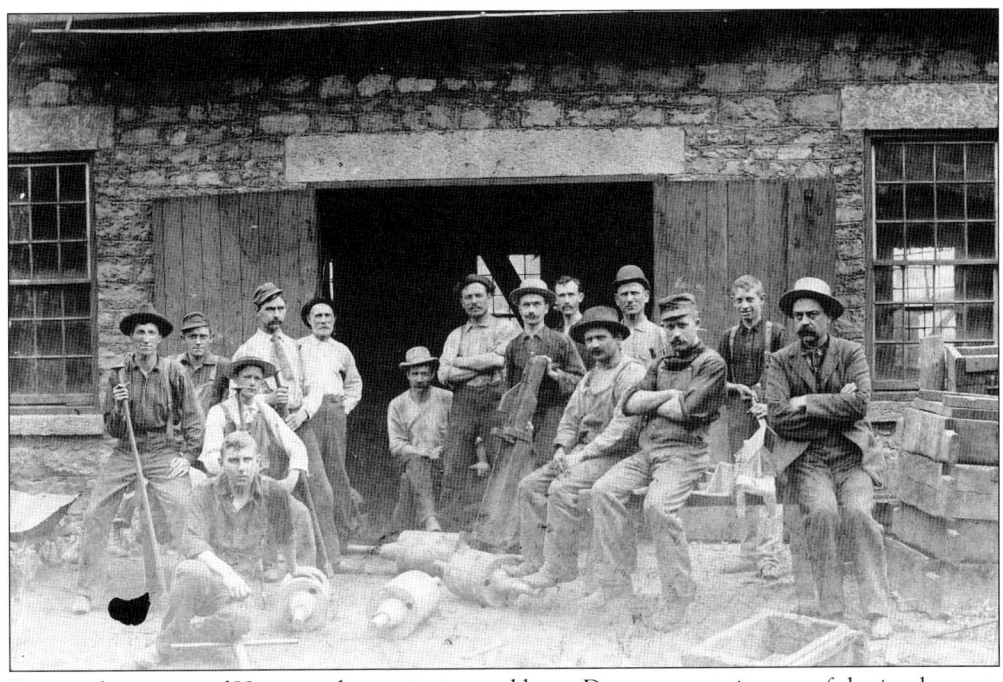

Yet another group of Hoyt employees is pictured here. Do you recognize any of the implements some of them are holding? The stone work in the building was probably quarried nearby.

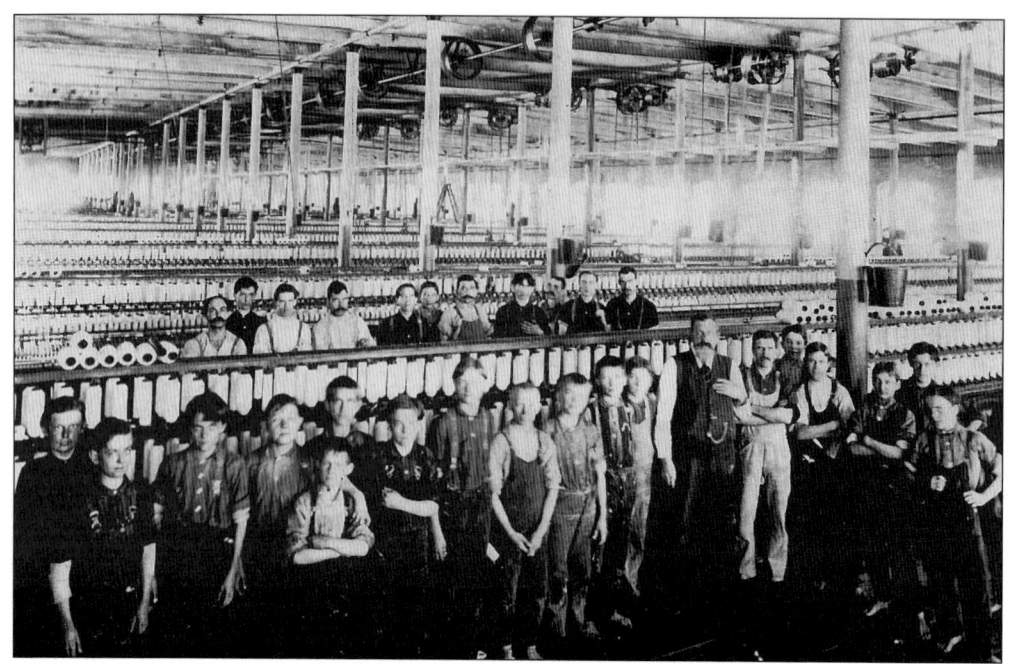

Hobbs built a cotton-batting factory that was destroyed by fire in 1881. The following year the owners organized and built the Aurora Cotton Mill. It had 6 acres of floor space in four stories with more than five hundred looms and 20,000 spindles. By 1908 the factory employed some four hundred boys, men, and women and had doubled the capacity of its mills.

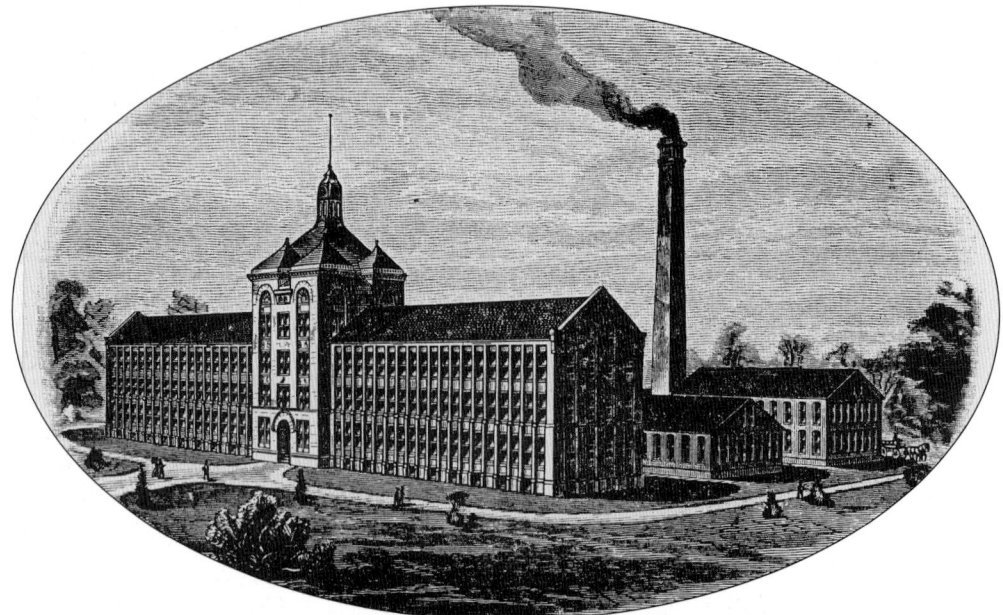

The Aurora watches, which had good reputations as timekeepers, were made in various grades, and fit Elgin-style cases. The Aurora Watch Company was making one hundred watches a day with two hundred employees in 1888. This business began in 1883 in Chicago but was moved to Aurora in 1885. The company was reorganized several times and finally taken over by the Hamilton Watch Company.

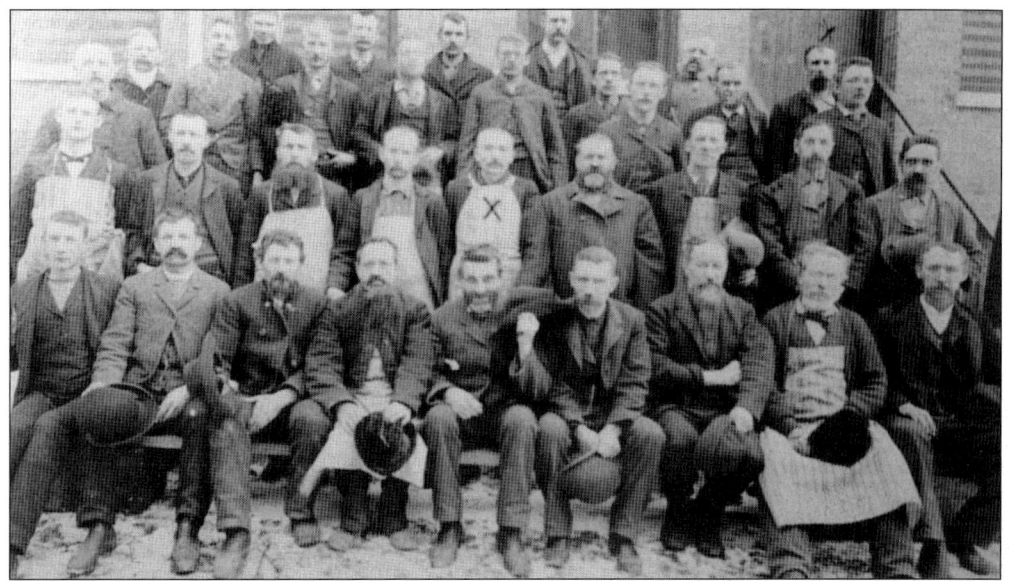

Frazier carts and buggies were sold all around the country and were advertised in *Harper's Weekly*. The two Frazier buildings are still in downtown Aurora located on River Street.

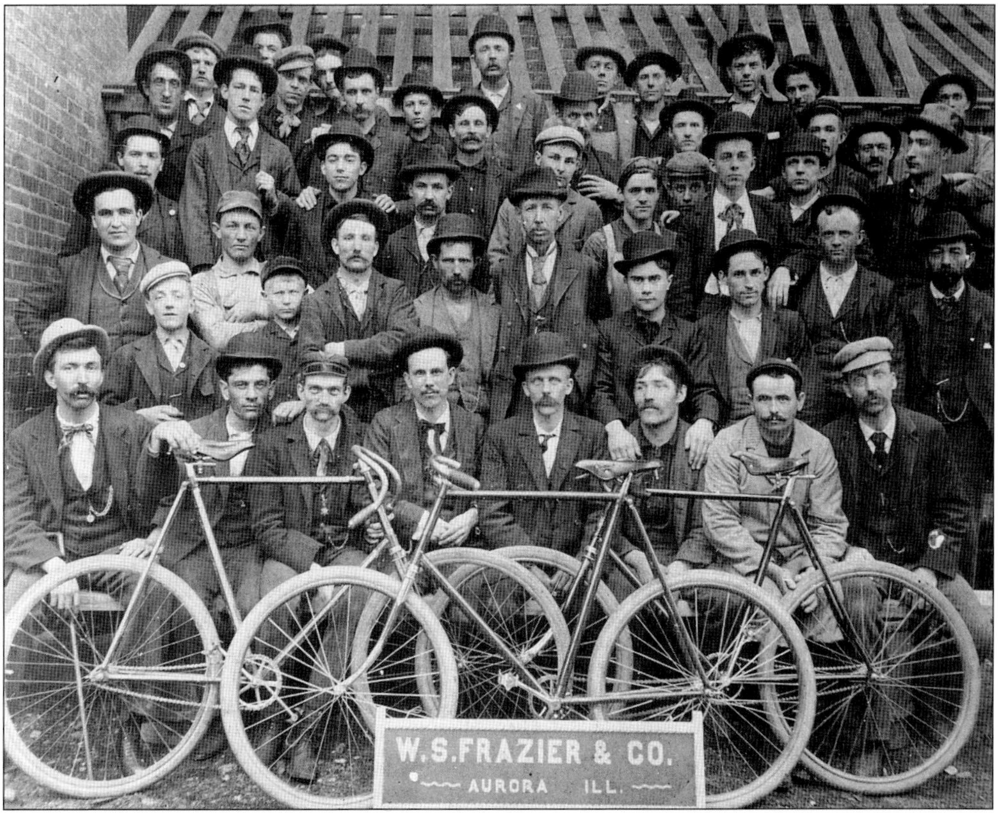

W.S. Frazier & Company made buggies, racing sulkies, and bicycles. This picture features the workers and their bicycles. Bicycles were all the rage for the well-to-do class of people in the 1890s.

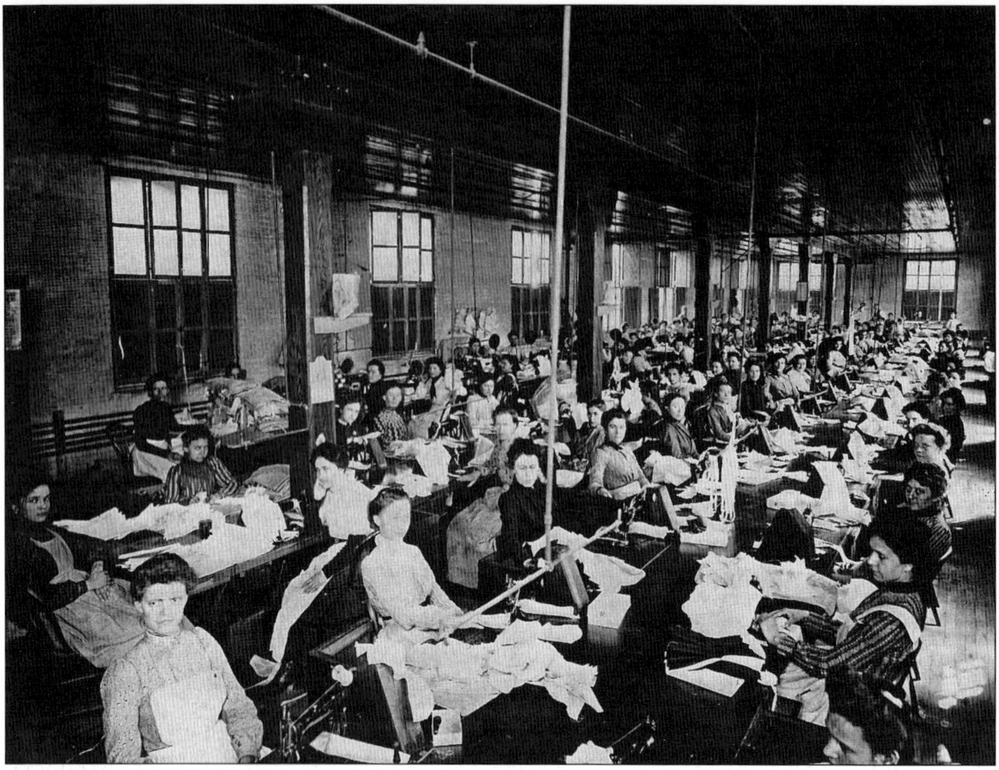

The Aurora Corset Factory, founded in 1895, employed girls to make the corsets stiffened with whalebone in order for women to have an hourglass figure. It manufactured a complete line of figure-molding garments under the trade name Henderson.

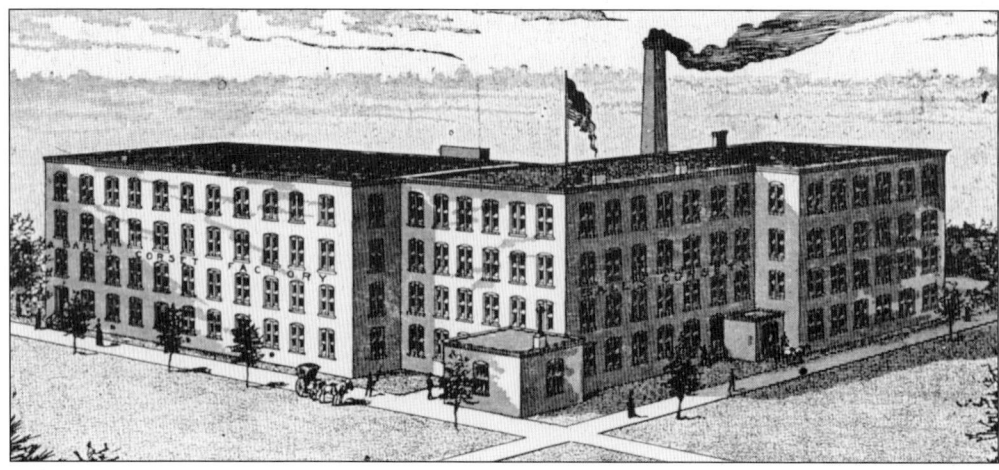

Ball's Corset Factory was the second largest corset works in the world. The Aurora factory was started in 1883 and began production with two hundred employees. At its peak, six hundred employees, mostly girls, worked there and produced nearly 2 million corsets annually.

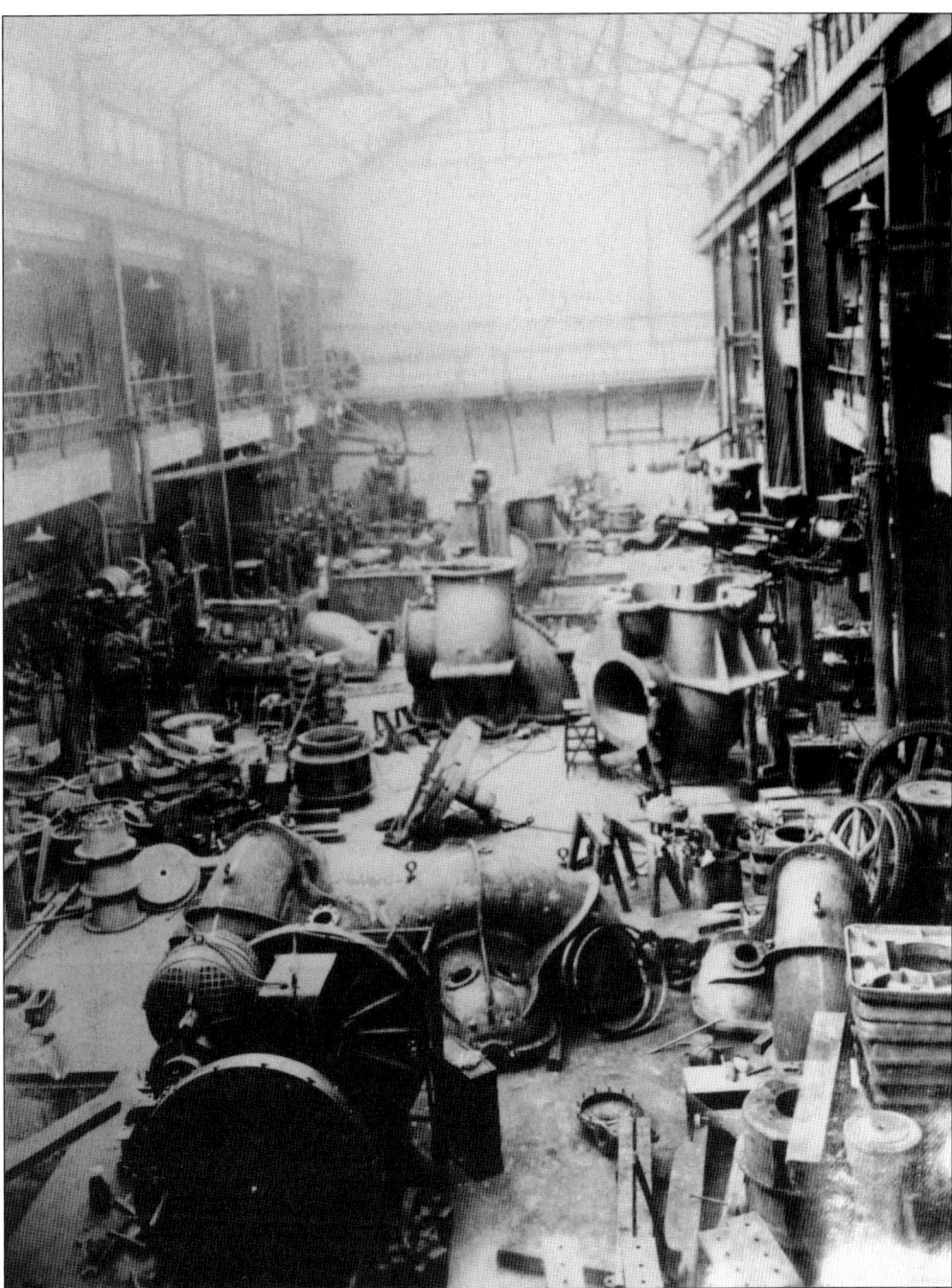

As the American pioneers spilled over into the last frontier, the prairies there developed a huge demand for well-pumping windmill heads and fittings for drilling shallow wells. In the cities, the demand was for deep well equipment. American Well Works made it all. In 1890, they became the world's largest manufacturers of well-sinking machinery in the U.S. From this photograph, they do not seem to be mass-producing parts yet. Some of the custom fittings shown in this view were as tall as 20 feet. These components were used as deep-well casings by cities and large factories. The factory seems to be lit both by electricity and by natural light.

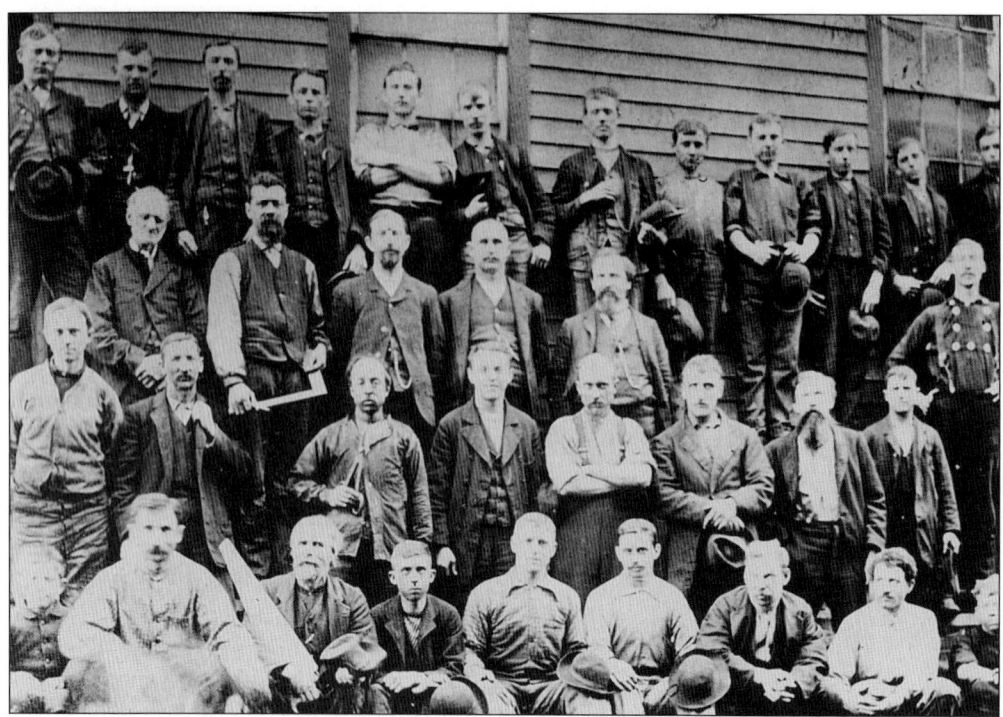

This 1878 group of men, both common laborers and foremen, younger and older, inexperienced and experienced, blue and white collar, worked side by side as a team. Several men are holding the tools of their trade.

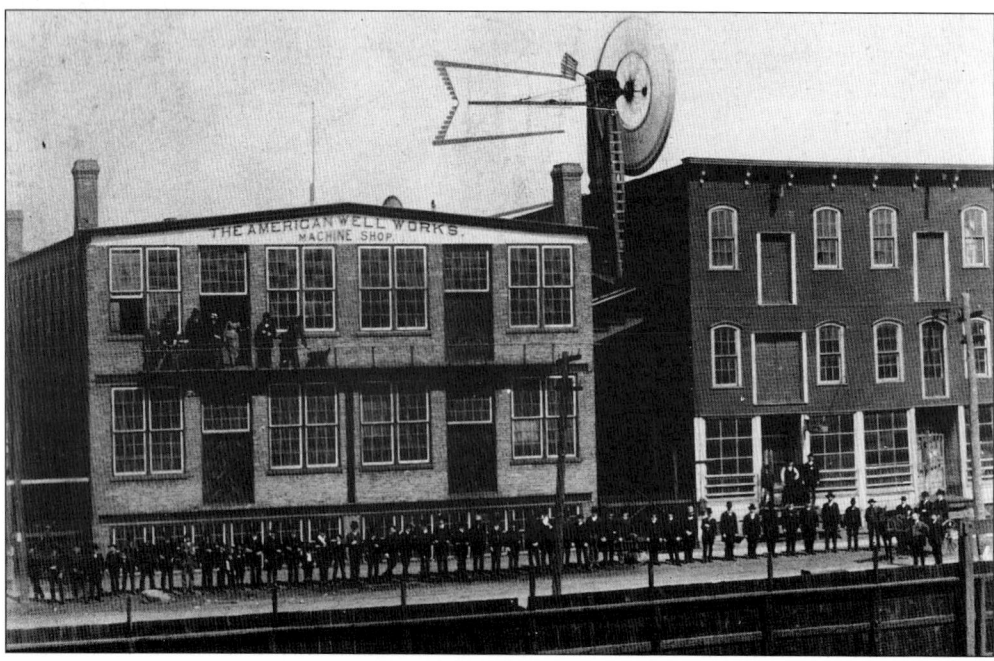

Here the workers are lined-up outside a plant that has a windmill on top. The well works was using its own windmills to drive machinery in the pattern shops and machine shops. American Well Works products were patented as the "American" line of deep-well machinery.

This ad for a pumping windmill head appeared in the 1872 city directory. Great Western Manufacturing Co. on N. Broadway was run by the Chapman Brothers. They did a general business in brass and iron turning and gas fittings.

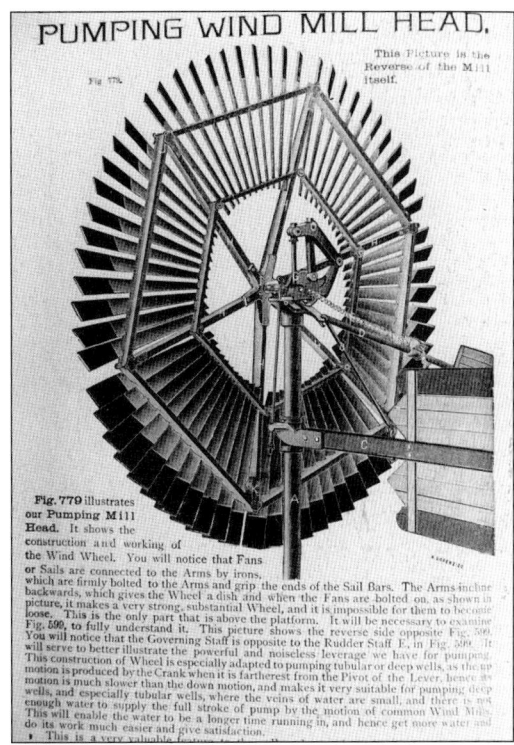

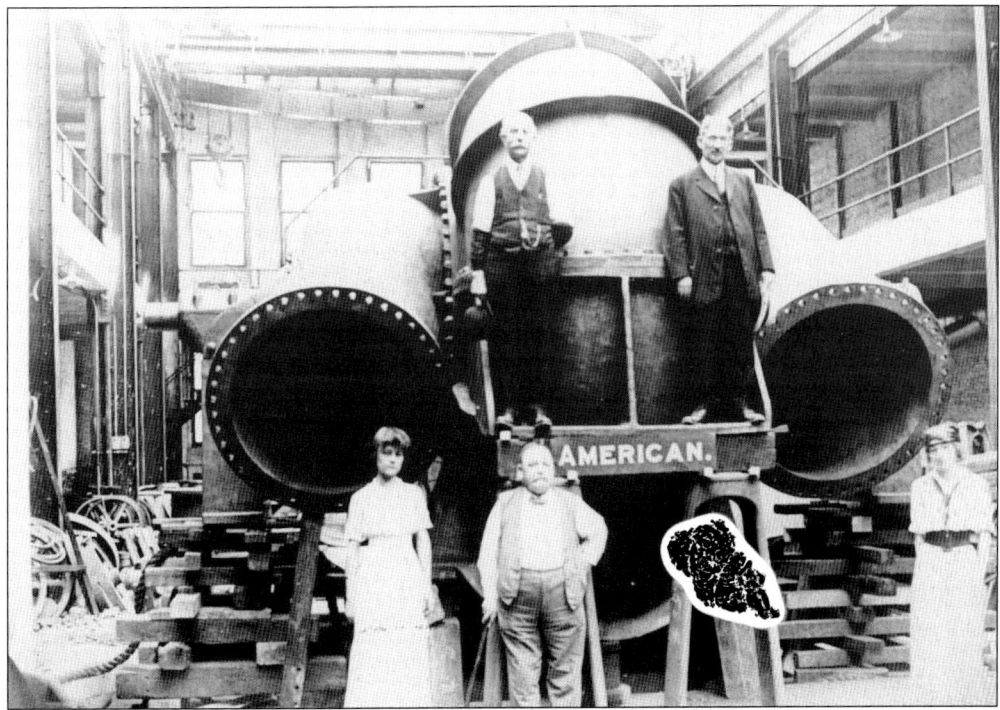

Here, on and in front of one of the parts they have made are (center bottom) Matthew Chapman, (above him) Mark Chapman, and John Sears. The unnamed women may have been secretaries.

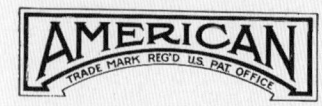
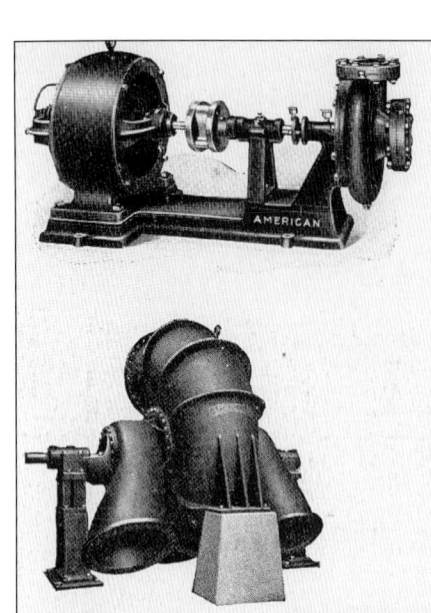
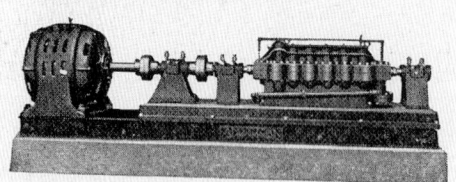
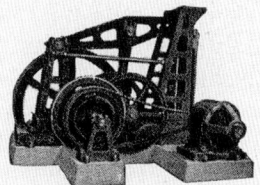

The *"American"* Line of Centrifugal and Deep Well Pumping Machinery Gives Satisfaction Wherever Used

Manufactured in a large variety of styles and sizes to suit a variety of purposes.

The American Well Works
AURORA ... ILLINOIS

This ad from Aurora East High School 1918 yearbook shows the American line of centrifugal and deep well pumping machinery.

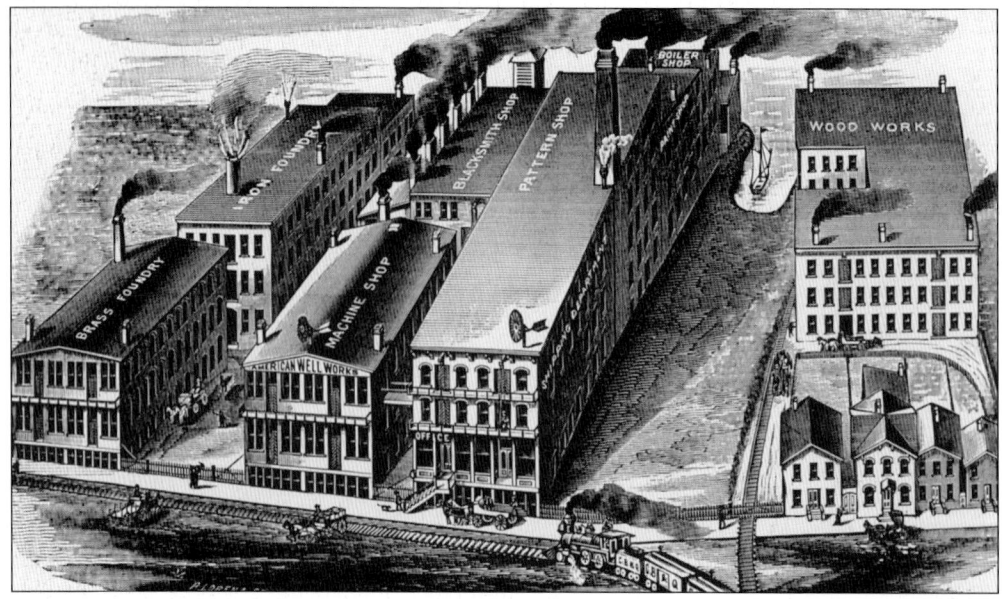

Here is a drawing of the American Well Works factories located at 92-126 N. Broadway. The company was founded in 1869 and enjoyed an international business. The factory covered 75,000 square feet and employed 150 to 170 men.

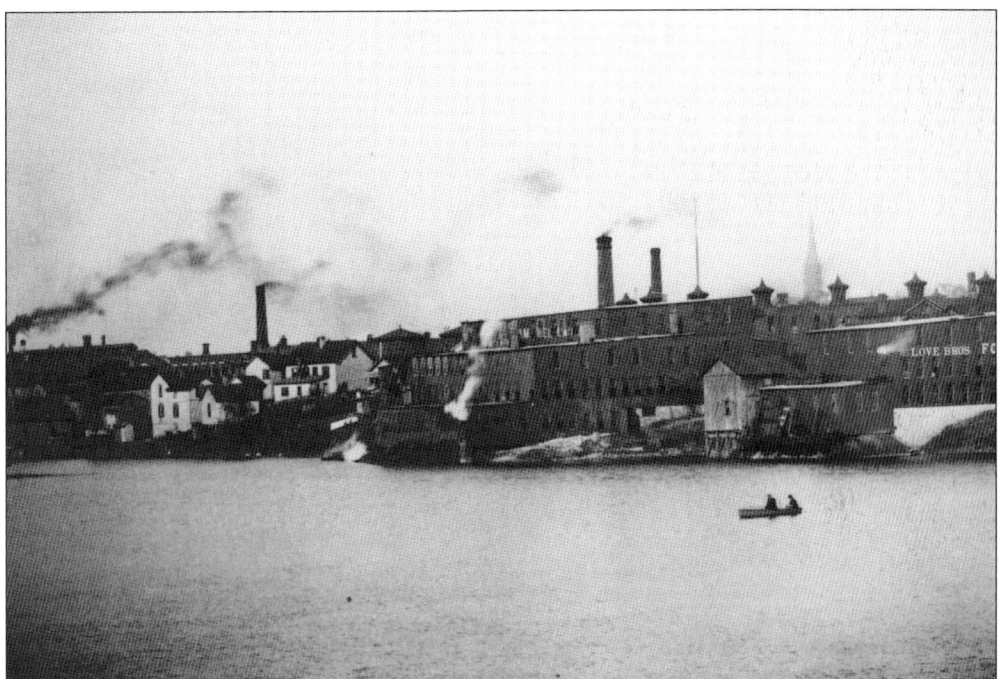

Love Brothers Foundry was, for many years, one of Aurora's largest industries. It was founded by two brothers, Joy and John P. Love, in 1876. Their first foundry was in a little building on Pierce Street. The little foundry soon grew to such proportions that in 1882 it was moved to Clark and Water Streets where, under the name of Love Brothers and Company, it developed into the largest industry of its kind in the city. Love Brothers and Company is shown at the far right.

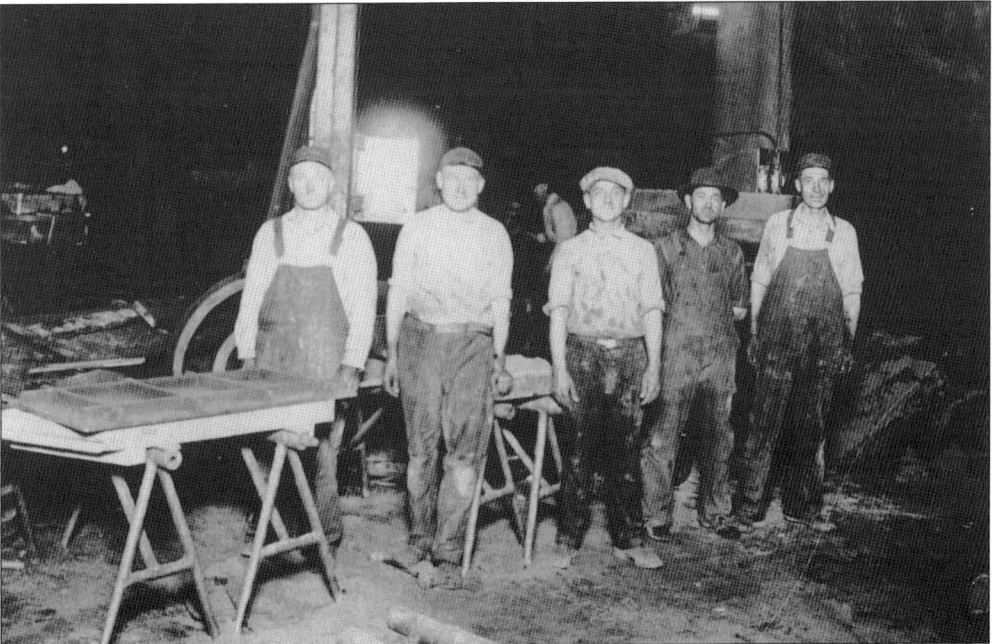

For many years, the company supplied structural iron for buildings in Aurora and throughout the Midwest. The business expanded rapidly and buildings were added from time to time.

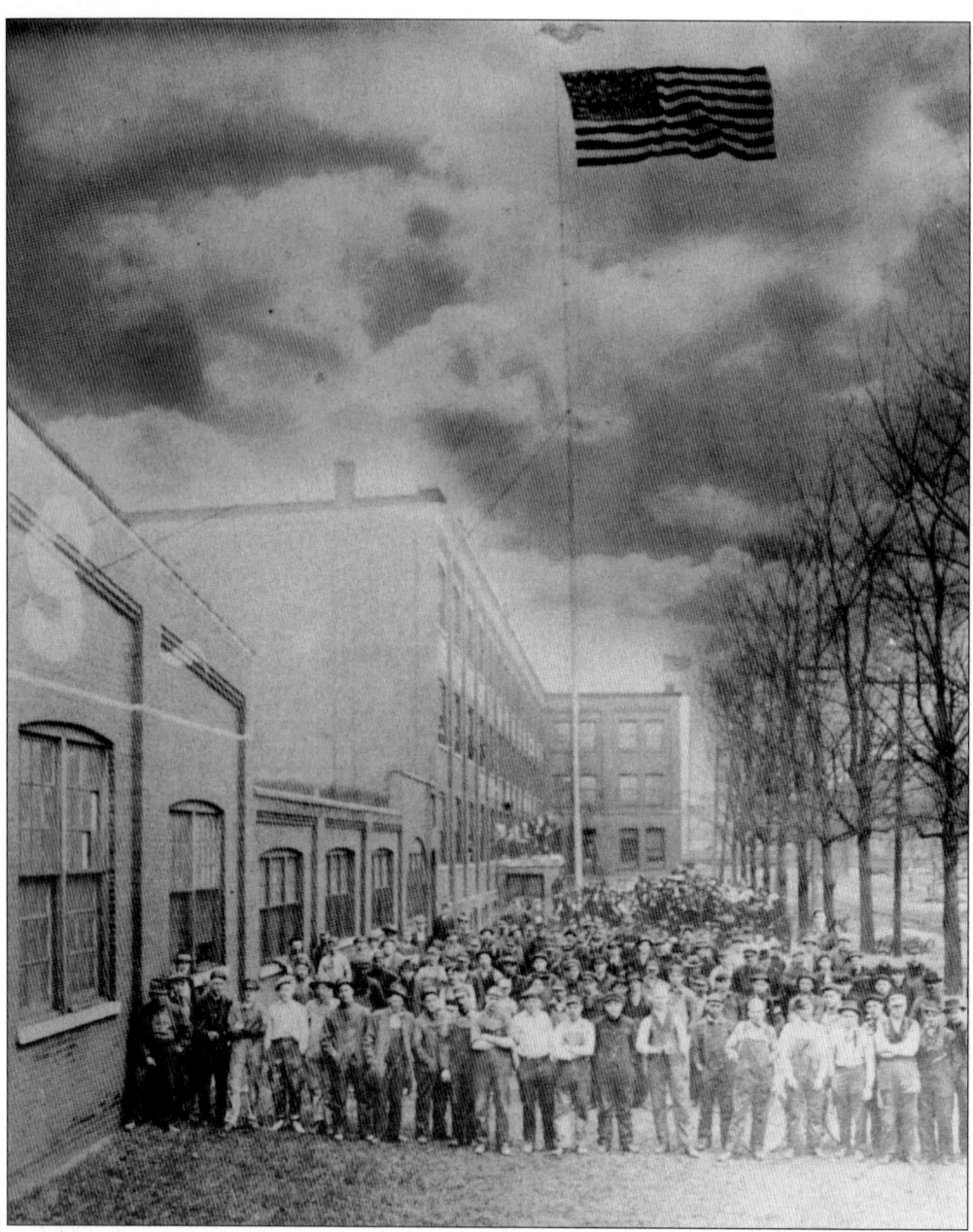

In 1889, a committee of local citizens was appointed to negotiate with Rathbone, Sard, and Company in Albany, New York, who was seeking a midwestern location for a branch of their stove works. The cities of Elgin and Joliet also wooed the company, but Aurora won out. The company began building stoves in the summer of 1890. Unique at this time was the fact that the city had developed the "Aurora Plan" whereby the city secured options on 150 acres of land along the CB&Q railroad south of town. Fifteen acres were to go to the stove works, ten for other possible manufacturers, ten for rail sidings, and the rest cut up into five hundred city lots to be sold for $200 each. The first half of these lots sold within 30 minutes, and the rest sold by the next day! This revenue would bring in $100,000 and offset the $60,000 offered to the stove company.

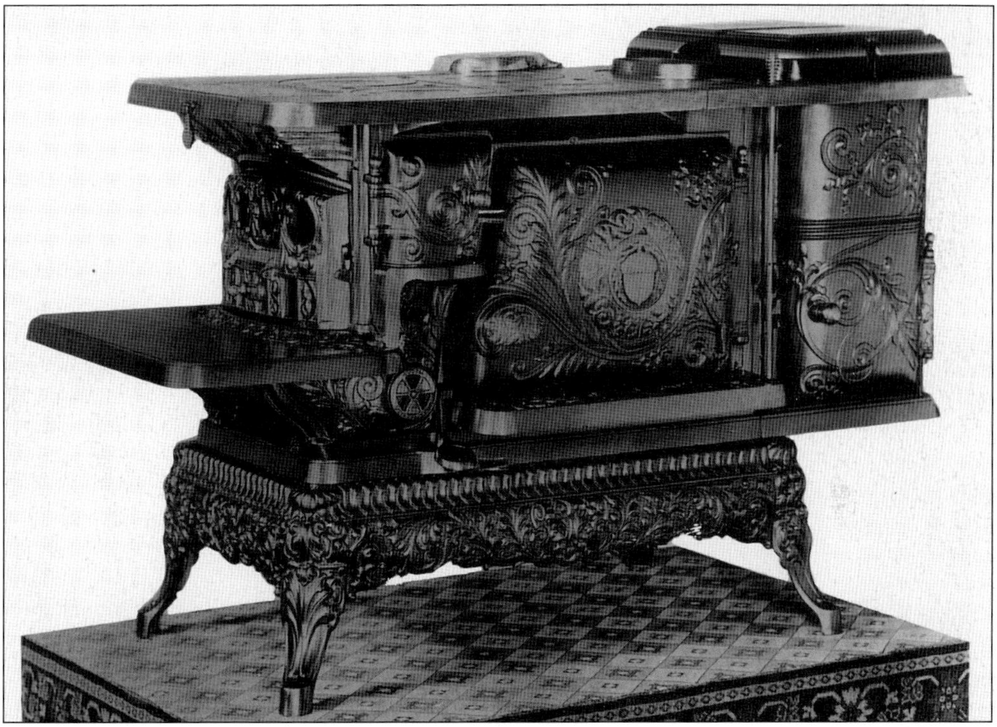

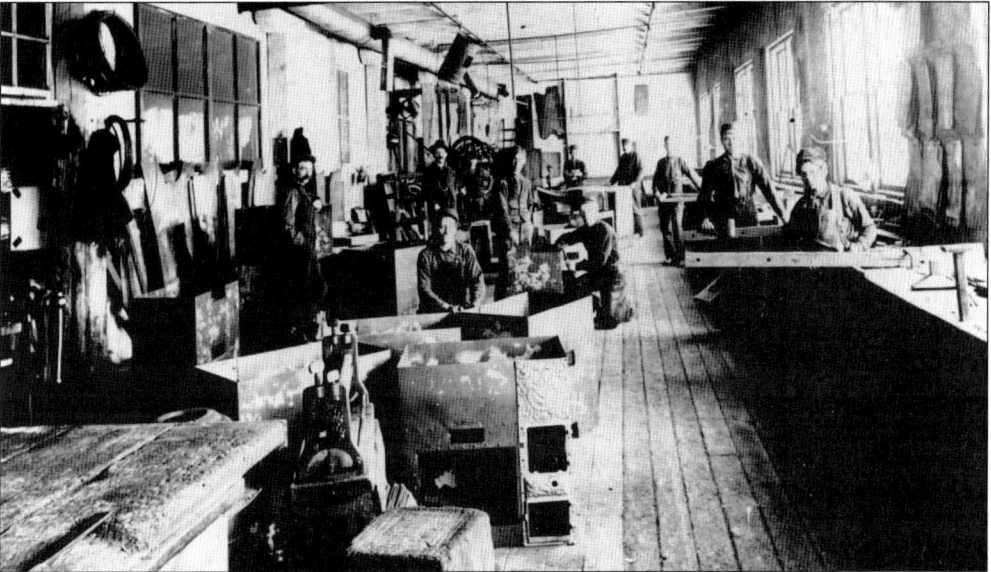

Their line of Acorn stoves ranged in price from $3.50 for a wood-burning stove to an elaborate kitchen range with a warming oven that sold for $50 in 1890. This picture is a variation of the stove that sold in 1890 for close to $50. Rathbone, Sard, and Company sold coal, wood, and later gas stoves for homes and commercial establishments.

In a letter written in 1890, the firm wrote of their reason for locating in Aurora. They wrote, "The people of Aurora are a law-abiding people. Industry and sobriety are their characteristics. The families can live in Aurora much better for the money than any other place we know of." Five hundred men and women worked there. The plant closed in 1925.

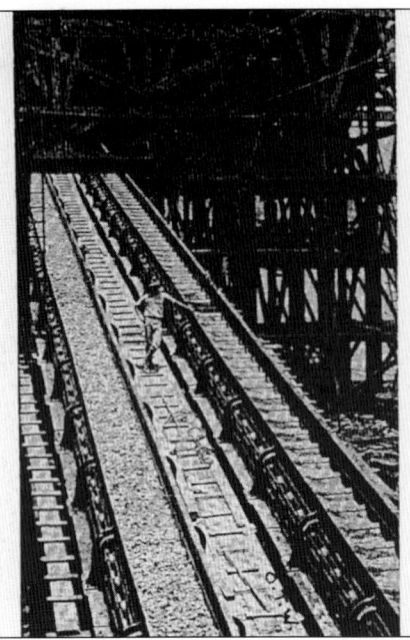

Is the greatest work of its kind ever undertaken in any age by any people. The successful carrying on of this work has been made possible only under the guidance of the United States government and by the application of modern methods and modern machinery. The locks and dams are the largest ever built, and to supply material for the work in sufficient amount to keep pace with the other work, it was necessary to build a plant especially for this purpose.

The Great Crushing Plant at Porto Bello

Which is located twenty miles from the canal, furnishes all the stone for the concrete work. This plant has a crushing capacity of 3,000 cubic yards per day. Conveying Machinery, which could handle this immense quantity of stone in a way satisfactory to the Government Engineers could be obtained only from an Aurora concern. All the conveyors and elevators for this plant, approximating $100,000 in value, were designed and manufactured in Aurora.

The pivoted bucket conveyors used here are the largest ever built and the plant itself is one of the largest ever constructed.

This plant is but one of many in all parts of the world designed by Aurora Engineers and equipped with machinery built in Aurora.

Stephens-Adamson Mfg Co.

W.W. Stephens (Vice Pres. and Gen. Mgr. of Webster Manufacturing Co. of Chicago), David Pierson (who worked for him), and Frederick G. Adamson (secretary and treasurer of John Metcalf Co. of Chicago) formed Stephens-Adamson. They made machinery and appliances for mechanical handling of material in bulk or in packages—conveyors, bucket carriers and elevators, mining cars, and coal-handling equipment. The plant covered 17 acres and employed two hundred men by 1908.

Aurora, Elgin & Chicago R. R.

THE GREAT THIRD RAIL LINE

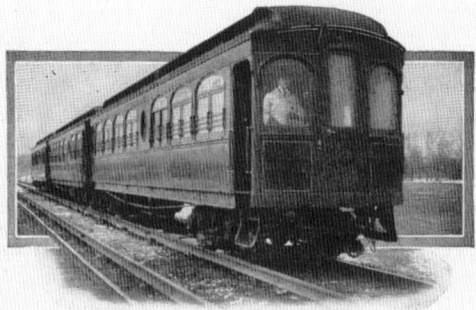

Unexcelled Transportation Facilities to Chicago - Frequent Service
Express Trains at Convenient Hours - Buffet Parlor Cars - Low Rates

The electric railroad played an important part in Aurora's development and growth. The city was once the center of a great network of inter-urban lines running in all directions. Many inter-urban rail systems were third rail, called so because of an added rail that conducted over six hundred volts of electricity. Downtown, the danger was too great to run a third rail, so the trains were powered by overhead electric line.

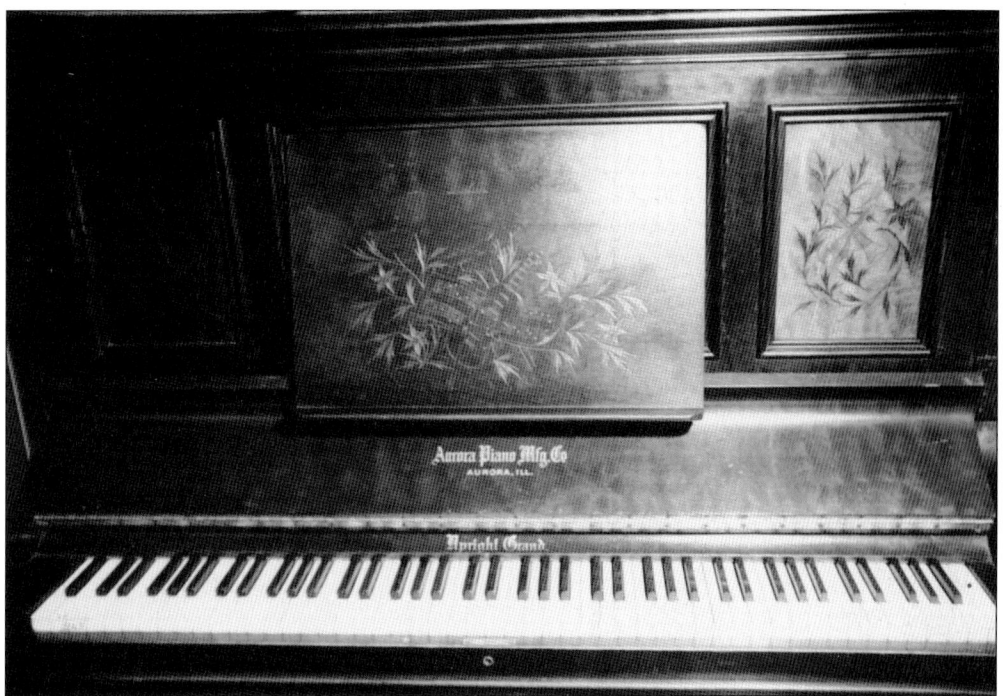

The Aurora Piano Manufacturing Company was located at 23 S. Broadway. They manufactured pianos from 1893 to 1904. They ceased manufacture just before the player piano boom days.

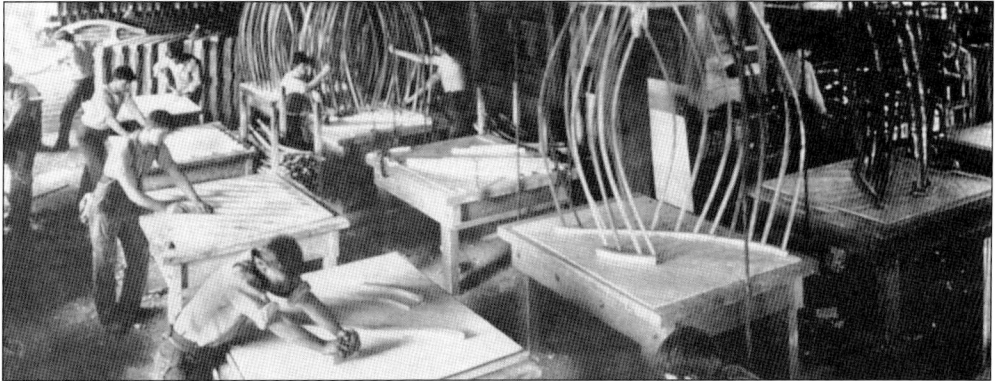

Here the piano workmen are preparing wood for the sound boards. Making pianos was a labor-intensive business. Not much was done by machines, and the assembly line was a human one.

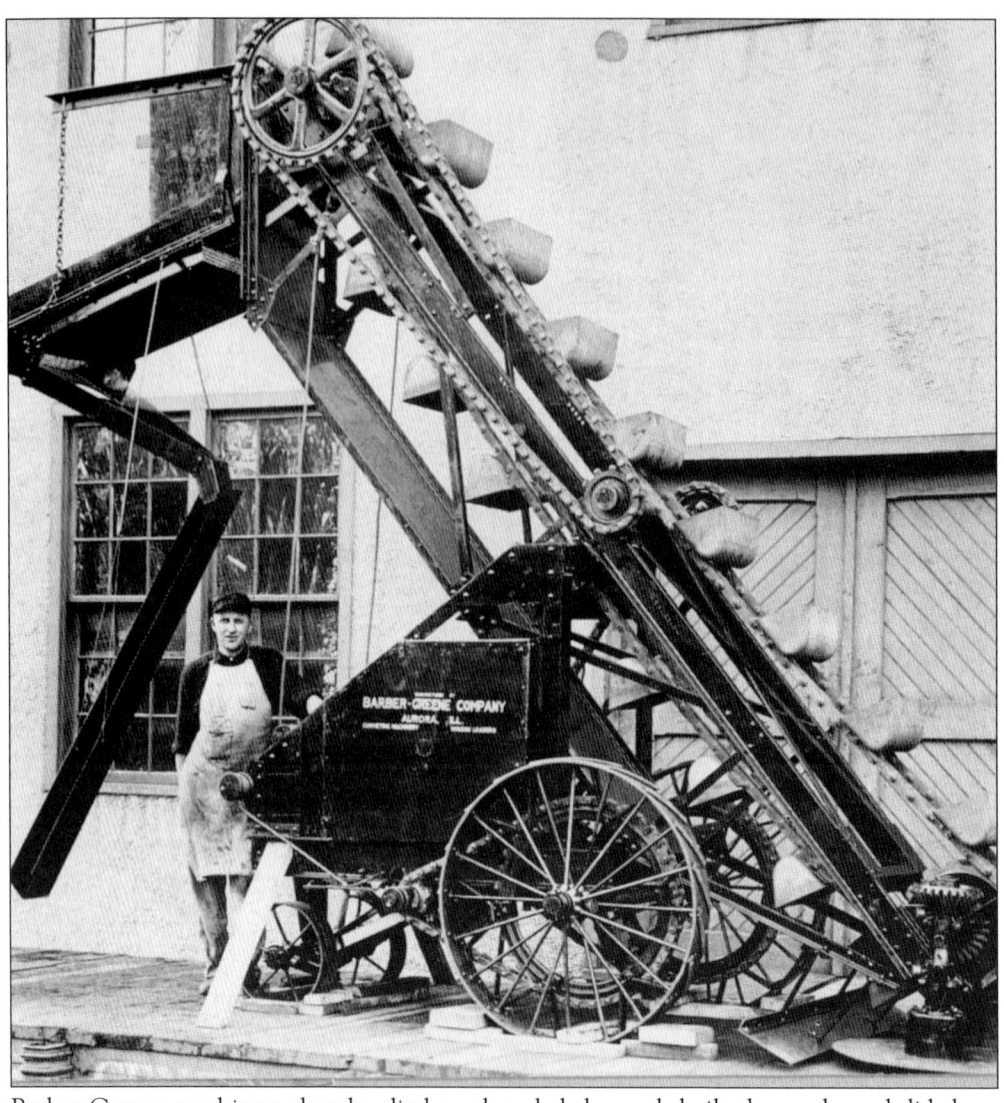

Barber Greene machinery dug the ditches, shoveled the coal, built the roads, and did those dirty, rough heavy jobs formerly assigned to the newest immigrants. In the beginning, Greene worked with W.S. Frazier & Co. whose horse-drawn carriages were becoming obsolete and whose racing sulkies could not make up the slack. They had available shop space, and they would manufacture, as subcontractors, items designed and sold by Barber and Greene. First built was a portable belt conveyor to install at Lilley Coal Company, across the tracks, to use as a demonstration unit. The coal company continued to be the place where the new designs were tested.

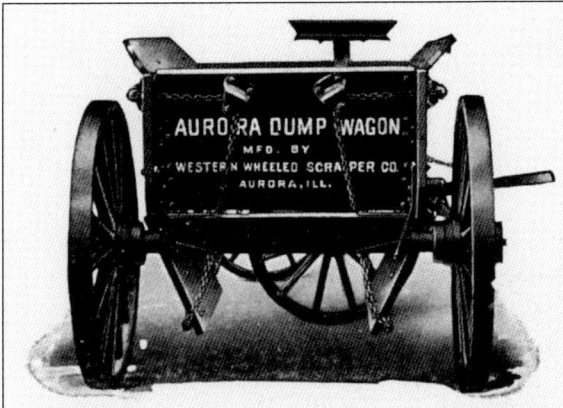

Western Wheeled Scraper Company, now the Western-Austin Company, was brought from Iowa and located at the eastern edge of the city. By 1908 there were six to seven hundred employees, making it the second largest industry, the Burlington being first. It furnished much of the machinery for the Panama Canal. The Scraper Company was the second largest employer of the Mexicans who came to Aurora beginning in the 1920s.

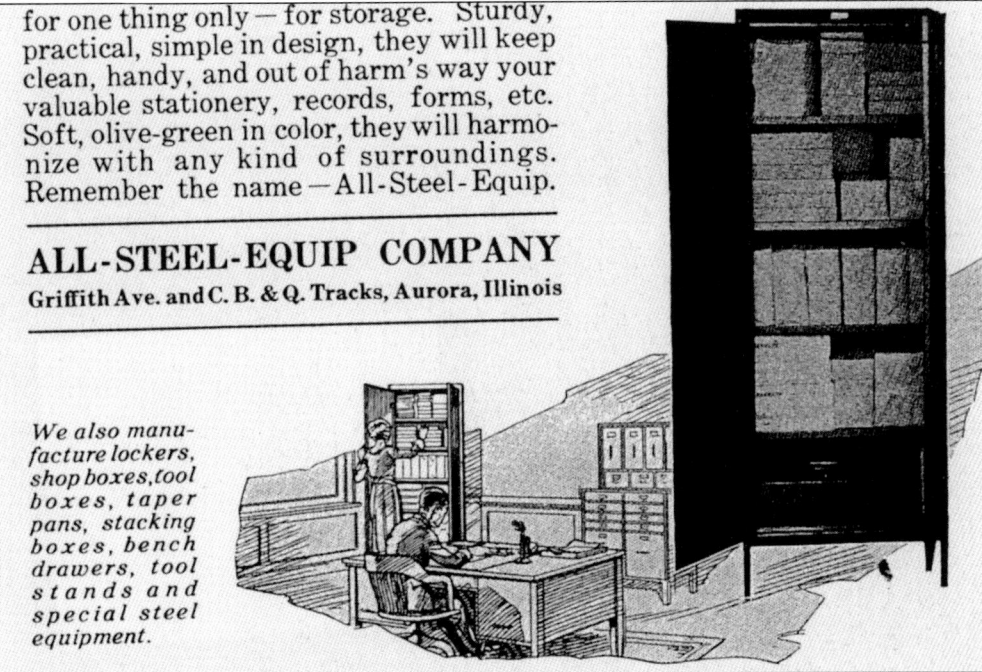

This story of the founding of the All-Steel-Equip Company was published in Aurora's centennial book. Axel Nelson, Charles Lembcke, and George Herteau worked at Lyon Metal Products Company. In December 1911, they wanted to open their own factory. They had about $2,500 and wanted to borrow an additional $700, so they went to the Old Second National Bank for a loan. D.W. Simpson, a director of the bank, was present while the meager financial statement of the three men was being examined.

"What are you installing for office fixtures and furniture?" Simpson asked.

"Two kitchen tables and two kitchen chairs brought from home," was the reply.

"Let them have the money," said the astute manufacturer and bank director. The All-Steel-Equip Company thus had been born.

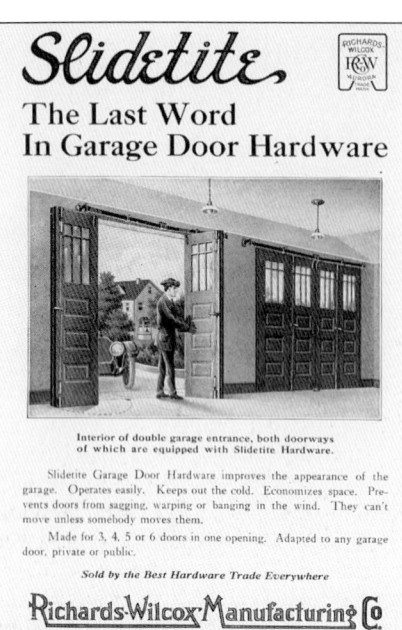

The Wilcox Manufacturing Co., incorporated in 1880 as makers of carpet-sweepers, was reorganized in 1894 to produce sliding hangers for parlor doors, and soon after expanded to manufacture other door hangers, elevator gates, and hardware specialties. The Richards Manufacturing Co., incorporated in 1880, erected a factory in 1903 for the production of door hangers, door hinges, etc. The two combined to form Richards-Wilcox in 1910.

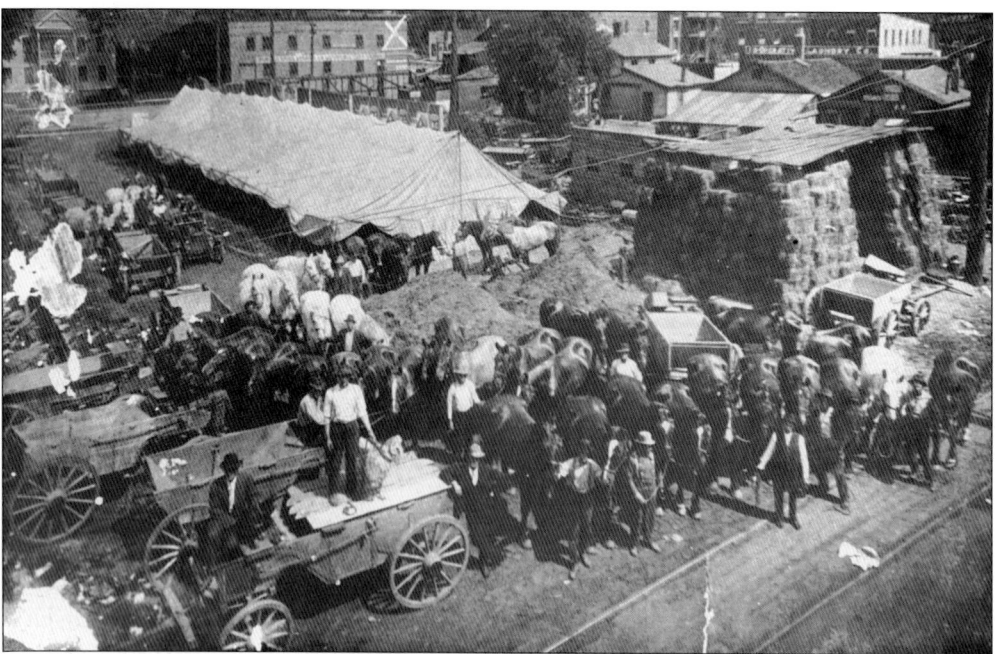

The following quote is from the history of the First Baptist Church: "McCarty Company came to Aurora to build the new bridges. This picture shows the horse tent, wagons and men used in building of the bridges. The site shows the S.E. corner of Lake and Galena where the original McCollum Wagon Factory (marked x) and McCollum home (left in the background) [were located]. The early Baptists once used the McCollum home to change their clothes after being baptized in the Fox River. The McCollum shop was the oldest wagon manufactory in Aurora. Mr. McCollum moved to Aurora in 1837 and started a wagon and plow manufactory."

Five

Picnics, Violins, and Front Porches

By the year 1900, interest in leisure-time activity was at an all time high. It had been growing slowly since the Civil War. What contributed immensely to making leisure time activities yet another American "business" was the shortening of the week from seven to five or six days. Just as the Civil War unchained the African American, industry unchained its workers and set them free on weekends. New sports and professional teams saw the results of their matches on the front page of the newspaper in red ink along with the serious news of the day.

The first place that people enjoyed their new found leisure time activities was right in their own homes and gardens. Checkers, chess, and reading were popular home activities as well as music making, various card games, and the new 3-D stereopticon. If you were lucky enough to have a large garden, you could engage in one of the two most popular sports crazes of the period, croquet. Aurora once had a special croquet field on the west bank of the Fox River. The other craze was bicycling. After the invention of the "safety" bicycle in 1895, ten million Americans hit the roadways. Communities, churches, and schools also began organizing leisure activities such as sports and music.

Relaxing itself, possibly with a hammock stretched across a wide verandah, was a most therapeutic leisure time activity. Porches were where one could sip real lemonade and contemplate the bright future for everyone lucky enough to live in "modern" times in Aurora, Illinois.

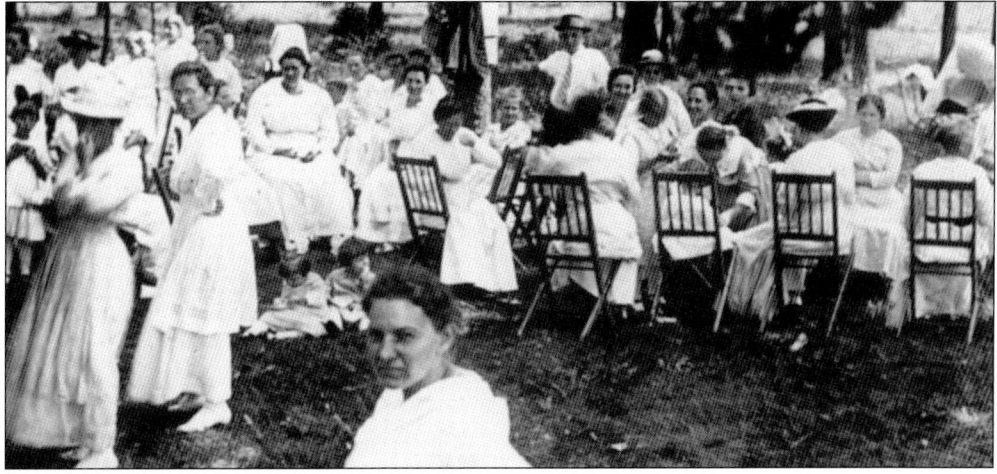

Members of St. Paul's Lutheran Church take to the outdoors for a picnic under the trees in this 1890s photograph. There are few men in evidence. Could the rest be off playing ball?

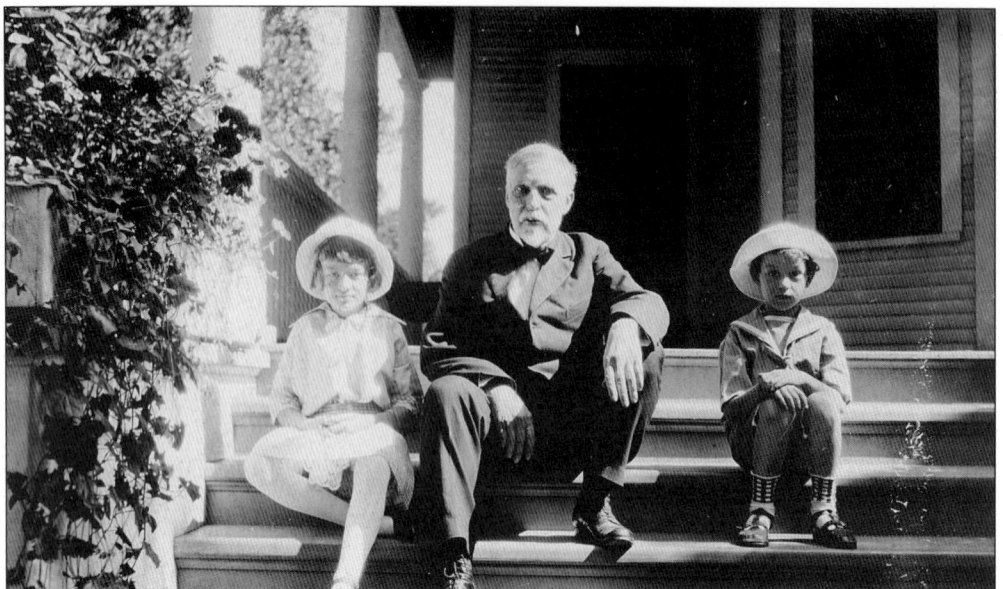

Victorian homes, for all their exterior immensity, were chopped up into many small rooms with 10- to 12-foot ceilings. Tall bay windows helped light come into the interior rooms of the house, but curtains, draperies, and a multitude of other Victorian bric-a-brac crowded out all but a pathway in some rooms, such as the parlor. Photographing people at home was best done outdoors when the photographer could capture a good image of the people.

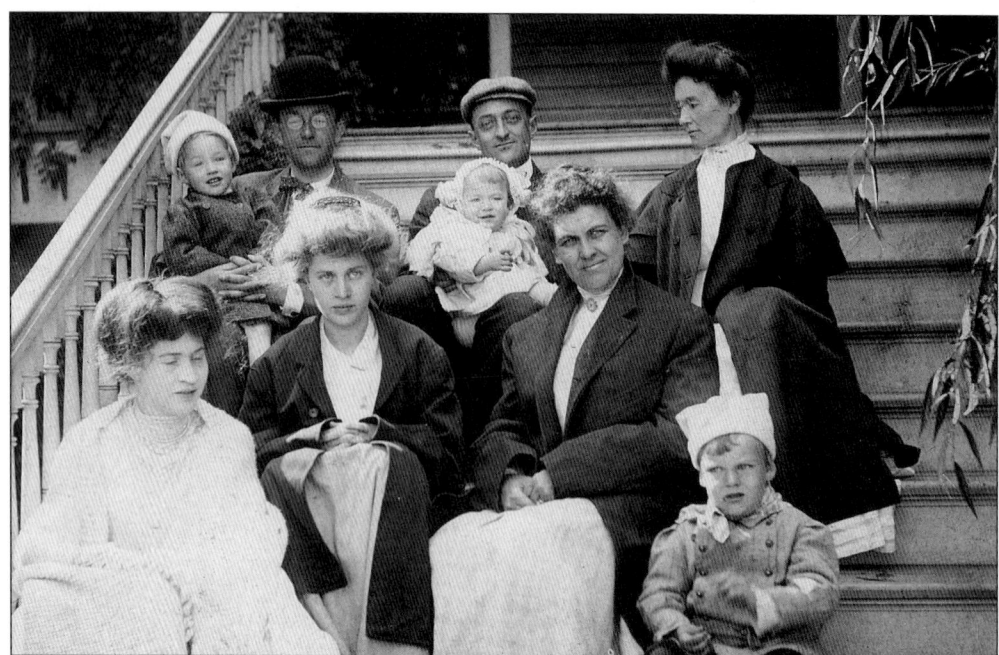

In this homestead, the porch is ten steps off the ground making room for a raised basement living area. The photograph was evidently taken in the autumn. If we could digitally enlarge this image, we would see in the gentleman's right lens of his eyeglasses the reflection of the photographer and his camera.

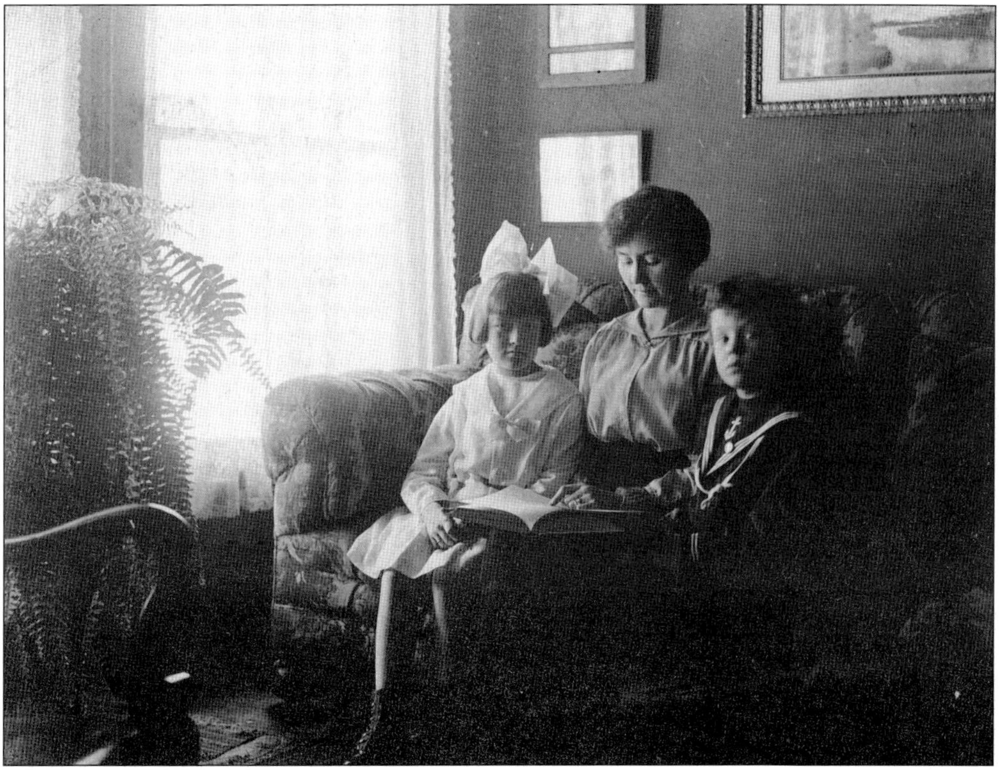

Victorian interior images are scarce because of poor indoor lighting conditions. Here the photographer has captured (with natural light—no exploding powder to aid him!) a mother doing what in those days every middle-class mother did, reading to her children. It seems as if, in this glimpse, the children resent the presence of the photographer who has interrupted a wonderful story. Was father the amateur photographer?

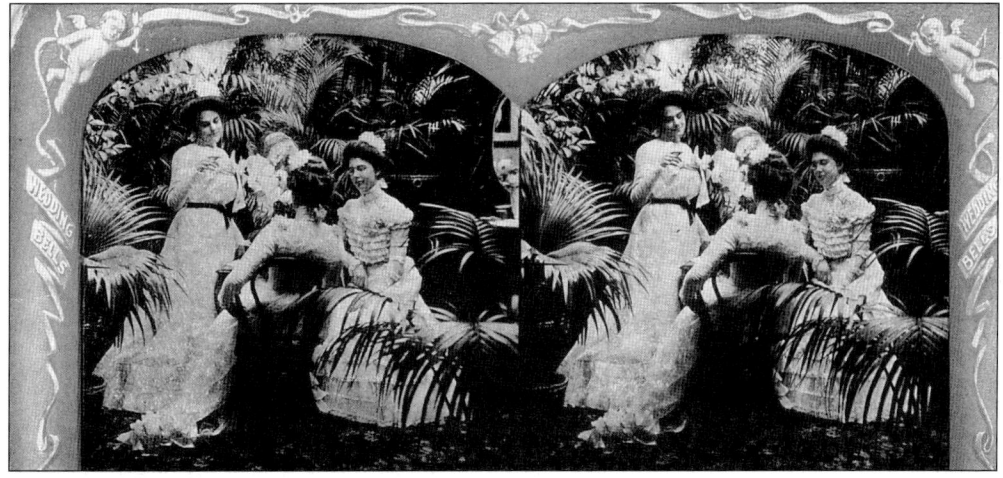

In this 3-D stereopticon card, part of a whole series of views from courtship to the altar, women gather to view the new engagement ring of one of the young women. Notice the almost laughable clutter of plants and chairs, and the cake-frosting-like dresses. It is hard to imagine how women were able to walk around their own houses and not bump into furniture!

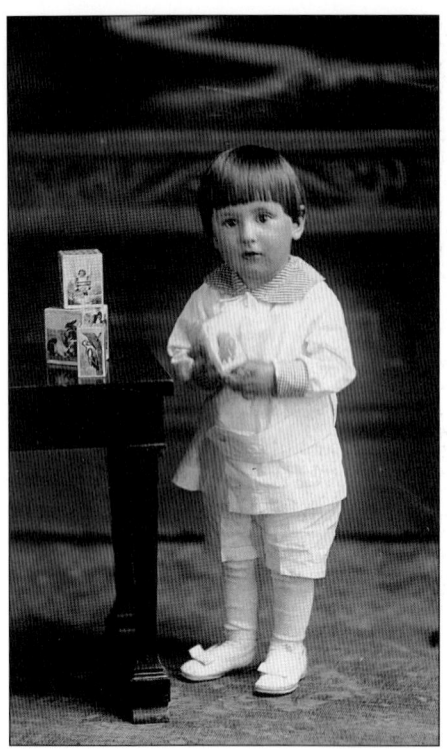

Children in middle-class Aurora played with entirely different types of toys than their 20th-century counterparts. Toys of the day included interactive mechanical iron banks, hoops and sticks, metal fire engines, and colorful hand water-colored blocks like the ones this young tike is carefully arranging on a piano bench. This scene was probably taken in a photographer's studio.

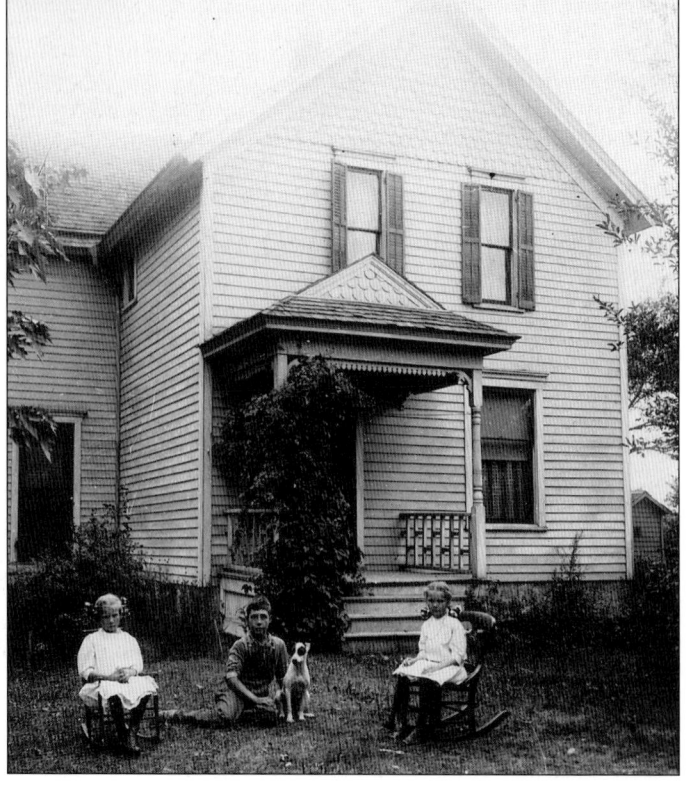

Children spent a lot of time outdoors messing up their prim Victorian outfits. Pets were in abundance, in and out of doors. Children played games such as marbles and pick-up sticks, but going all the way to the moon and back on the old swing attached to a strong tree branch was a favorite.

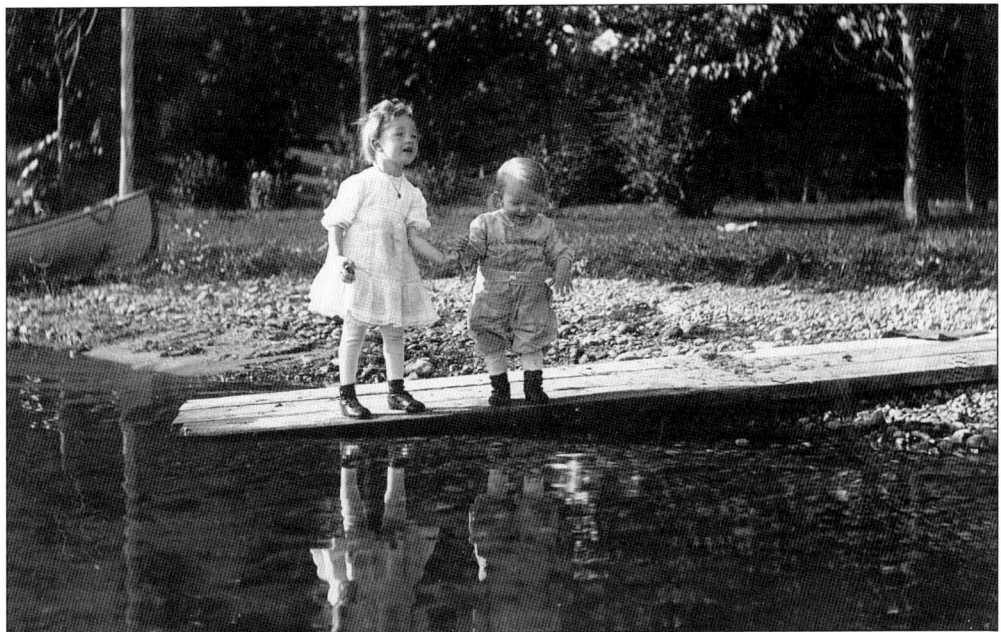

Children sought-out any body of water where they could fish or skip pebbles across the pond for many yards. Pleasures were simple in these days. A brisk stroll with your little brother to look at your reflection in the water was not an earth-shaking event, but it was enough to satisfy the children of one hundred years ago.

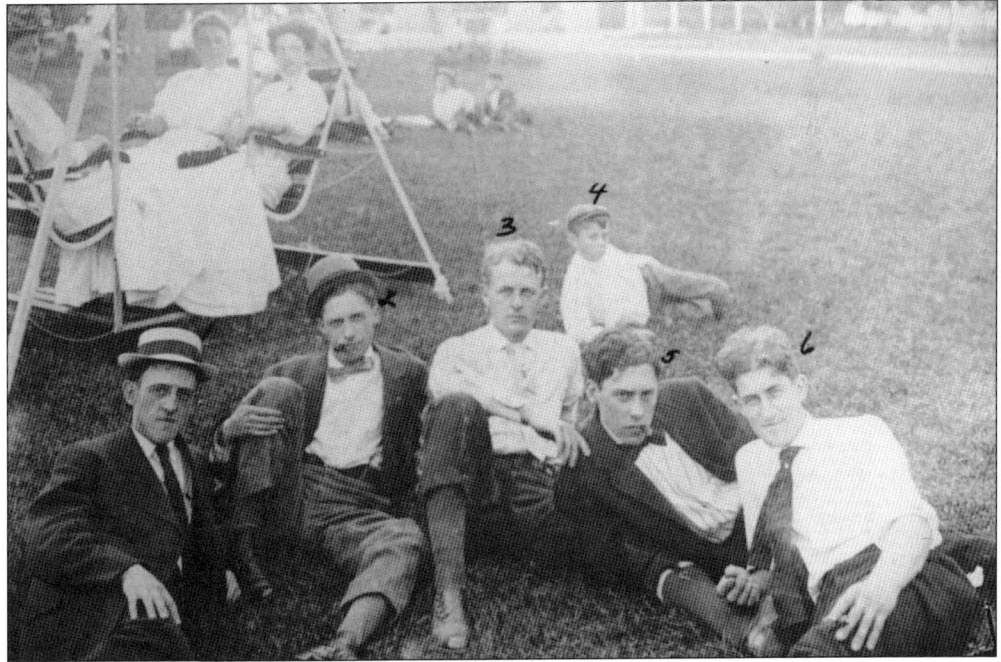

Picnics were popular whether they were held in the back forty or in a local park such as River View Park near Aurora. After the food was eaten, you could bet that at some time the girls and boys conversed separately. Pictured from left to right are: unidentified, George Sontag, Orin Menard, Erlenborn, unidentified, and George Taemans. The girls are not identified.

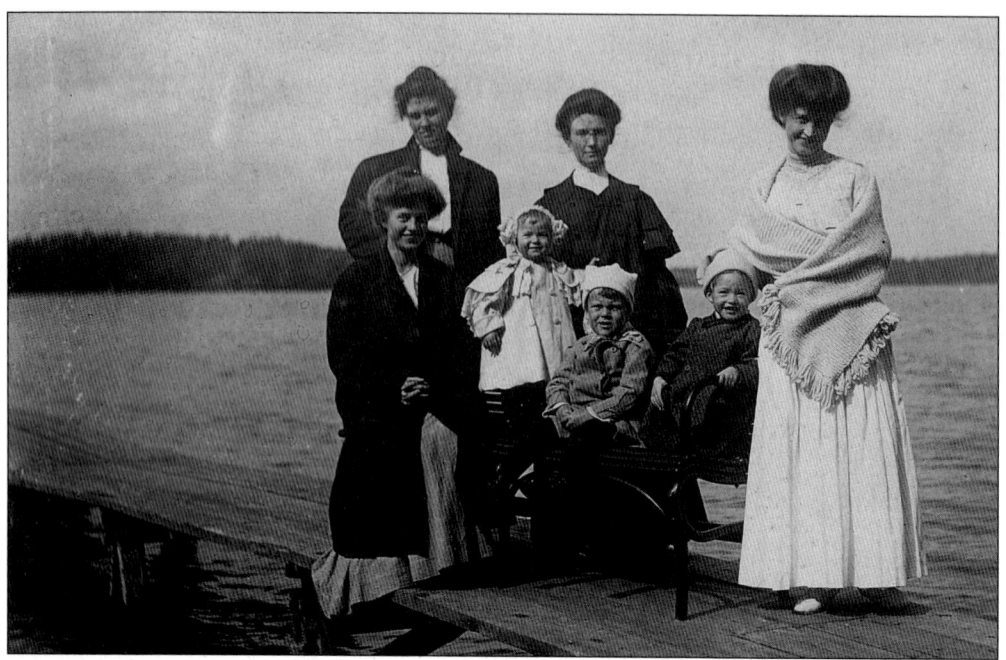

Fishing was as popular a hundred years ago as it is today. Numerous nearby lakes and rivers offered opportunities to a whole family on an outing. Men went fishing while women stayed on shore, watched the children, and had their photos taken.

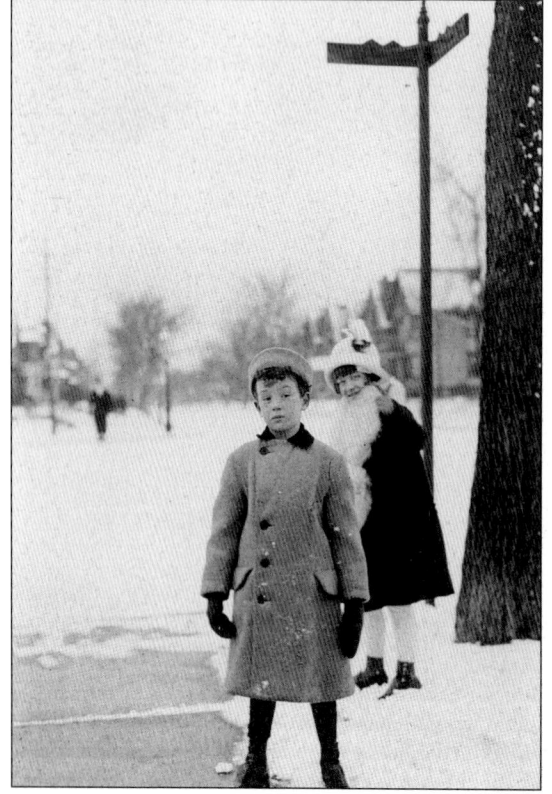

Winter time in Aurora meant snow and lots of it. A child could pull out a sled or toboggan and head out for the nearest hill. It wasn't much fun, though, to have your photograph taken outdoors when a sister was clowning around behind your back and making fun of you.

Children were expected to learn music so that the family could have inexpensive music "live." Countless young boys and girls suffered through hours of endless torture playing special "musicals" for visitors. Some actually thrived and went on to become world-class musicians. Such was Aurora's Maude Powell, who was billed as America's First Virtuoso Violinist.

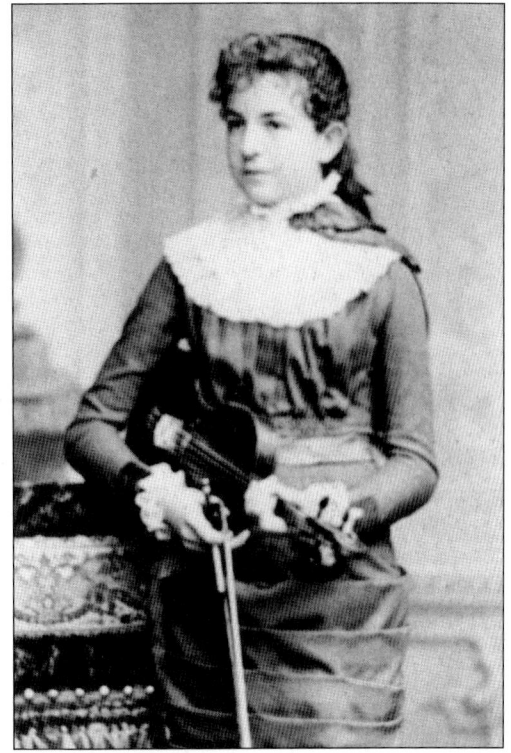

Maude recorded for Victor Phonograph and Record Company. She toured the United States many times as well as Europe, and she was at her peak performance level around World War I. Maude played with Arthur Loesser, one of the most gifted pianists of his day. Here she is seen autographing one of her recordings.

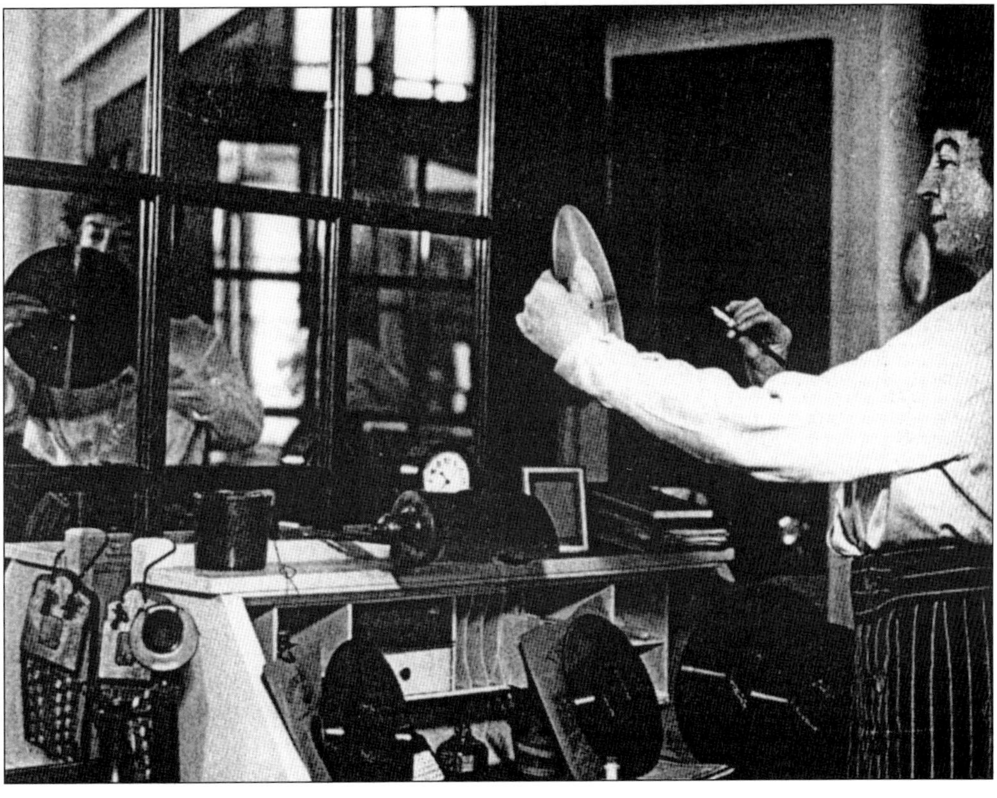

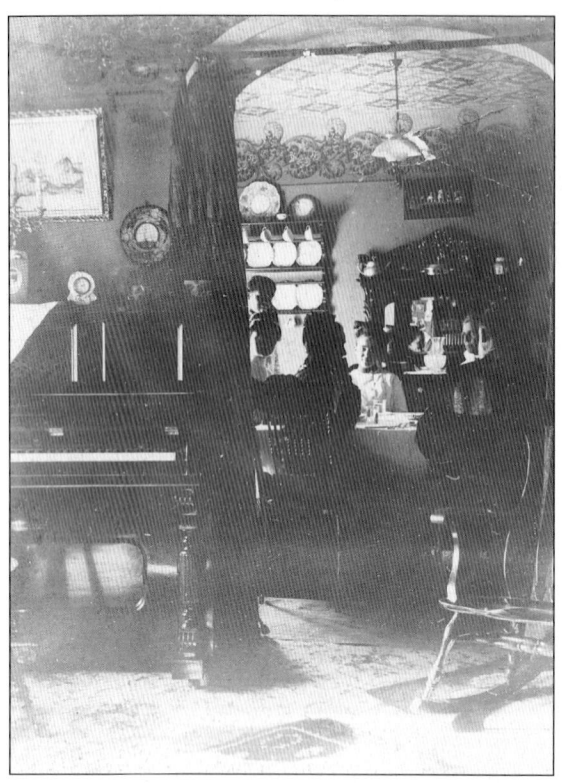

Homes of the day often had melodeons, pump organs, or pianos. Sheet music was 5- to 10¢ a copy, and one could take home the latest ballads or rags to have a family sing along or an impromptu dance. Most families also spent hours relaxing around the dinner table chatting and gossiping about the latest news or scandal.

The accordion that came to America from eastern Europe was regarded by many as a perfect, whole orchestra captured between two palms. Others called it the "curse from the east." Aurora, and the whole Chicago area, was awash with the sound of thousands of children practicing and dozens of polka bands playing until the middle of the 20th century.

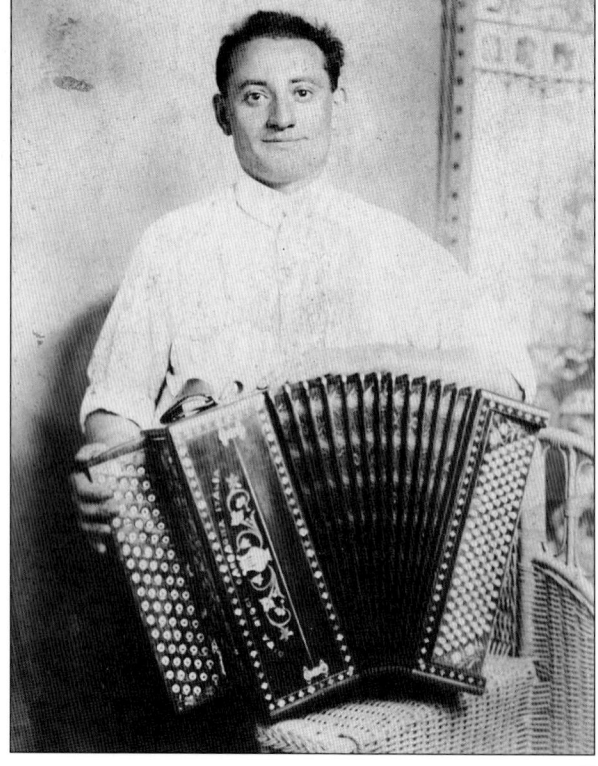

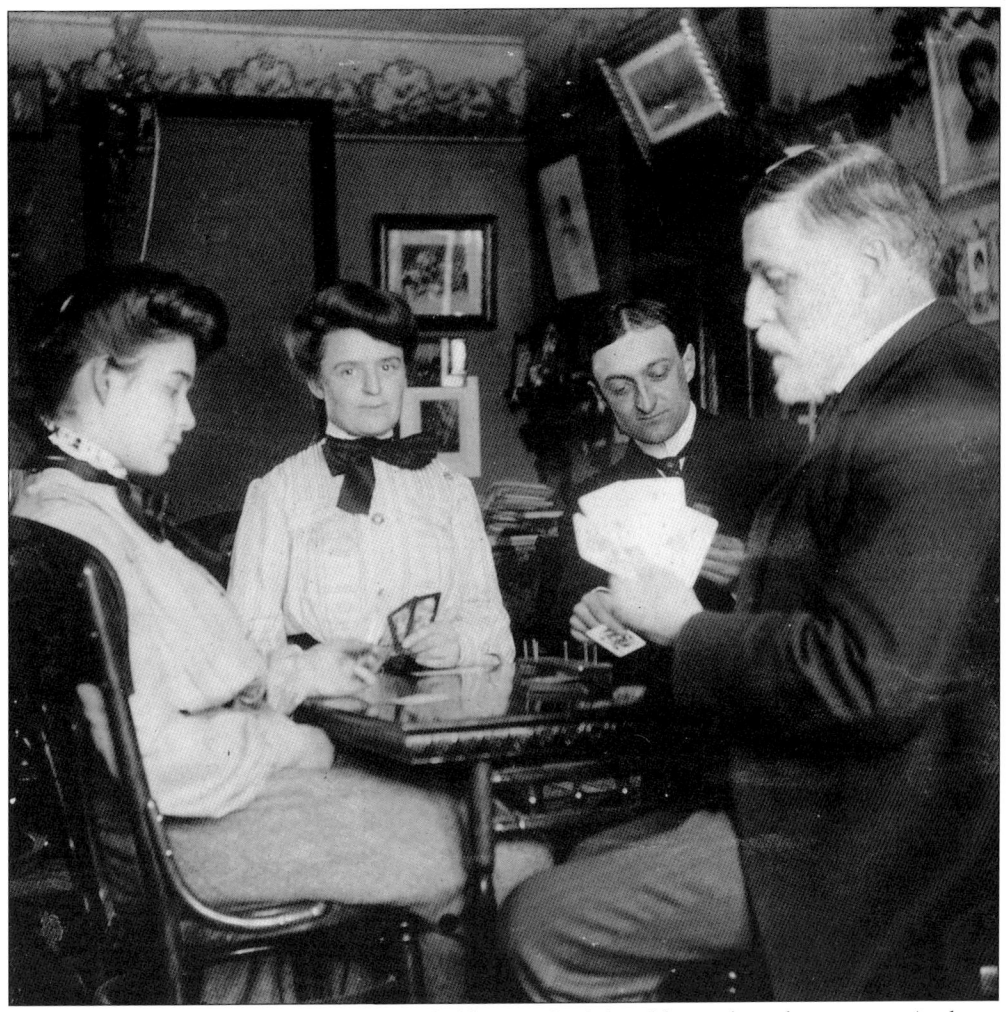

Card games were popular pastimes for children and adults alike with such games as Authors, Old Maid, and Snap. Adults were also fond of card games that could be played with members of the opposite sex, such as Whist, a game where one took tricks. This was the Edwardian predecessor of bridge.

Not a spot on these walls seems to have been spared from being filled with pictures. Note also the flocked border band around the ceiling. The well-dressed couples may be two sets of marrieds or a young courting pair engaging in good relations with future in-laws. They do not appear to be having a barrel of fun, or else they are really concentrating.

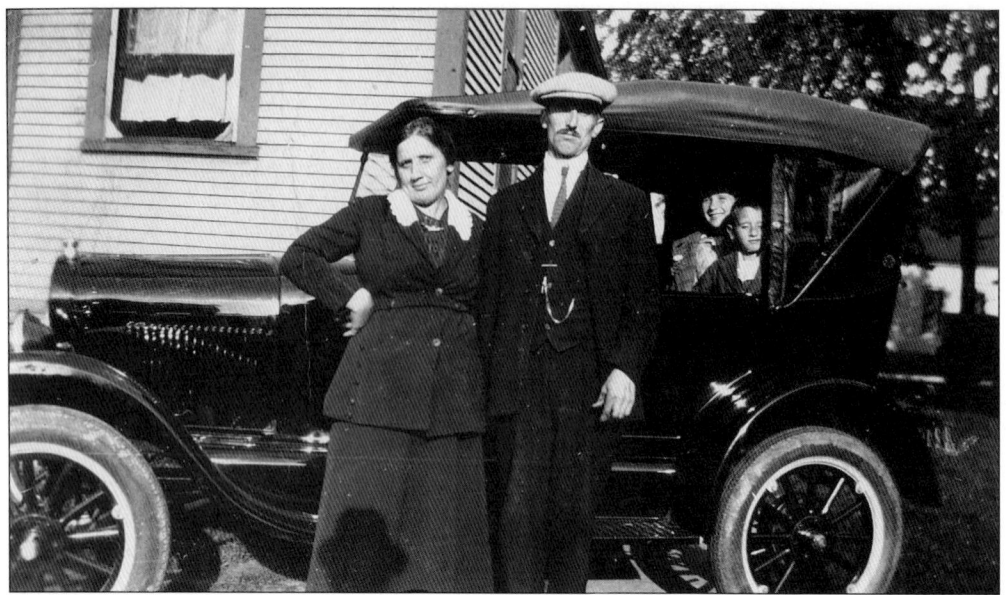

The lure of the open road proved irresistible. This Aurora couple and children appear to be off for a "Sunday spin" in their early touring car. The first Ford model T was produced in 1908 and cost a whopping $850. The introduction of the assembly line in 1913 cut assembly time from 14 to 6 hours. Prices plunged, and Aurora lined-up to join the automobile revolution.

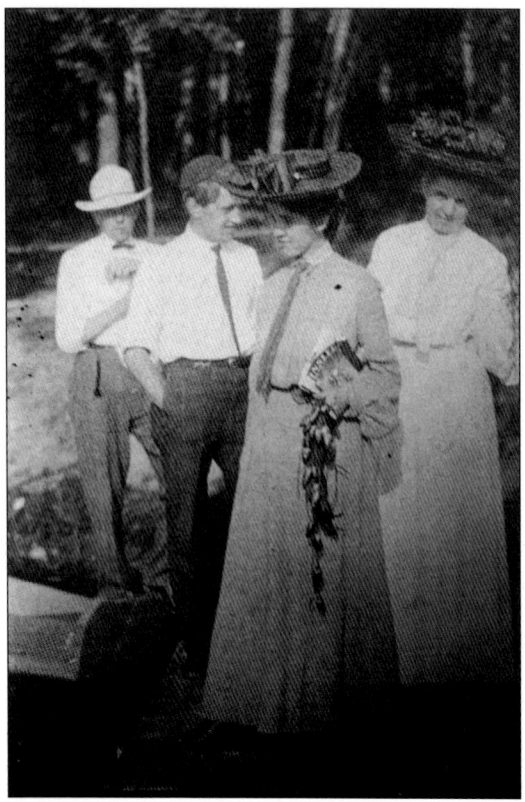

Boating was a popular pastime during all of the 19th century. Here one could escape the tortures of every day life, fish to your hearts content, or engage in recreational boating with the opposite sex, removed from the scowling of an aging chaperone too afraid to board the boat.

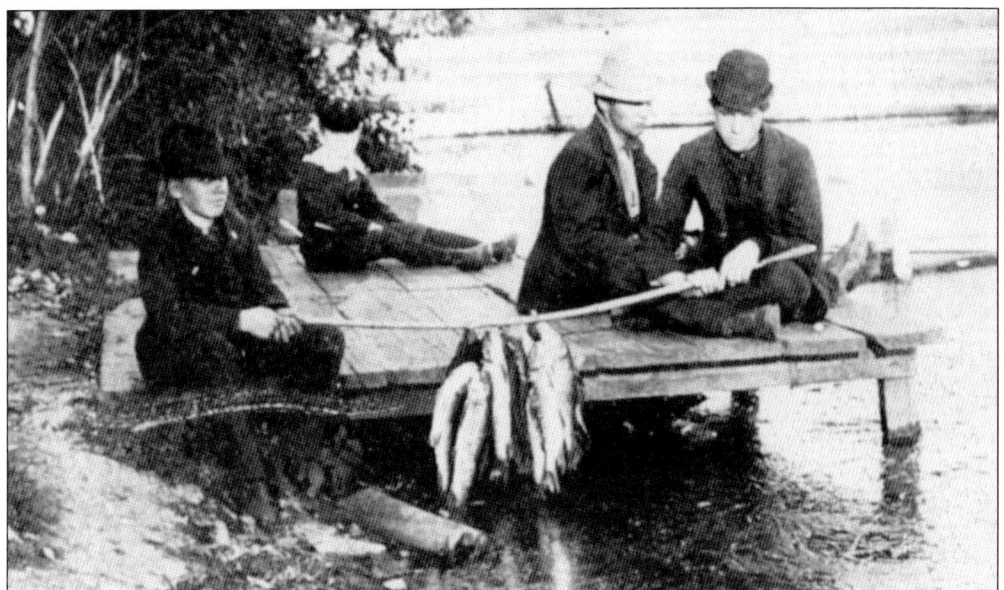

These extremely successful fishermen are fishing from a dock on the Fox River about 1900. Fish were plentiful and healthy until industry crowded the banks of the river and began to use the Fox like a public sewer. Some fish species died and others became unfit to eat.

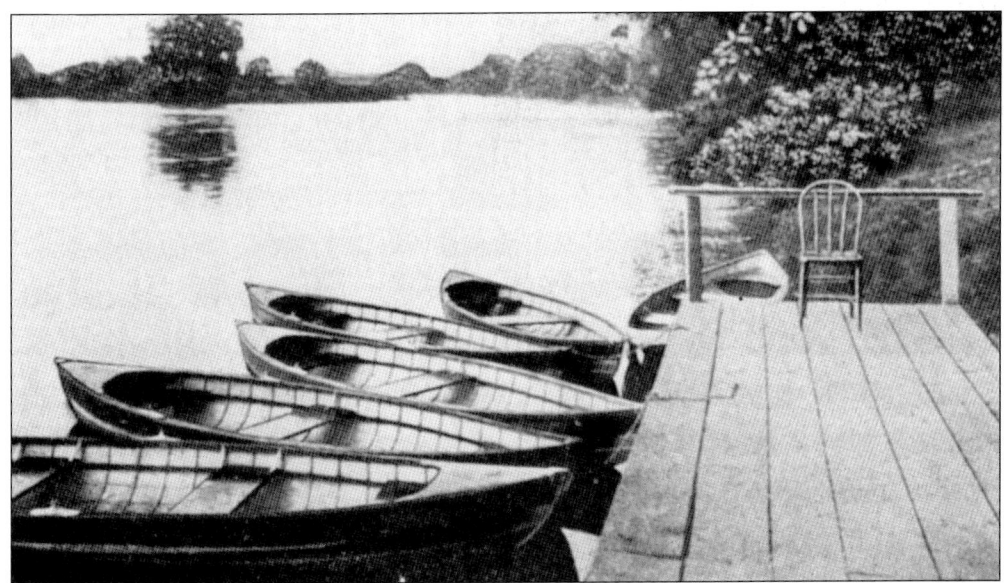

This tranquil photograph shows deserted boats and the Fox River banks mostly devoid of settlement. Once too many people arrived in the valley and river footage sold for homes and factories, the whole character of the river changed and became an unfriendly place until the environmental clean-up efforts in the later 1900s.

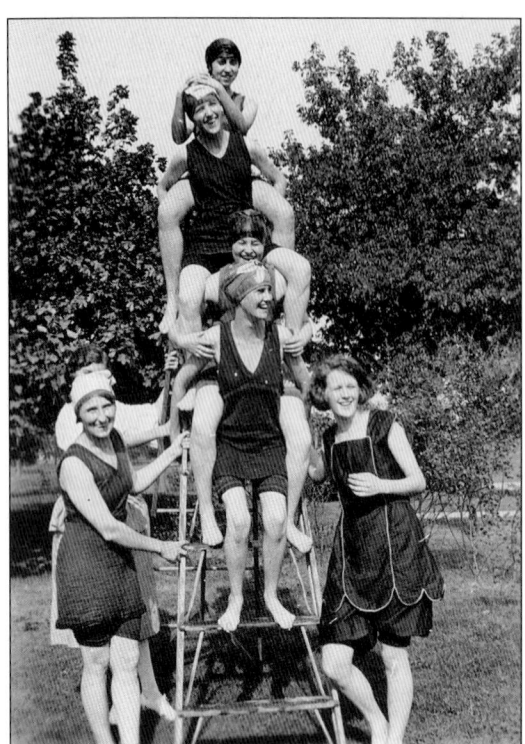

Swimming in abandoned quarries, water holes, and the river was never questioned. People were safe from the contamination that would later follow. This group of Aurora College girls is very much into water sports, and the girls are wearing the latest one and two piece outfits that revealed the arms and legs. Their grandmothers would never have shown so much flesh when they went bathing in public.

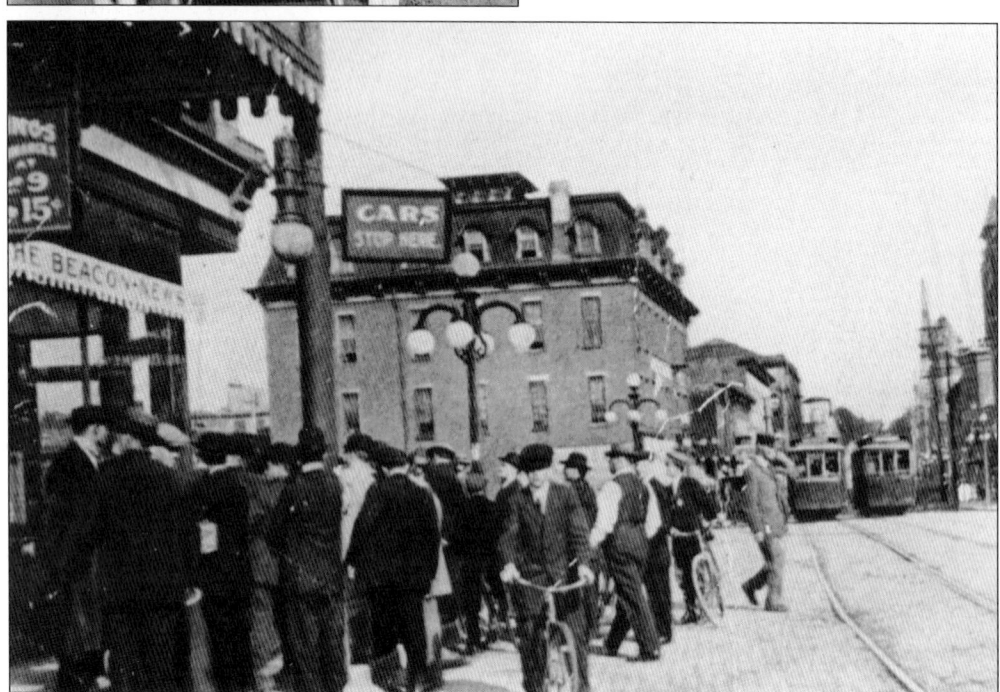

Men had some private pleasures of their own in Aurora. Besides being virtual economic dictators at home, able to smoke everywhere in the house, and able to engage in serious talks with other males after dinner, they could follow the latest baseball scores posted outside the newspaper offices.

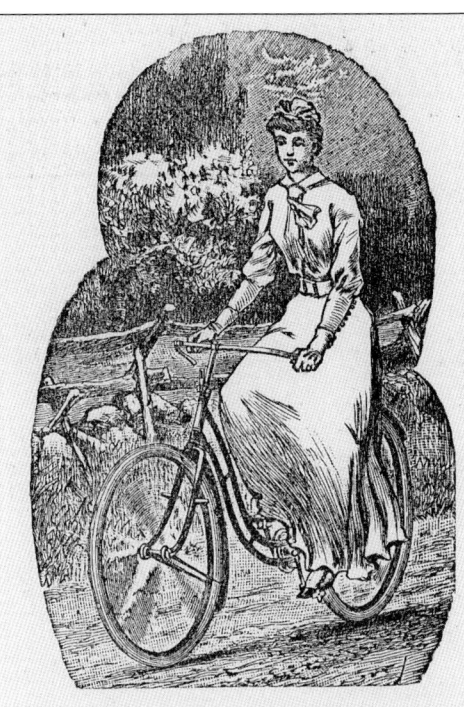

In the 1890s, manufacturers in Aurora, such as Frazier, and Chicago, were quick to capitalize on the American craze for bicycles. The new high-tech bikes featured two equal-sized wheels and frames that were smaller and safer than their big wheel predecessors. By 1896, bikes were being built on assembly lines in Chicago in this $60 million industry.

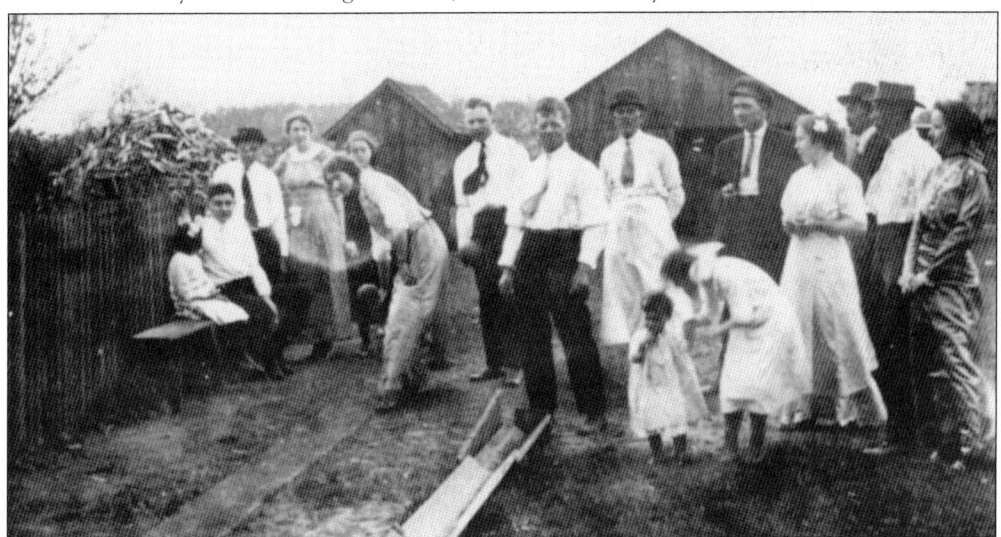

For the blue-collar working class, there were not so many leisure activities available. The workers at the Q shops were full of hard-working Luxemburgers. When the workers' real wages began to increase and their workweek only lasted 59 hours, there was time to engage in bowling. Here is a picture of a homemade three-pin bowling alley about 1900.

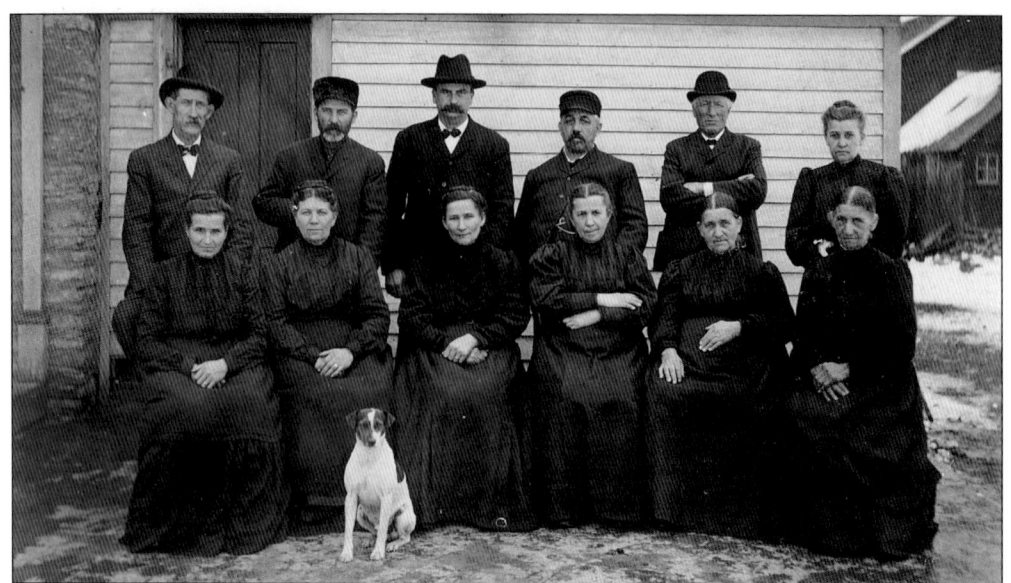

Death was as much a part of life as living. A funeral was one time when people took time to come together. Here, members of the Lies family gather to commemorate the family after their mother's funeral in 1907.

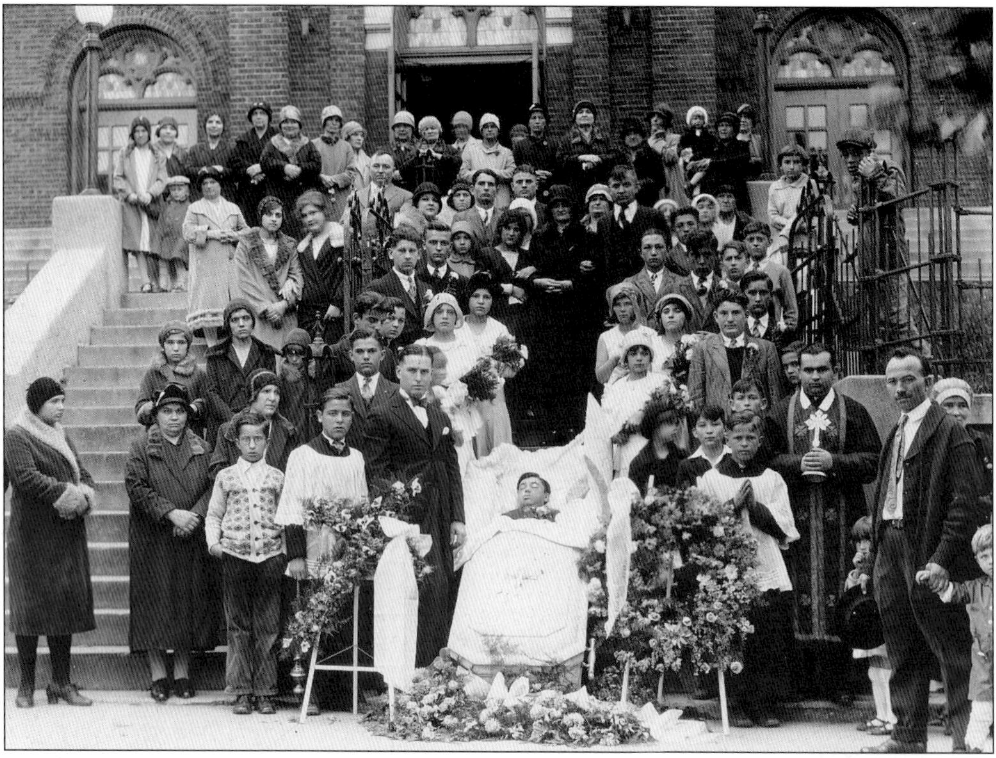

In the tradition of many Eastern European countries and cultures, the Romanians of Aurora gather outside St. Michael's Church for a funeral tribute with the deceased in this 1912 photograph. Notice in the upper right-hand corner, a curious African-American boy is looking on as the photographer captures the scene.

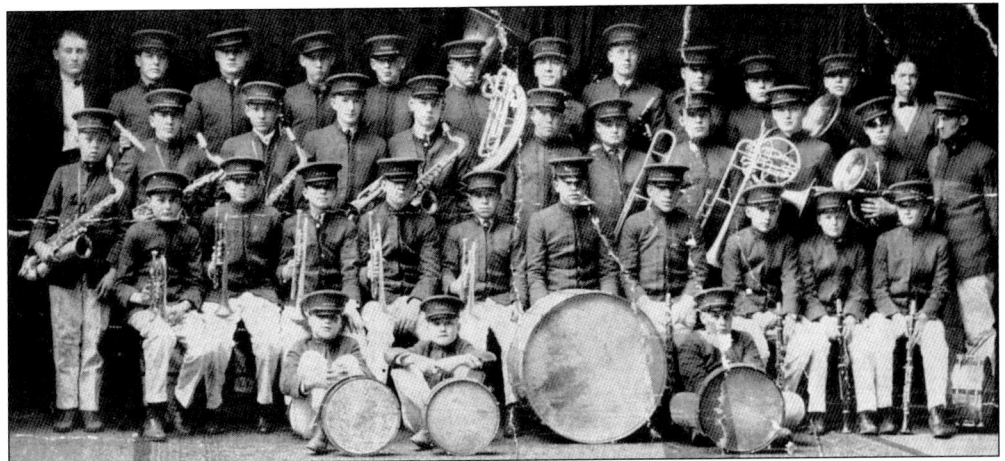

Strike up the Band! Bands were everywhere. There were cornet bands. There were brass bands. There were symphonic bands. One could hear them in public and parochial schools, factories, fire departments, and even in churches. John Philip Sousa and his sousaphone probably started the craze. Soon the streets and public parks were full of the sounds of music from bands such as this early 1900s Aurora School District 129 band.

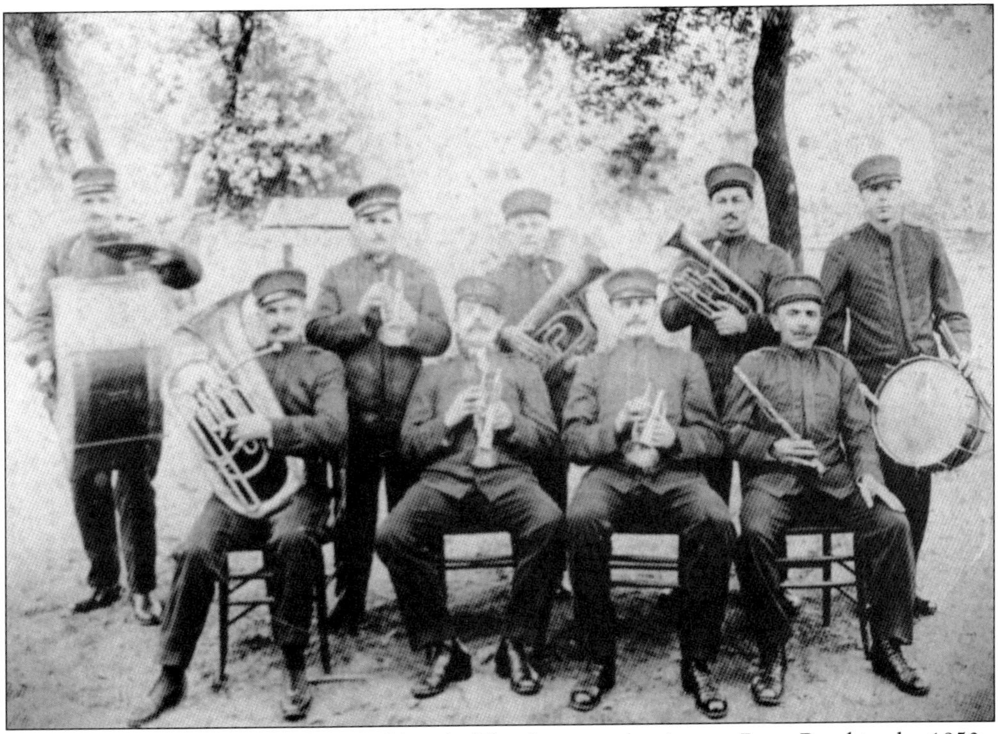

Aurora had many public professional bands. The first was the Aurora Brass Band in the 1850s, and in 1866 the Aurora Cornet Band was organized. By the 1890s, Aurora had a philharmonic band. This group appears to be a turn-of-the-century marching band.

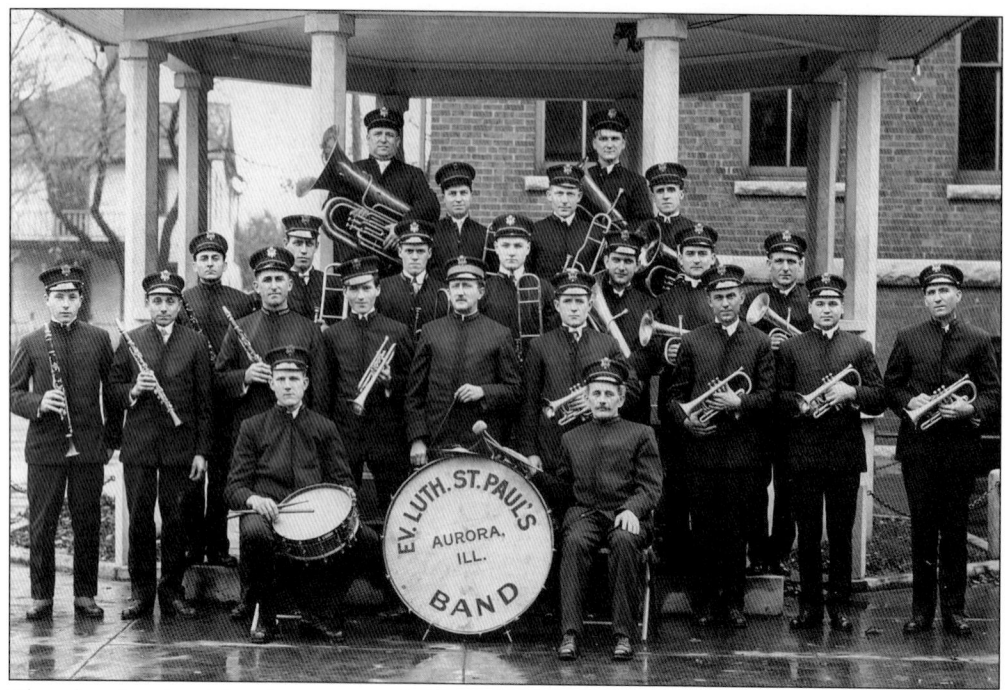

The church school band was a marching testament to their religious faith and fervor. The repertory may have consisted of many hymns to be played in the fashion of the most famous Salvation Army Bands. This ensemble is heavy on brass with cornets, baritones, and trombones with only a sprinkling of clarinets, drums, and a lone tuba.

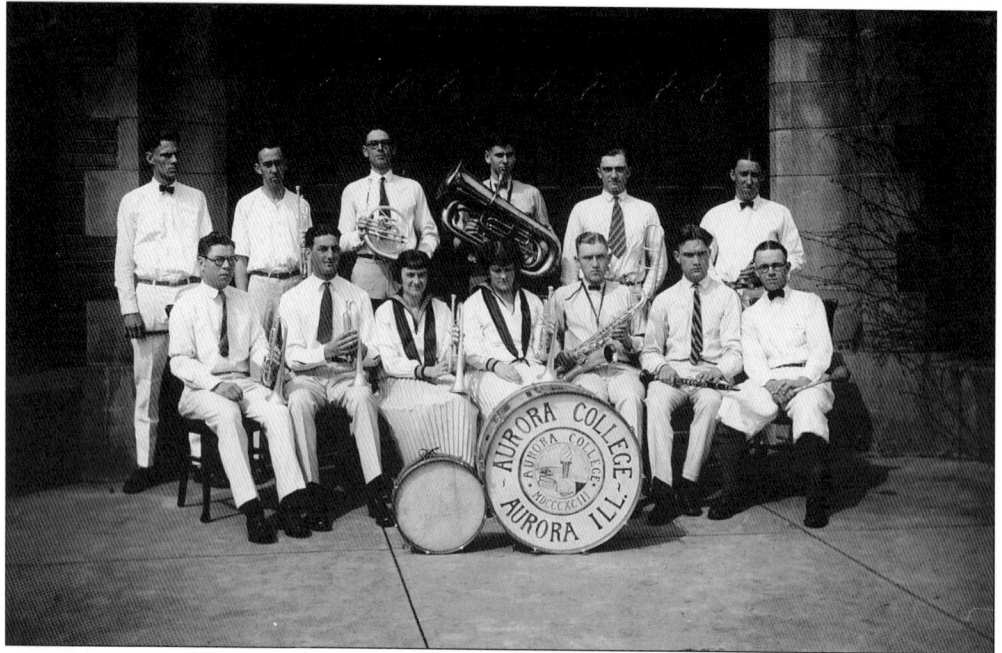

Rag time music and the fox trot, a fast step, were hot in the Fox Valley! The saxophone was a relatively new instrument, and its wailing sounds along with a slippery clarinet ushered in the sounds of the 1920s when the music was "runnin'-wild."

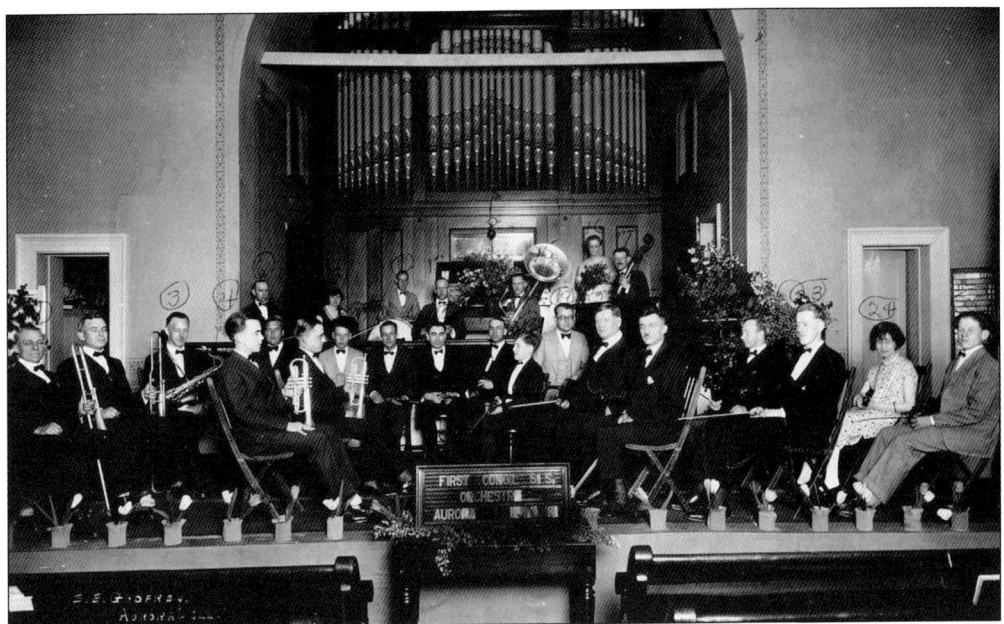

The old instruments were brought to the valley from New York and northern Europe along with a love of the great symphonic and choral music of Handel, Beethoven, and Mozart. The new immigrants from southern Europe made America go opera-mad, at least in New York City where rival opera houses slugged it out like competing Hollywood studios of the 1990s. Churches such as the First Congregational Church organized their own symphonies and orchestras to bring the classics and great liturgical music to their followers.

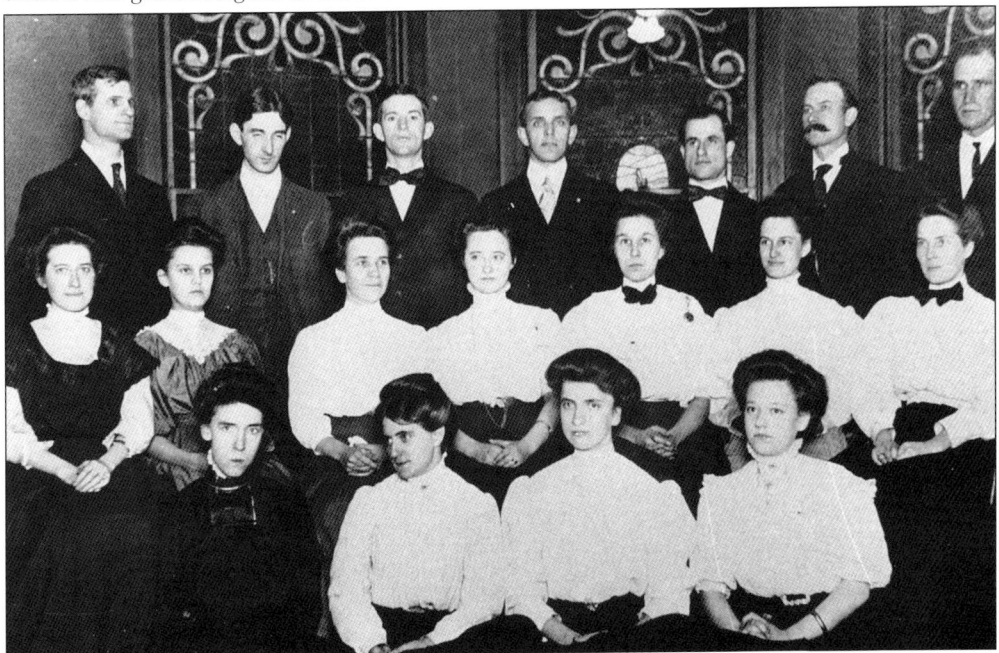

Not every church in Aurora had an orchestra up its sleeve for Sunday services, but they all did have musical groups that required no unnatural instruments, only voices. This is the eloquently dressed First Presbyterian choir of 1908.

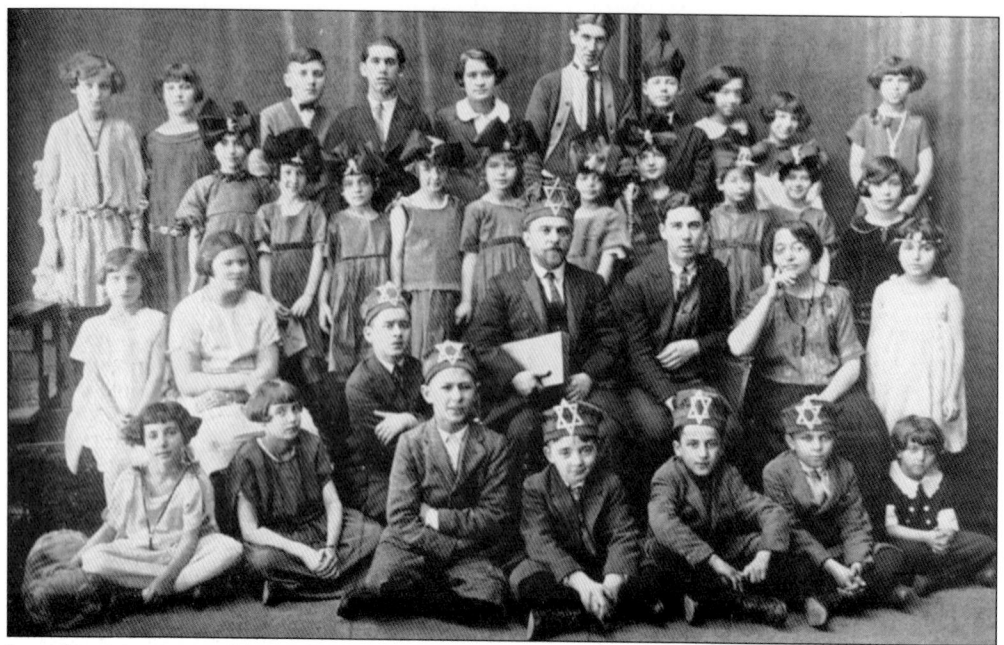

In order to attract and keep their young people, churches and temples not only provided music and instruction in religious truths but also organized good parties with plenty of fun. This group of young Jewish children and their adult director from Temple B'nai Israel in Aurora seem to be commemorating an event with a play, complete with young actors.

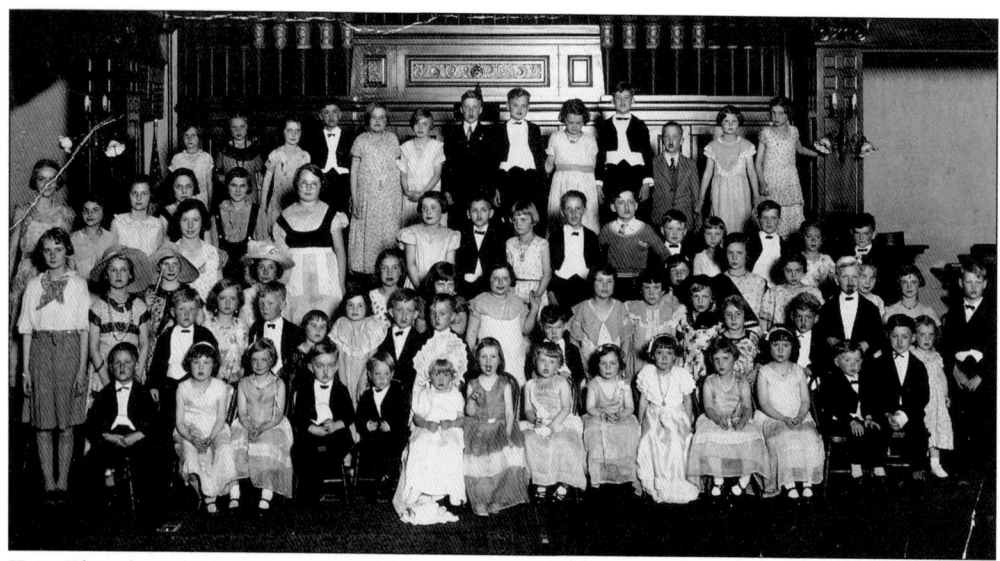

Tom Thumb weddings were a favorite treat for the adults as much as for the children at the First Baptist Church in the 1920s. By the time this photograph was taken, many of the children seem to have concluded that a few minutes of marriage is all they can handle. Luckily, at the end of the party, the innocents are spared and they are all divorced.

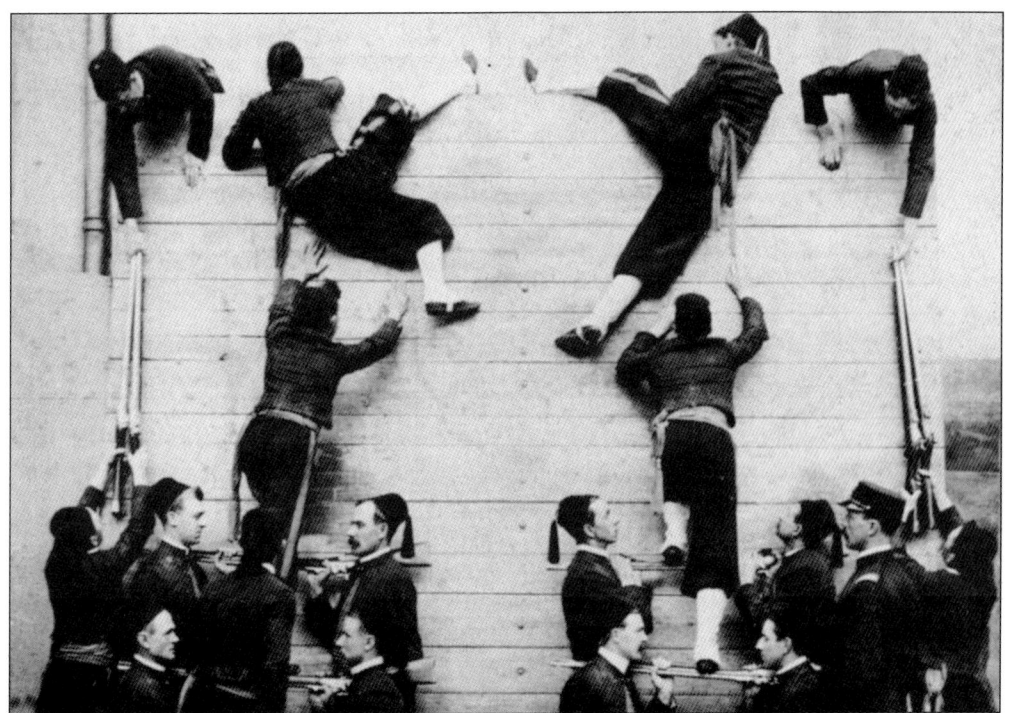

The most spectacular group of performing Aurorans to hit the international big time was the famous Zouaves who were the toast of London. They were supposedly the world's greatest precision drill team, and in 1896 they took the world championship to prove it. The climax of the 16-man act was their scaling a 12-foot wall in 11 or 12 seconds.

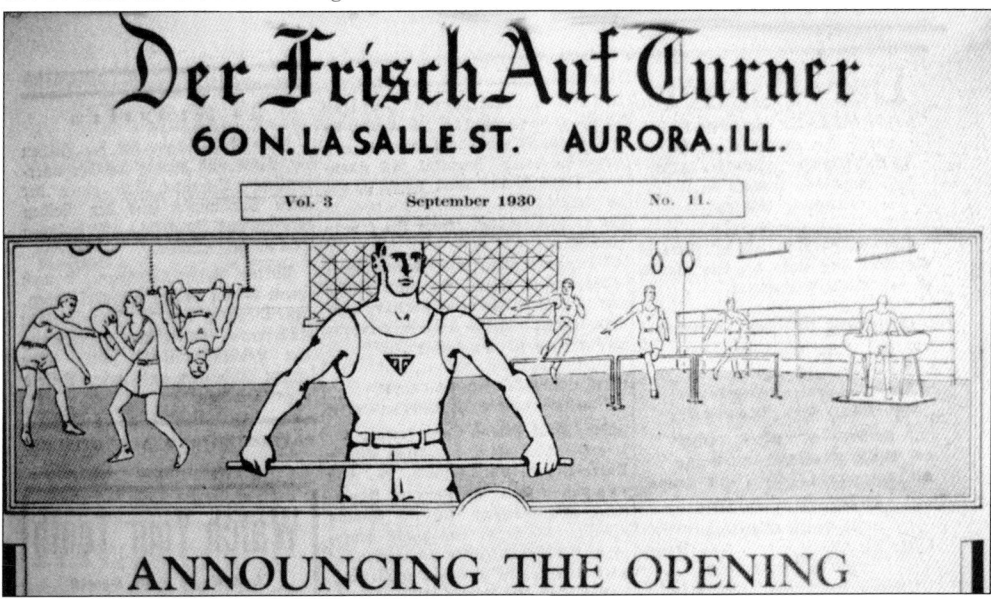

Immigrants from southern Germany migrated to the United States at the end of the 1840s. They brought with them the Turner Society and its gymnastics programs. The Turners performed at the World's Fair in 1890. The first Aurora Turner group was founded in the 1860s and practiced in the Rutishaushers Building.

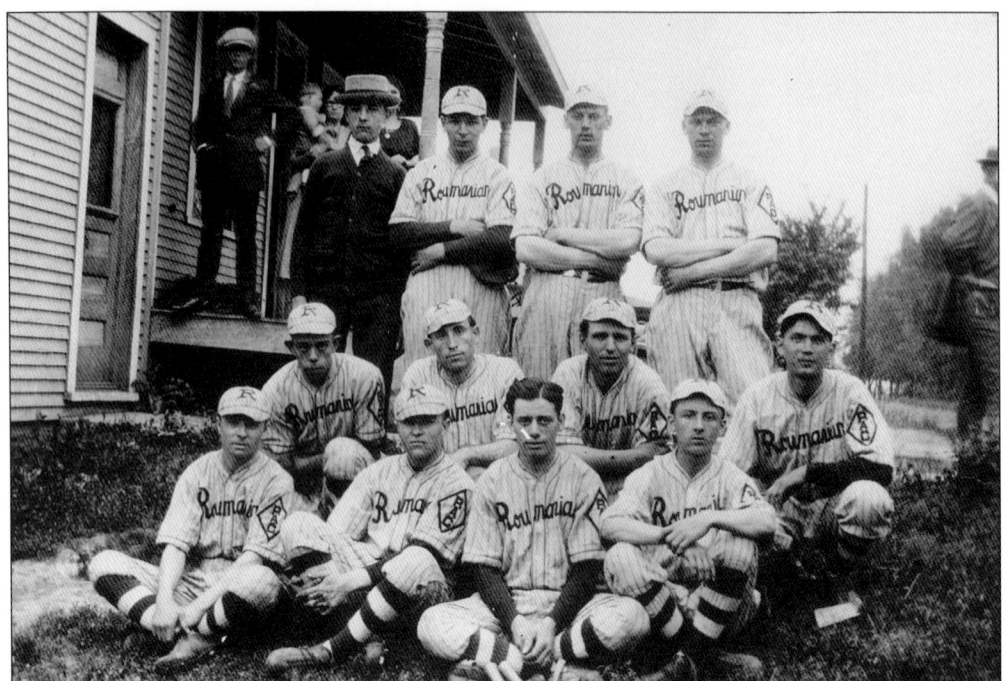

Abner Doubleday really started something with a new-fangled version of an old-English game called "rounders." Baseball is pure and simply America's most beloved sport. Churches such as St. Michael's enjoyed the friendly competition of baseball.

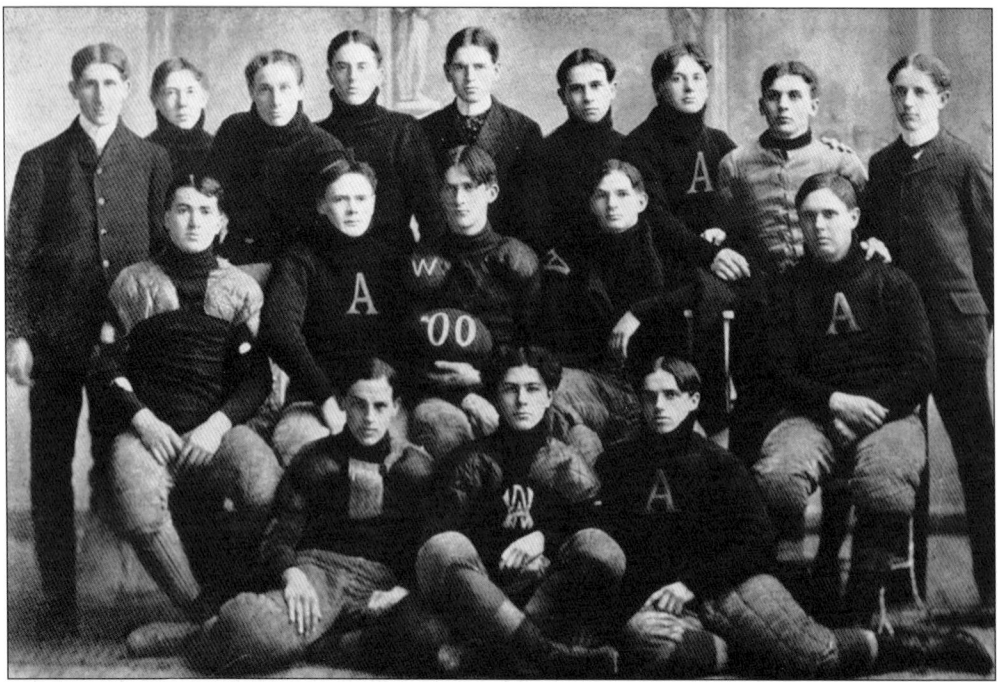

Football, the other American game, soon became the most popular sport in high schools and colleges across the land. In this manly game, one gets to physically pound the life out of your rivals. This is the West Aurora team of 1900.

Six

OUT AND ABOUT: ELEPHANTS, PARKS, AND SCHOOLS

Where did the people go to spend all their extra money between 1870 and 1890 when the per capita income went from $770 to $1,164? Where did they go to get away from the roar of machines in the factories? The answer is not so surprising. They were fascinated with the machines used to create excitement. Amusement parks, factories of fun, sprang up all around the country. The Aurora area had River View Park, Exposition Park, and the Driving Park. The machinery and events at these parks were designed not only to make people happy but also to frighten them. People loved to be frightened! Where else could you go to see two 90-ton locomotives crash into each other at full speed? Making people happy and frightened had suddenly become a very profitable business. People, all across the land, were having fun on the Ferris wheel, the merry-go-round, the steeple chase rides, and the biggest and scariest marvels of the day, roller coasters.

Exposition Park and Central States Fairgrounds featured the dueling locomotives, Siamese twins, the largest swimming pool and log cabin, and the 1920 craze, dance-a-thons. Whew! Racing was expanded to include the automobile.

Schools curriculum by now had advanced far beyond the basic three R's to include leisure time activities. Young girls were taught to sew, not so much as a vocation but as an avocation. Schools became mini cultural centers for the masses to learn music, drama, art, and physical culture. Aurorans took their amusements seriously. Never before had a society worked so hard to make sure they had fun!

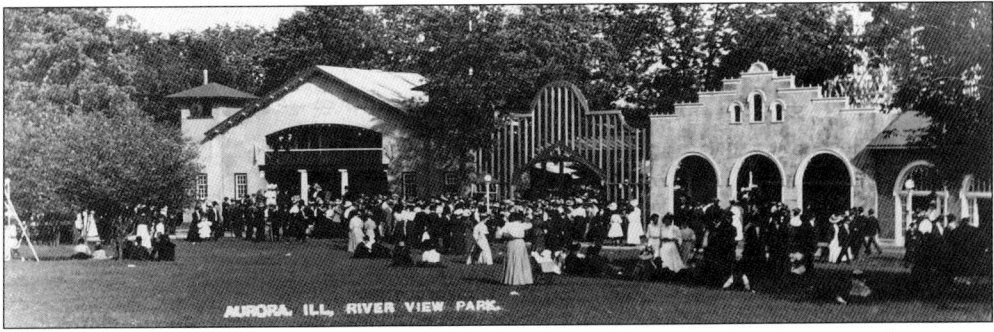

This is a panoramic view of River View Park in Aurora showing the entrances to the various attractions featured in the park.

At the turn of the century River View Park, later called Fox River Park, was Aurora's ticket to thrills and chills. But there was culture here too. You could attend an uplifting lecture at the Aurora Chautauqua Association. Season ticket holders could hear lectures by such famous speakers as William Jennings Bryan or Billy Sunday.

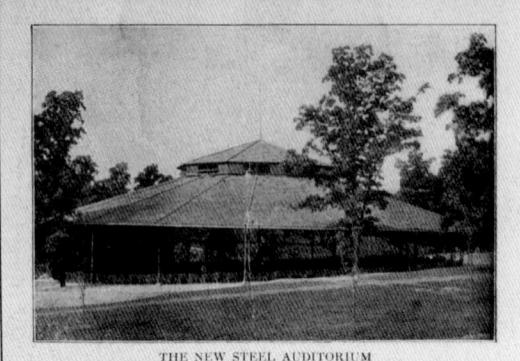

AURORA CHAUTAUQUA ASSEMBLY

THE NEW STEEL AUDITORIUM

Riverview Park, Aurora, Illinois
August 11 to August 22, 1909

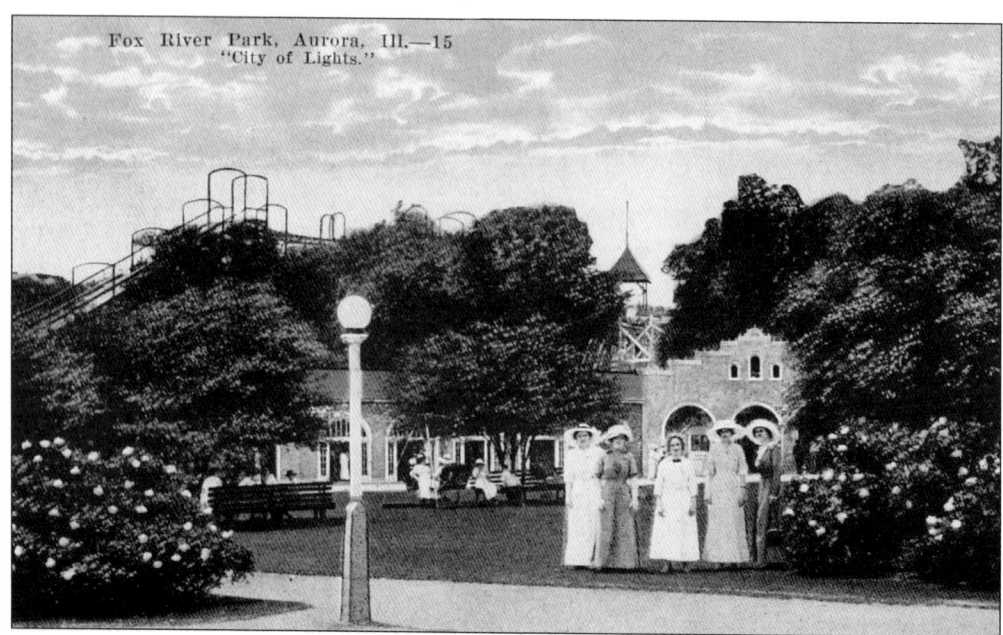

Fox River Park, Aurora, Ill.—15 "City of Lights."

One could also picnic or walk in the beautiful flower gardens and along well-manicured lawns with friends. The grounds were lighted for night use.

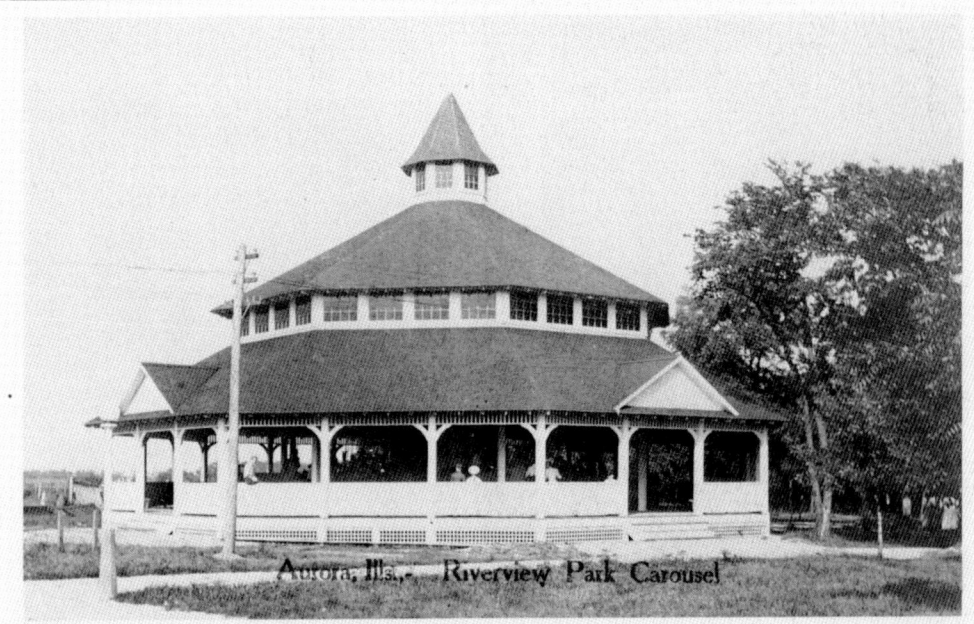

One of the most popular attractions at the park was a carousel ride, enclosed and protected from the elements. This was a large multi-rowed unit with lovely, colorful jumper horses and brightly painted sleds along with a menagerie of animals. There may even have been a Wurlitzer band organ in the center, loudly playing punched "book music." It is very likely that the animals were made in the workshops of the great carousel-maker family, Dentzel of Philadelphia.

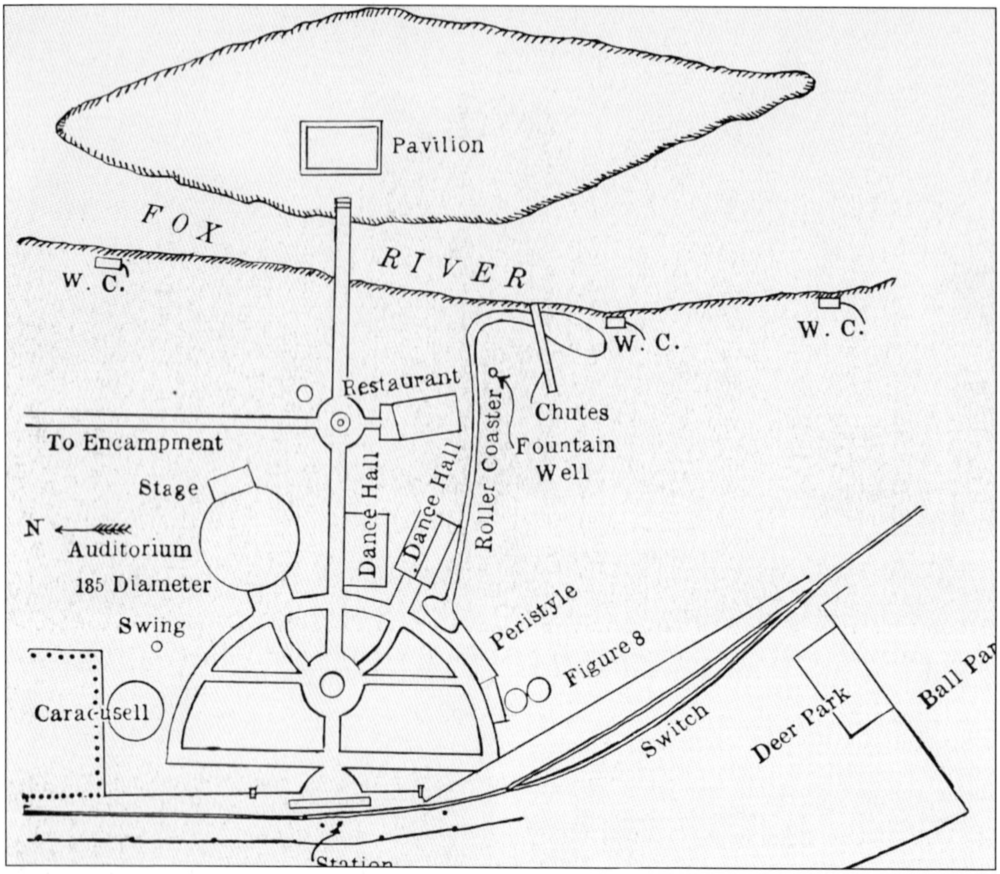

When the customers arrived by rail, they disembarked from a switch-line platform at the station and entered a grand land of fantasy, full of all the necessities of pleasure: a restaurant, candy sellers, and three centrally located "water closets." People paid for each ride separately, not at the front gate for everything.

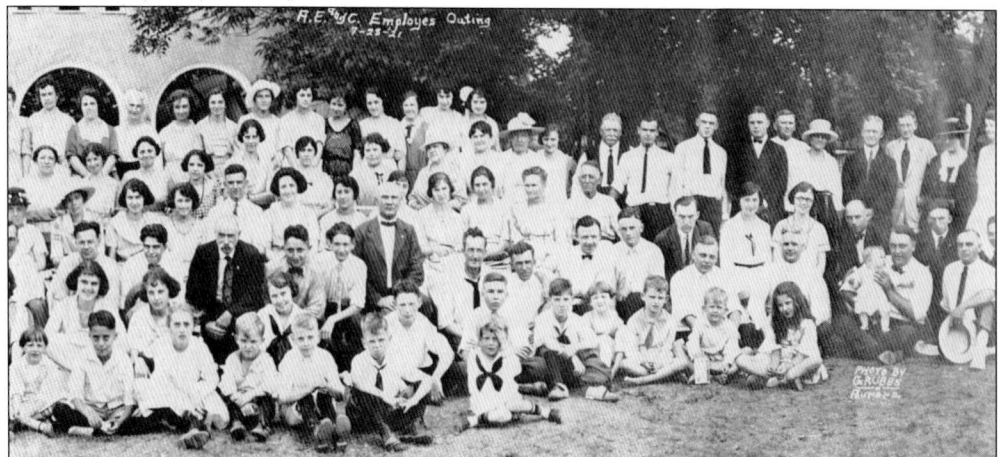

The park was perfect for church outings and company picnics. Shown here are the AE&C railroad employees, out for the day with their families. They could dance, take in a stage show, or take in some of the thrilling rides. Playing in or watching a ball game was also an option.

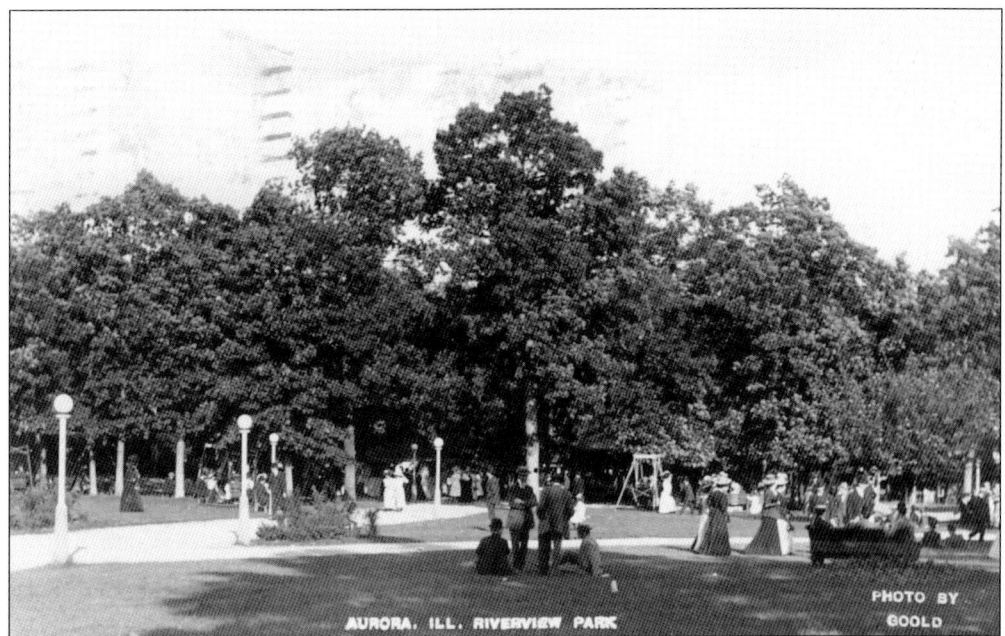

Many pathways wound all over the park, and there were swings for the children, benches, water fountains, and swing sets where four adults could comfortably relax and rock. Or, one could simply relax in the shade and have a picnic. At night the park came alive with one thousand lights that gave the park a fairyland appearance.

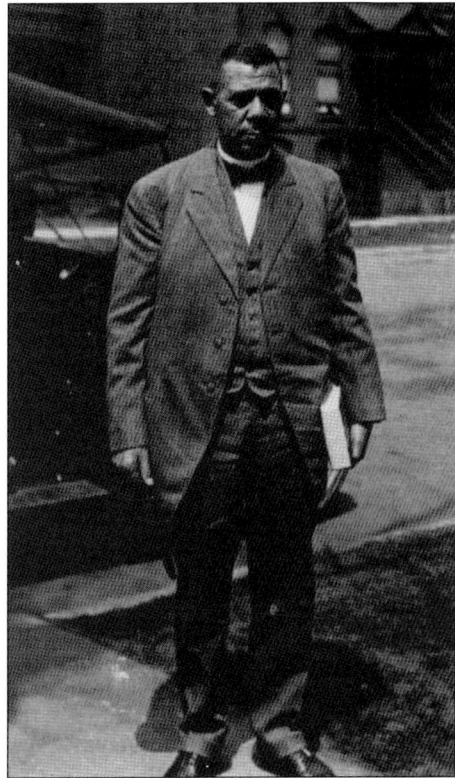

Once inside the park, visitors could walk along the facade entrances to the many attractions and head for an old favorite such as the "Giant Swing" or "Figure 8," or perhaps hear the famous educator and reformer, Booker T Washington, lecture as a part of a Chautauqua season.

91

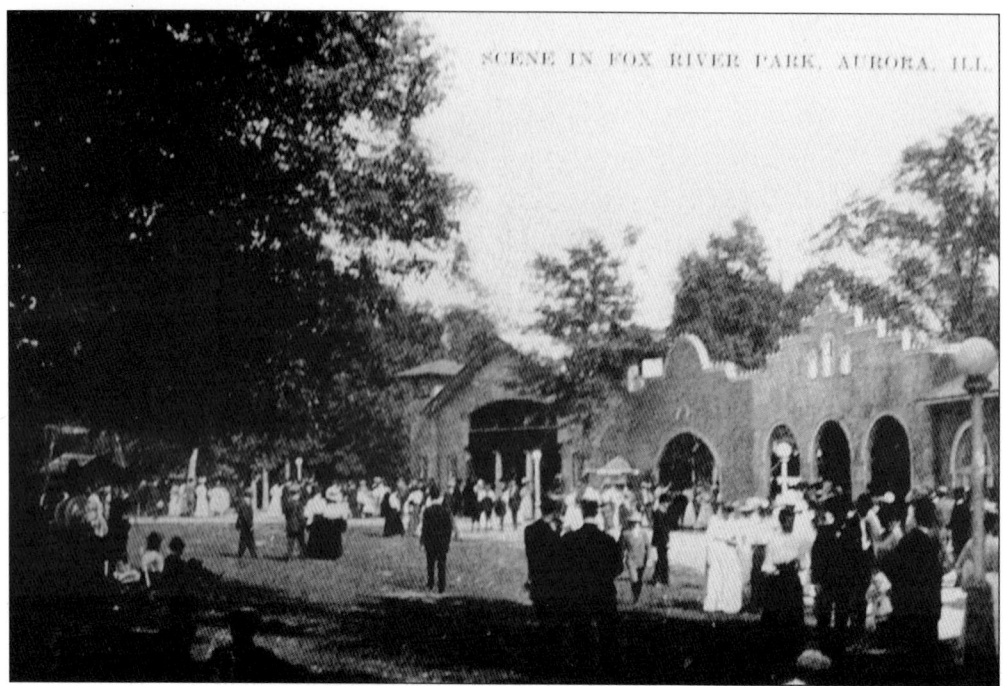

This postcard shows up close the architecturally unique entrances designed for each of the attractions at the park. On a hot summer day, women had to really work at staying cool, dressed up as they were in the typically corseted, multi-layered dresses. At least the popular wide-brimmed hat offered protection from the sun.

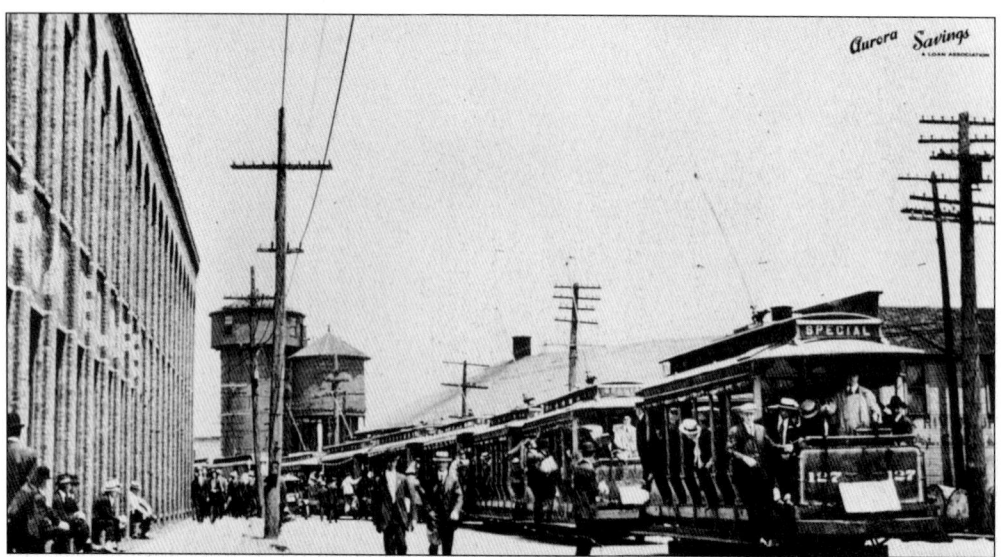

Good public transportation helped keep the park crowded. On weekends people came from up river and from Chicago on special open electric street trolleys. The railroads called these pleasure seekers "excursionists." The building to the left was the Western Electric plant in Montgomery.

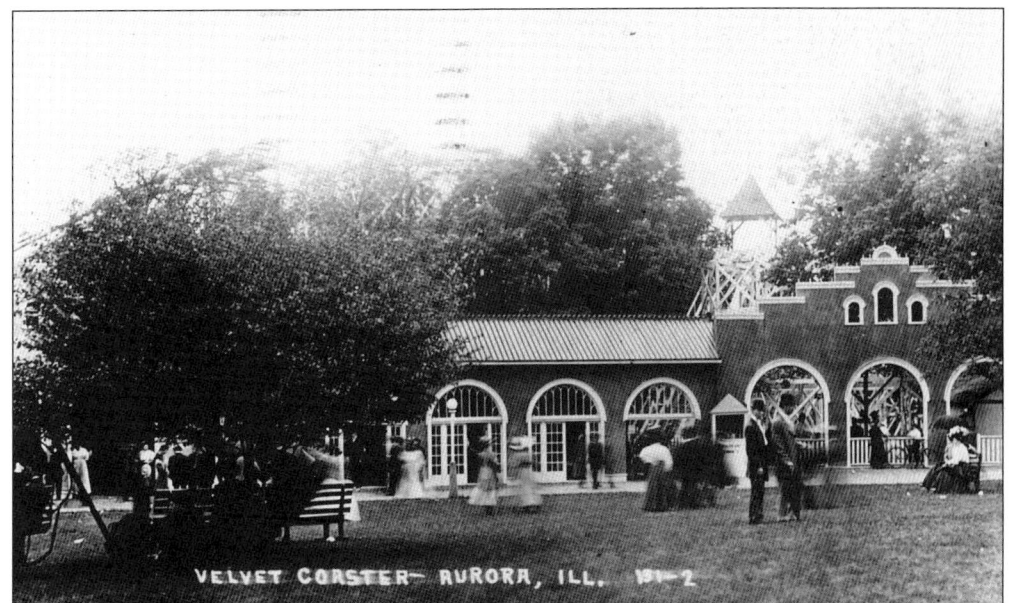

"Roller Coasters" and "Tunnels of Love" were the biggest attractions at amusement parks at this time. The roller coaster went by many names. River View Park's roller coaster was called "The Velvet Coaster." The wooden supports for the ride were behind the colorful and impressive facade. In the Victorian "age of manners" where else could you go to be hugged and hug back, and get away with it, in public?

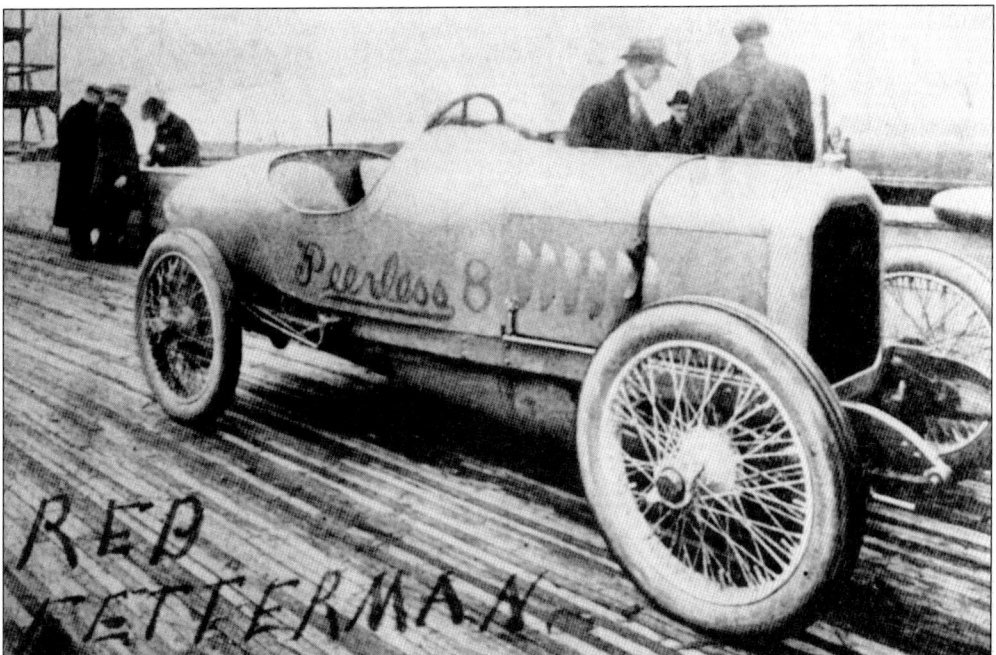

Races, baseball games, and special grand spectacle shows were to be found north of River View Park in Aurora in an area today called Riddle Highlands. Aurora's famous Driving Park was built here. Early racecar drivers, such as "Red" Fetterman, could bring home a trophy and an ego boost after racing in the Peerless 8.

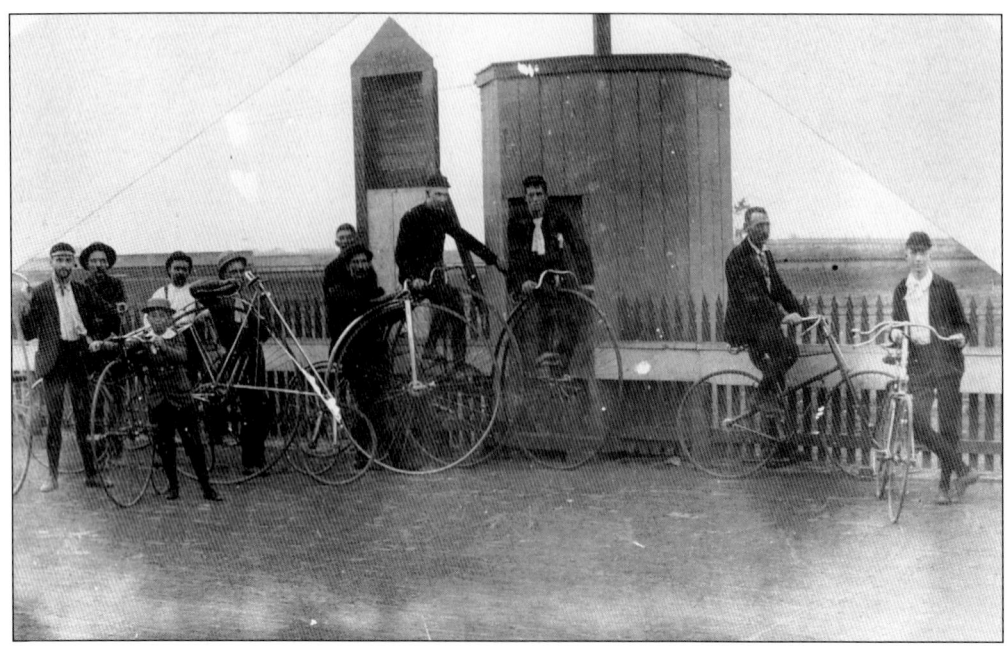

There were bicycle races at the Aurora Driving Park as well. Aurora even had its own bicycle club named the Hi Bi Club. The name no doubt was created when the front wheel of bicycles was indeed high. Shown here are "high" and "low" riders. Listed from left to right are as follows: J.M. Lillibridge, A.V. Brown, Henry Sperry, Axel Levedahl, Clarence Rogers, John Taylor, Dr. Geyer as a boy, Sam Lilley, Marsh Webb, and Fred Olson (on the fenced track).

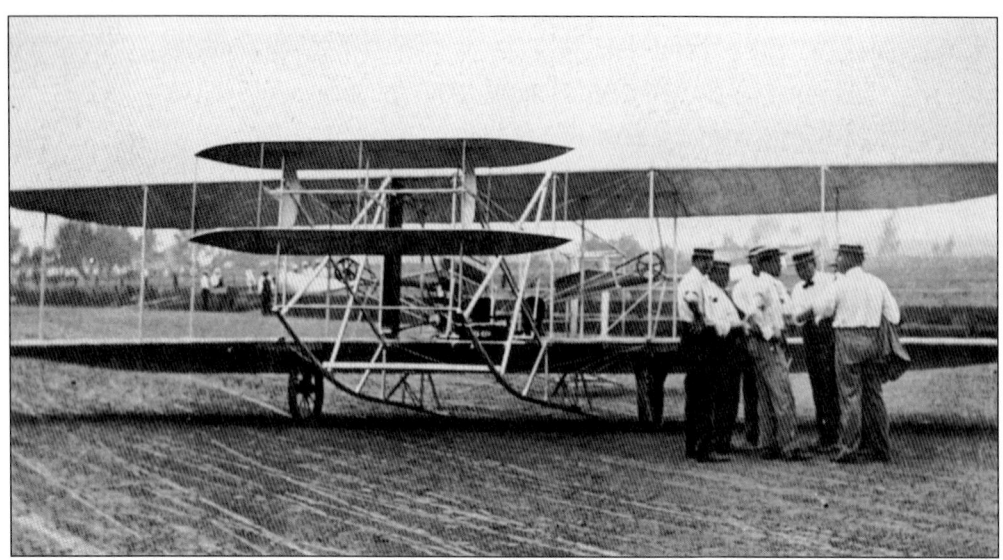

Aurora's first airport was Driving Park. Frank Thielen, on his way to the state fair in Springfield, went to Dayton, Ohio, and arranged with Orville Wright to bring two biplanes, like the historic flight plane, for the Fourth of July festivities in Aurora. Orville even came to Aurora to set up the air show!

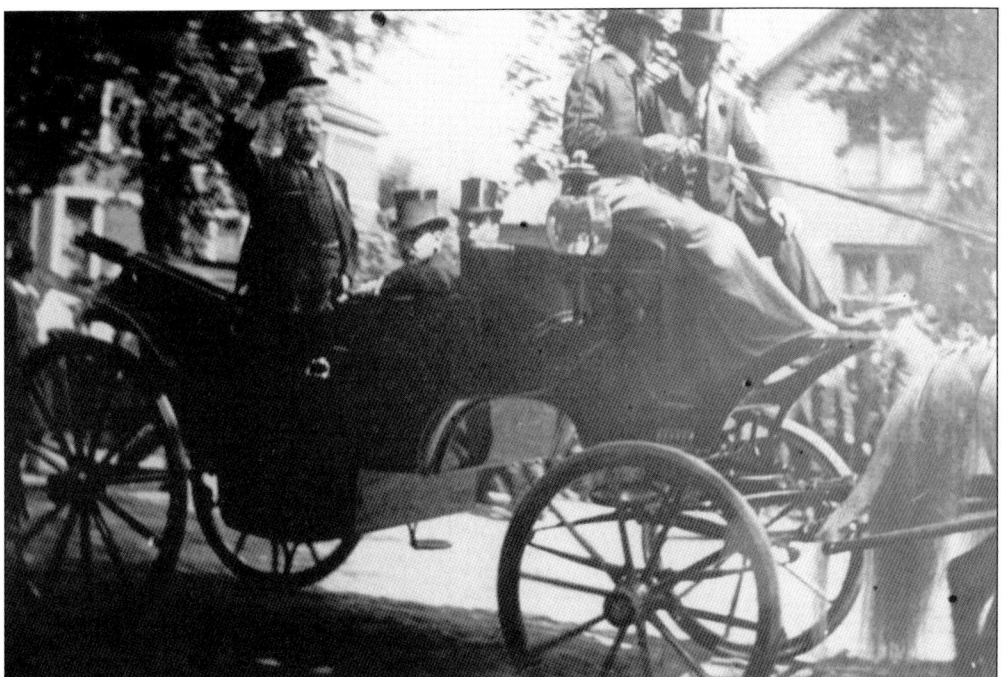

Downtown Aurora also had plenty of fun during the year for its citizens and visitors. Notable people dropped by ever so often, such as Teddy Roosevelt, who rode through the crowded streets of Aurora to visit Senator Hopkins in his home and make a speech at Lincoln Park (McCarty Park). This procession through town had 50 white horse-pulled carriages.

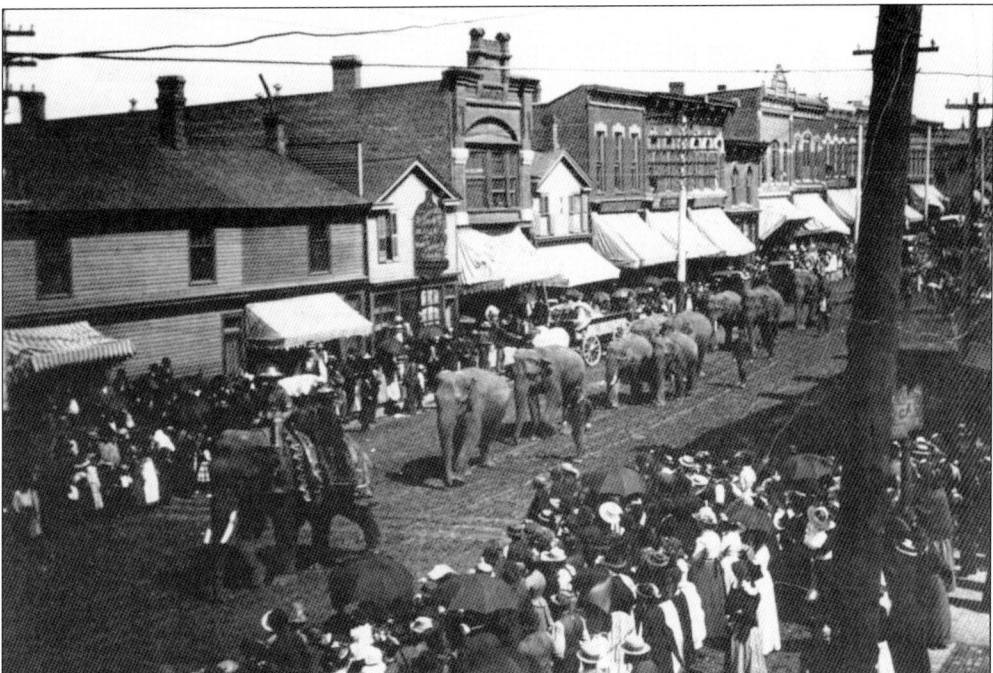

The circus came to town many times in the 1800s. This herd of monstrous pachyderms with colorful horse-drawn circus wagons is paraded down Broadway in Aurora in 1890.

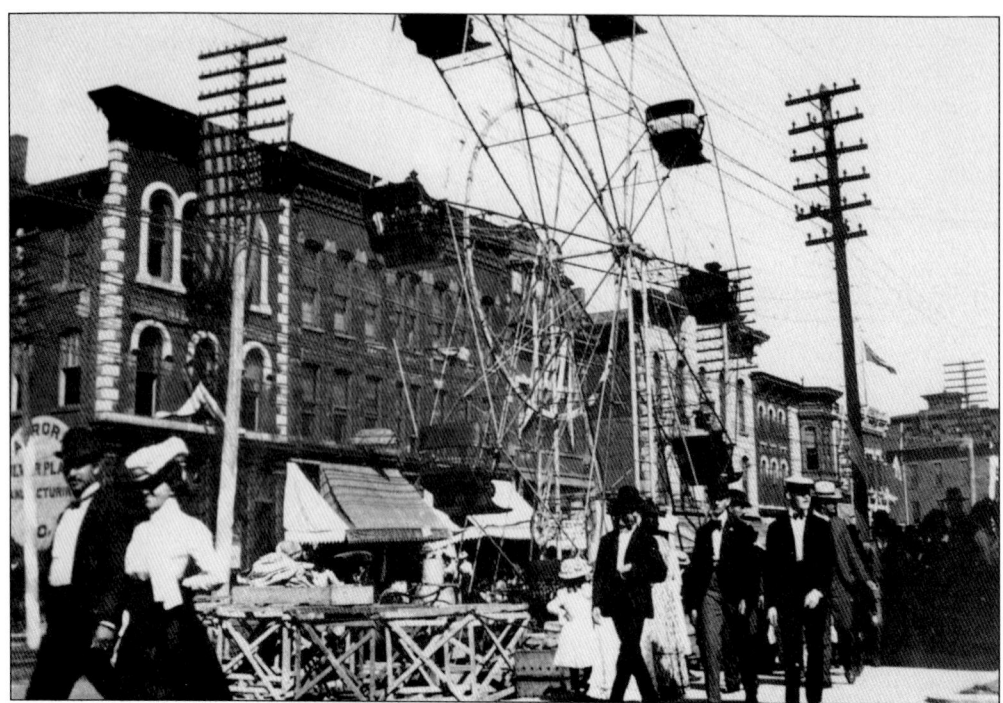

Carnivals drew Aurorans by the thousands to a prosperous downtown. Here we see a huge Ferris wheel as the central attraction during the Elk's Club carnival in Aurora at Downer and Stolp in 1901.

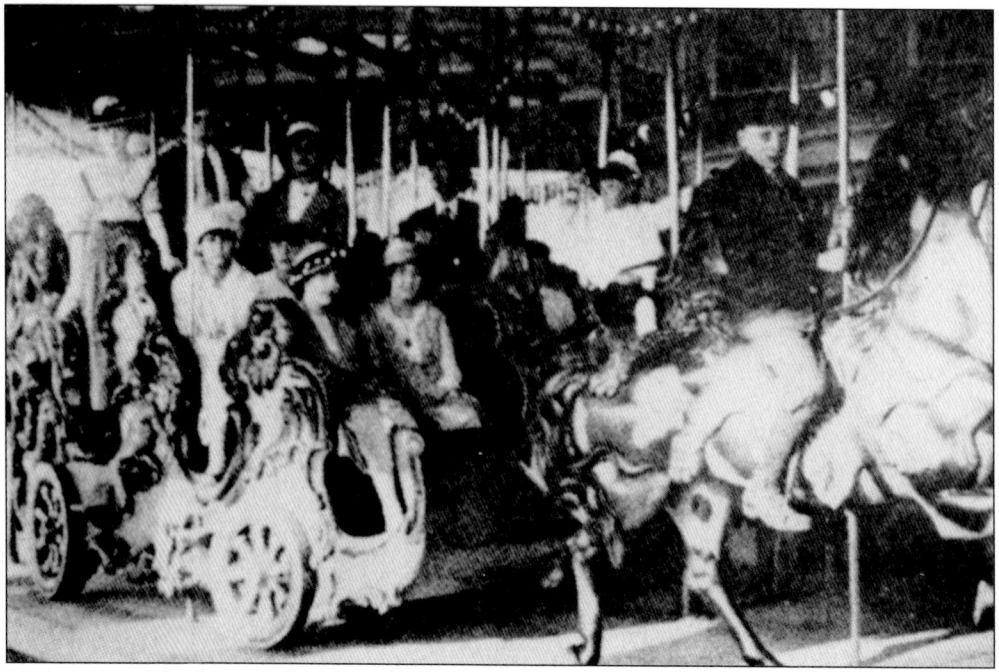

Most carnivals had carousels. The adults tended to babysit their children by riding with them in wagon-like sleds on the carousel while the older children rode the wood-carved prancing, rearing horses of this turn-of-the-century triple-row carousel visiting downtown Aurora.

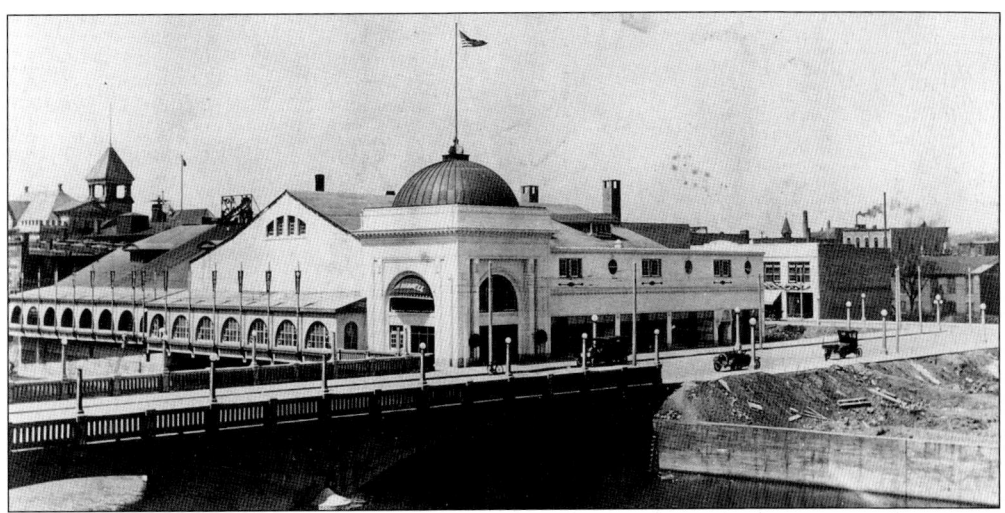

The jewel in the crown of Aurora's amusement area was a vast theater and amusement building, called Sylvendale, located downtown. It was a block long multi-building structure that had a promenade along the east facing the Fox River. Included in the 1920 complex was the newly completed Rialto Theatre.

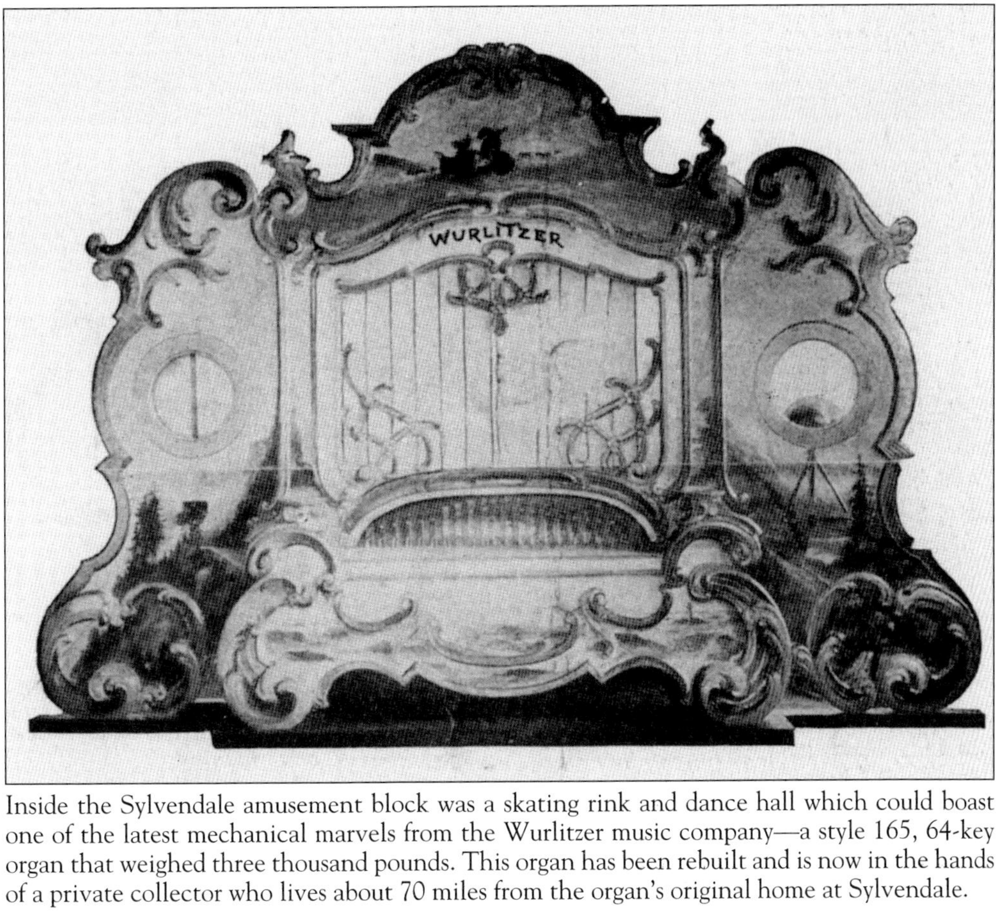

Inside the Sylvendale amusement block was a skating rink and dance hall which could boast one of the latest mechanical marvels from the Wurlitzer music company—a style 165, 64-key organ that weighed three thousand pounds. This organ has been rebuilt and is now in the hands of a private collector who lives about 70 miles from the organ's original home at Sylvendale.

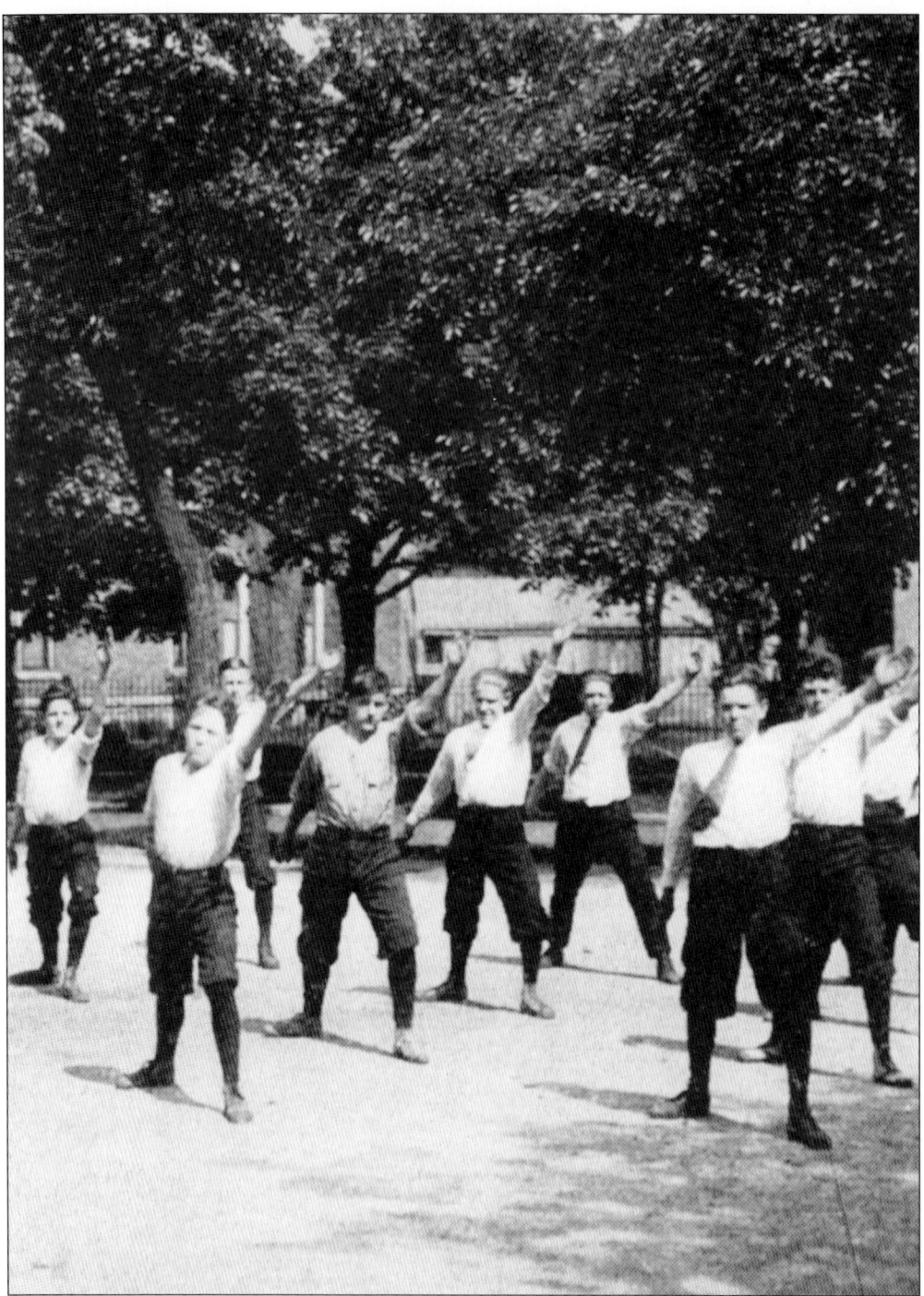
Schools from this period began to add to their curriculum, instruction in the technical trades of the day and courses in physical fitness. Not so strangely, this new emphasis in health-related exercise was also advocated by manufacturers who now became concerned that workers were not staying physically fit and healthy. This view shows students from Aurora's Oak Street School outdoors, practicing what was labeled "setting-up exercises."

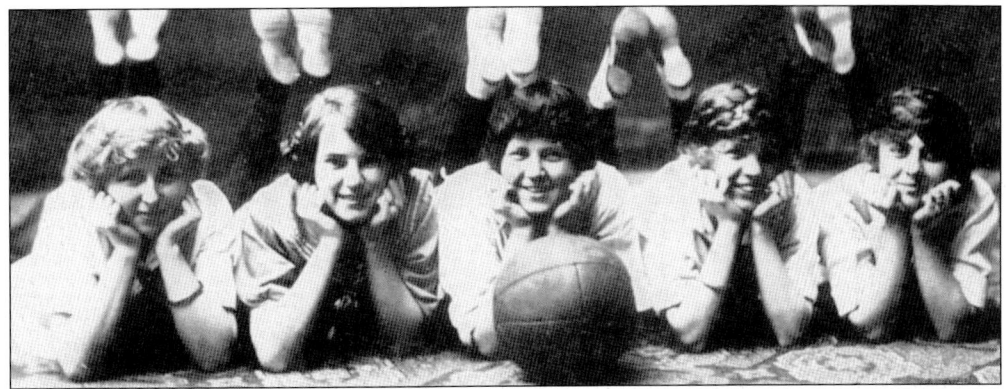

The school encouraged students not only to learn and excel but also to compete on the football field and in their classroom studies. Even girls were encouraged to join teams and compete with other schools on a selective basis. School girls from East Aurora High School posed for this girls basketball team in 1913.

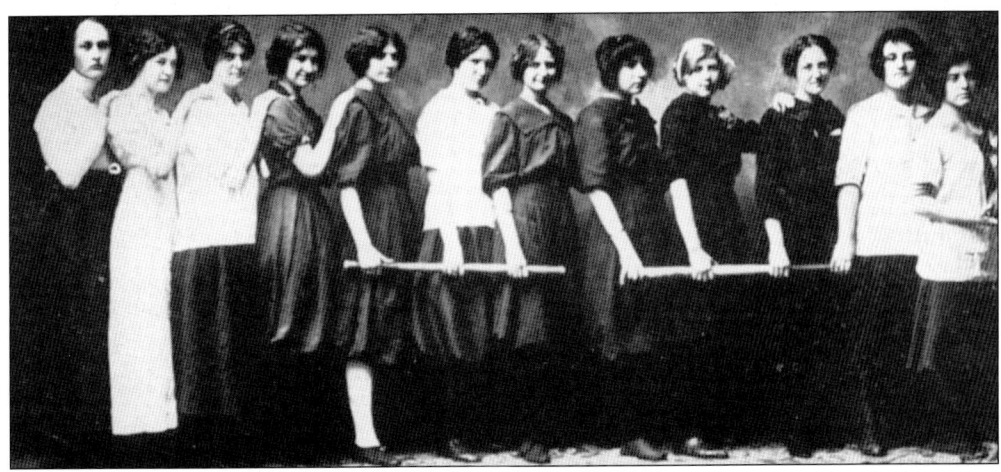

The community was not quite ready yet for girls to play the manly sport of baseball, so they kept the girls inside, softened the ball, and gave them skinny bats to reduce the possibility of breaking windows in the gym.

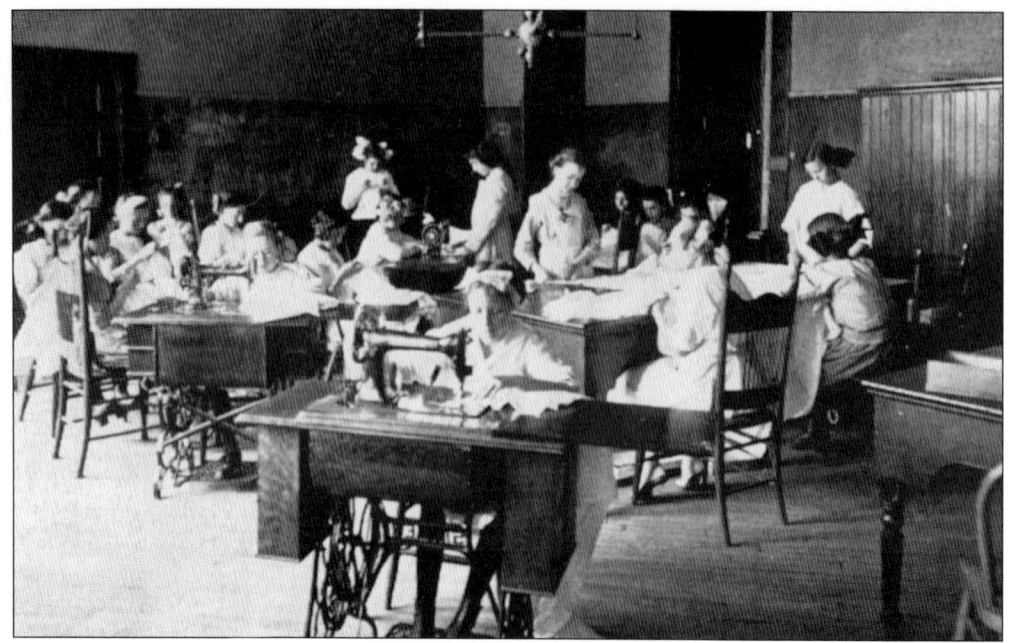
Many other new extra curricular courses were added to school offerings. At East High School in 1917, girls were encouraged to learn to sew. Sewing and the ability to play a musical instrument were valuable skills a young girl would want to have to attract a life companion!

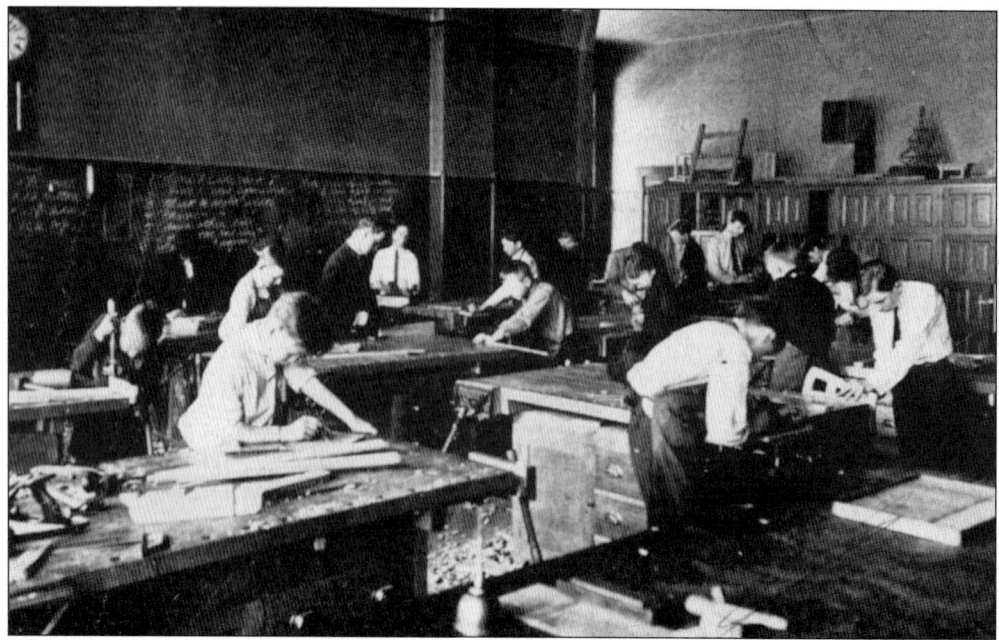
While the girls across the hall were making their sewing machines hum with activity, boys were busy creating sawing and buzzing noises in manual training class. Students mastered the art of the clamp, hammer, saw, and plane. No power tools are evident in this 1917 photograph.

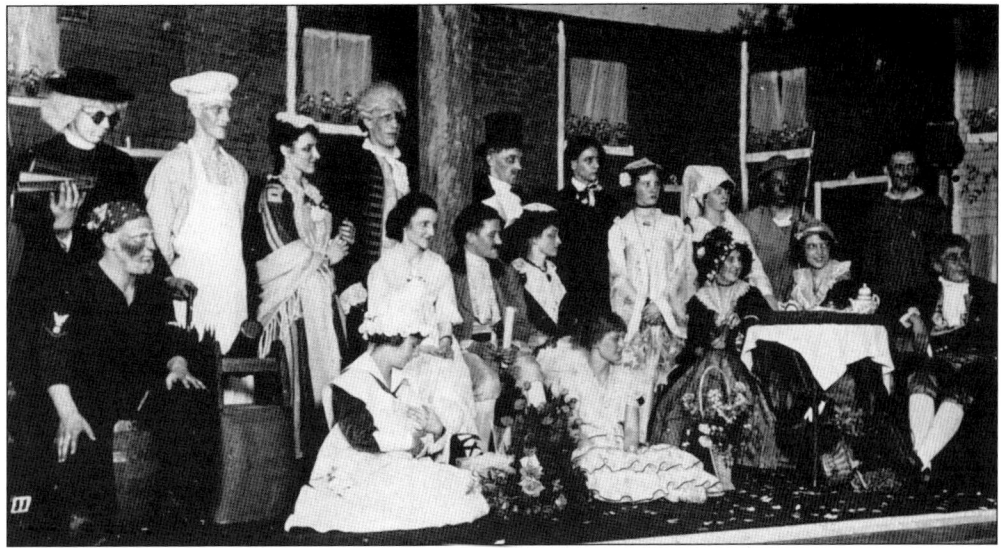

Luckily, schools in this period not only had a gymnasium for sports, but they also had a concert hall or auditorium where the arts and culture could flourish. Aurora's multi-ethnic people brought with them a love of dramatics. This group of high school thespians, magnificently costumed and hamming it up, performs in 1917 at West Aurora High School.

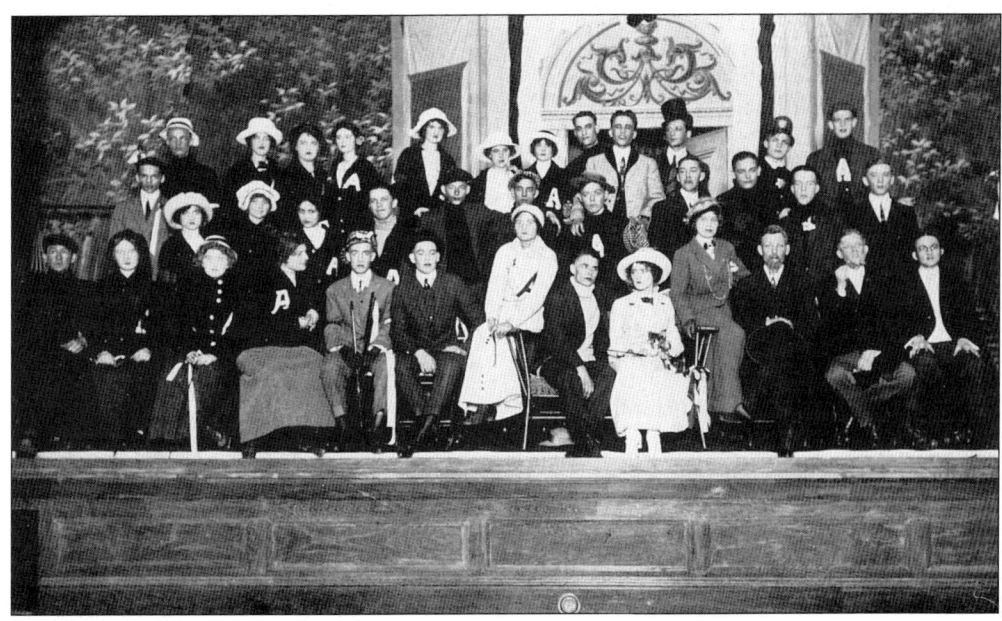

Across the river, at East Aurora High School, the budding actors were performing a contemporary piece in 1913 with the provocative title, *The College Widow*, that probably had more than a little resemblance to the plot of *The Merry Widow* opera.

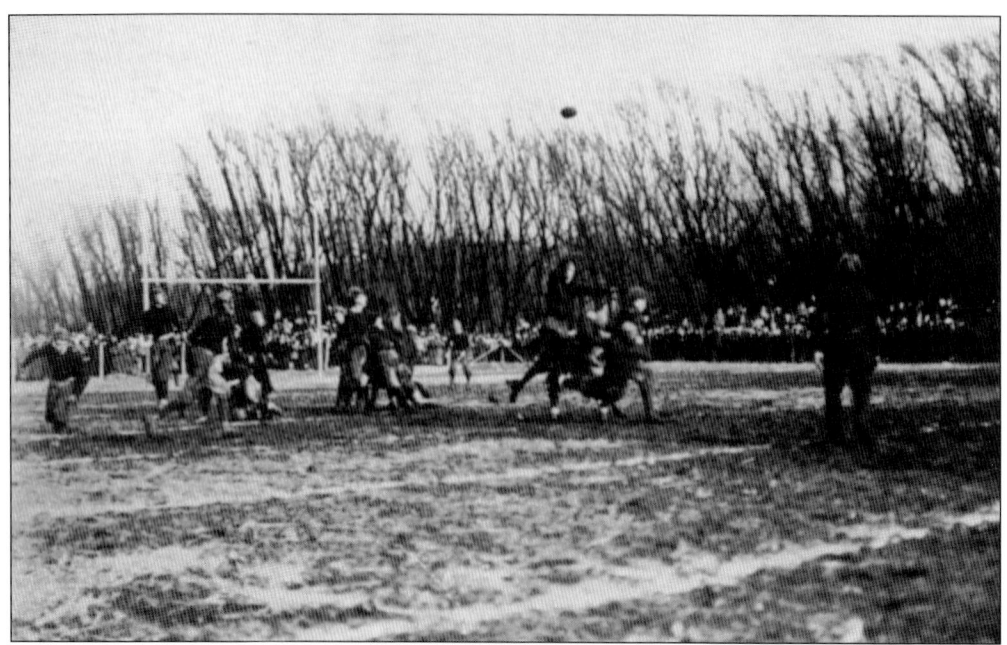

The eyes of the students at West and East Aurora had never shown brighter nor were fuller of excitement than when they played the "other side of the river" in football and won. The two high schools slugged it out in neutral turf. As with so many schools of the day, the athletic element of education began to overshadow the more basic pursuit of knowledge.

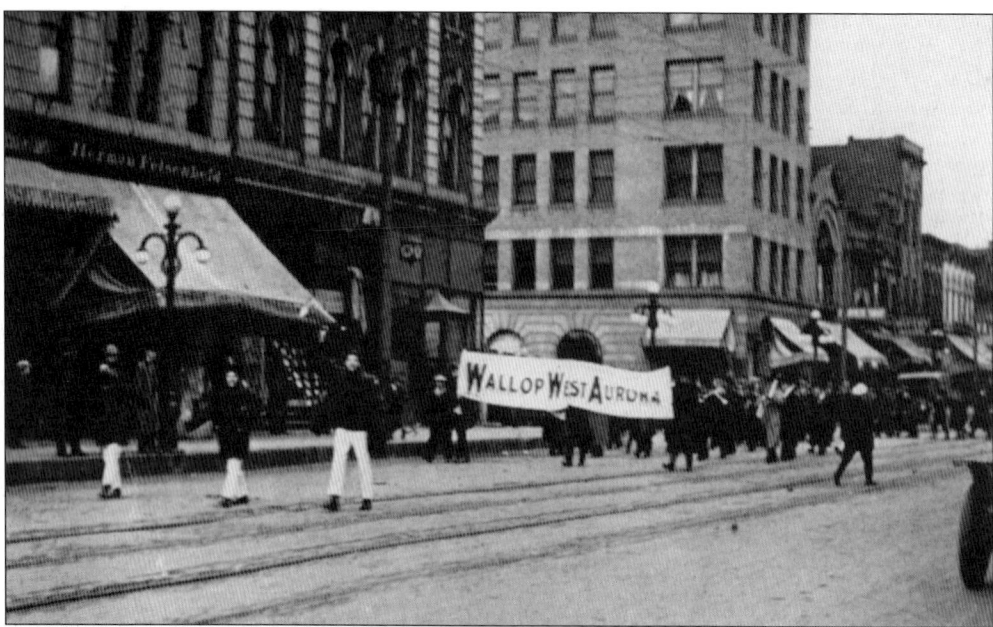

For the annual 1912 Thanksgiving Day confrontation, both schools paraded through downtown Aurora to create "spirit" and general pandemonium for the grudge match ahead. Bands played, floats were in evidence, carriages carried school officials, and the team and a huge banner flashed for all to see the watchword of the day, "Wallop West Aurora." Did they?

Seven

THE IMAGE MAKERS AND THEIR "DREAM FACTORIES"

Photography was elevated to a fine art by the people of the 19th century, and Aurora treated its famous photographers as community leaders and treasures. The photographers were responsible for recording moments from the lives of Aurora's rich, and not so rich, and those scenes of public interest. So it was these dauntless wizards of technology who battled with the fast paced, ever changing photographic field to capture and record life in Aurora to the best of their ability during a time of industrial growth and a rapid influx of different types of people.

When the Kodak camera came on the scene in 1888, amateur photography was born and the middle classes embraced photography almost as a responsibility of their rank. Photography then began to loose a great deal of its magic, for it seemed anyone with a camera could shoot a picture, have others print it, and come out a winner. Today the professional image-maker is still busy shooting cute shots of dogs in costume for fairy tale books, recording images for school yearbooks, producing ad copy for vodka, or posing formal wedding pictures. They are simply another merchant with a skill. However, in the past century, oh what a shadow they cast!

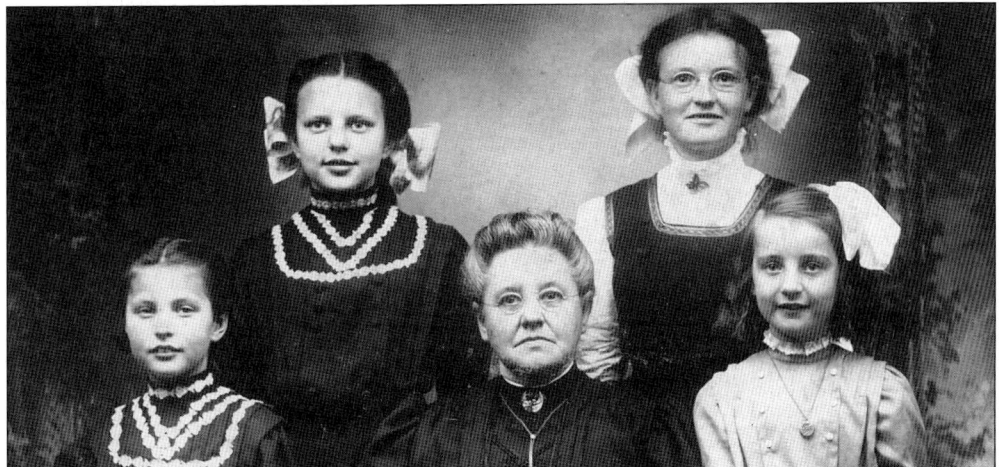

This photographer has captured the three female generations of a family. The warm smiles on everyone's face except Granny, and Granny's sober look, work together to convey the great pride and self-satisfaction of this long ago family. The unanswered question is "Why no men?"

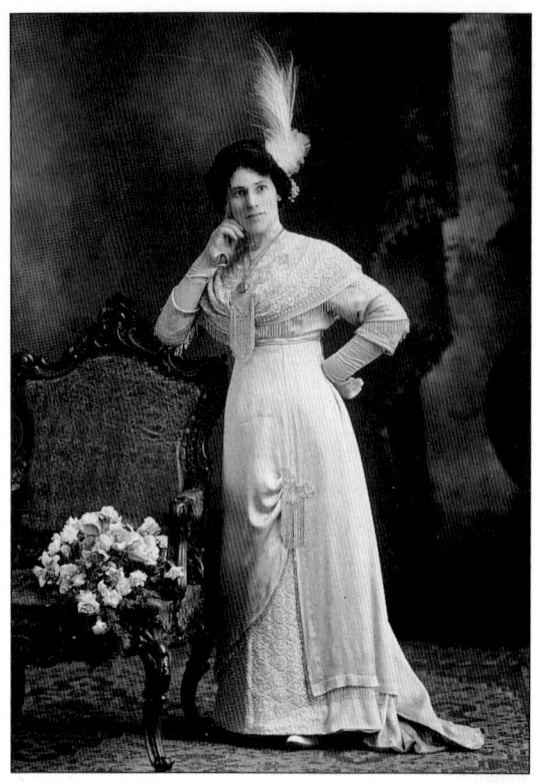

The image-maker was master of his craft in his studio. The tricks and special effects he would conjure up to please his clientele made his studio a somewhat Hollywood-like "dream factory." It was here that he could produce props to serve as colorful details in his views. With such magic at hand, he could make anyone look like a real lady of society.

Here is one Aurora couple's wedding photograph. This family photograph, shot on February 19, 1885, is of the J. Michael Lies family. John was an Aurora farmer originally from Luxemburg. Listed from left to right are as follows: John Lies, J. Michael Lies, his bride Mary Pettit, and Agnes Pettit. Notice that the bride is not dressed all in white but instead she's wearing a festive wedding head covering with a long train.

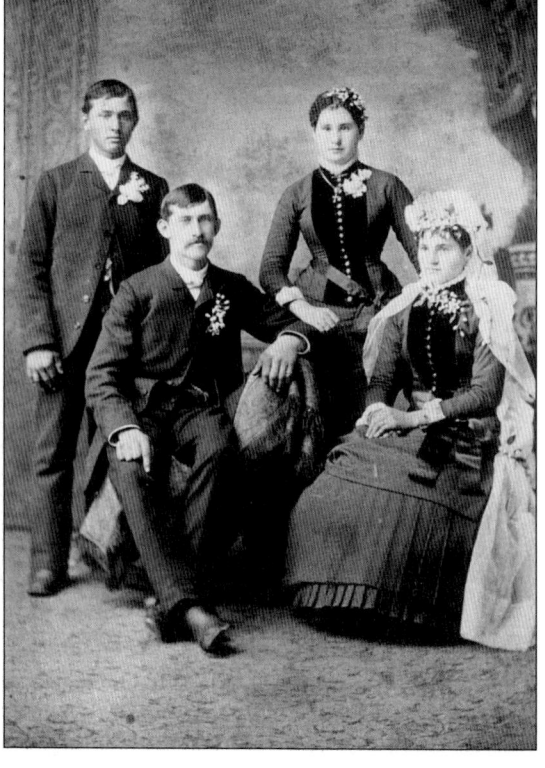

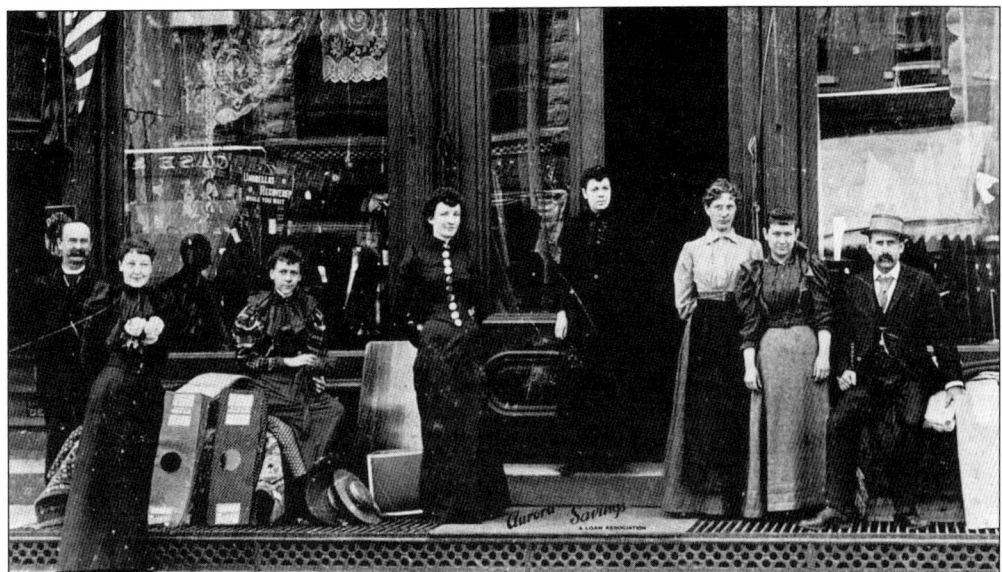

The photograph was limited in many ways in recording certain "views," a term popularly used in the Victorian era that today translates as "pictures." The problems were motion, poor light, and bulky camera equipment. That is why the photographer liked to work in the controlled environment of his studio. The workers in McMillian's Dry Goods Store, on the northeast corner of Downer at the turn of the century, was a most difficult scene to record.

Wiggling children were a photographer's nightmare in the 1890s, just as they are today. Metal rods with clamps were used to hold adult heads still but, for a child of this age, such a devise was useless. This photograph was by early Aurora photographer Samuel Taylor, who in 1883 had a studio at 33 S. River Street. In 1870 he moved to the corner of Downer and River but later returned to his old studio location.

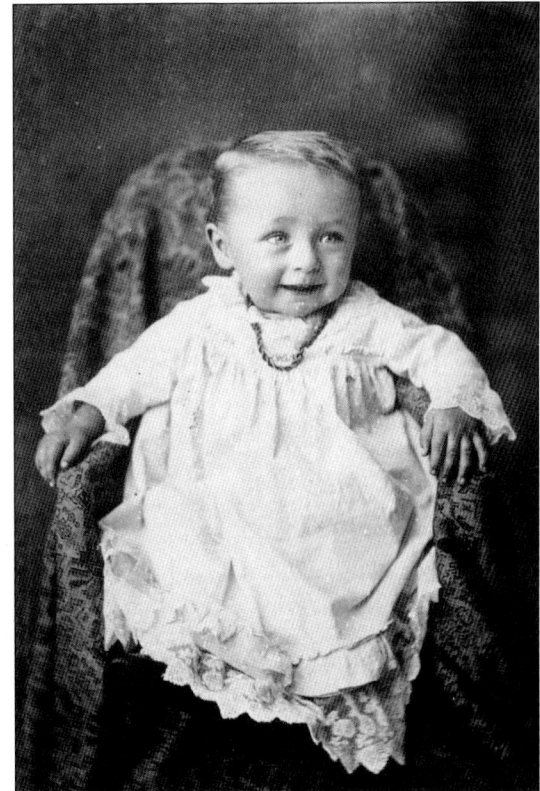

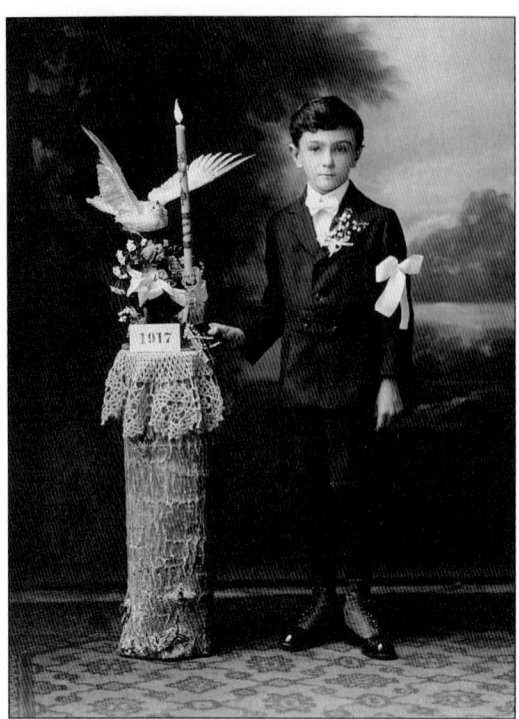

Families celebrated important religious milestones of their children with a visit to the local photographic art studio. Shown in this image is a young boy's entrance into the adult life of his church by his first communion. The event was recorded with pomp and symbolism. His Sunday best outfit is complete with spats, ribbons, floral, memorial candle, and a dove.

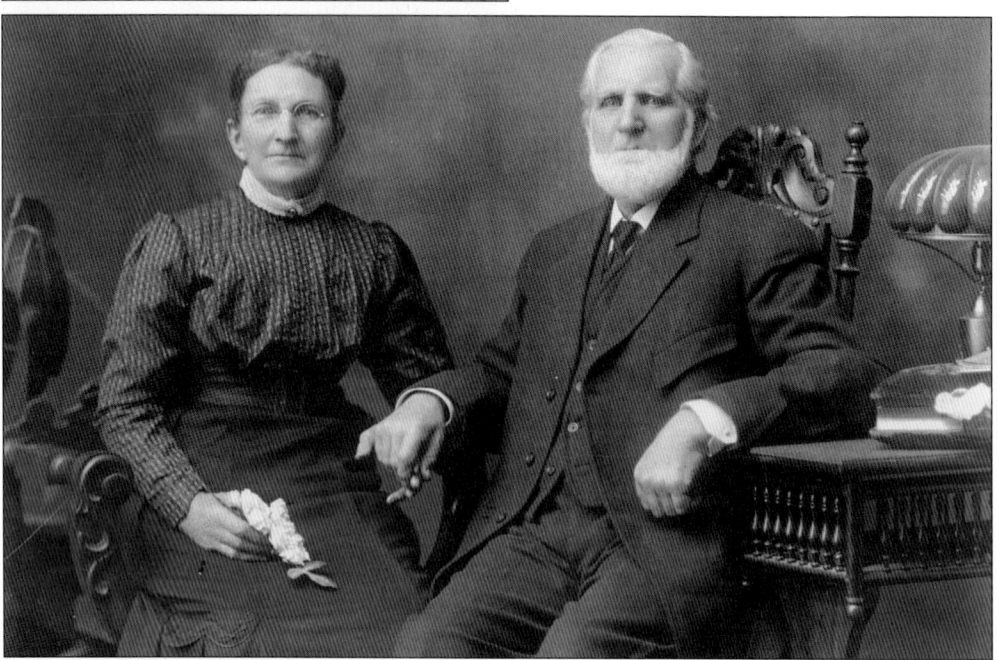

The image-makers also captured the twilight years of the marriage. Formality even in photographs, as in life, was wisely observed by subjects of the camera lens in Victorian Aurora. This extraordinary picture with the touching hands and the flower in the lace-covered hand of the wife boldly captures the physical reflection of love between two people who have been life partners. The photograph was made by Sigmund Benensohn who operated an "Art Gallery" in Aurora in 1904.

Dewitt Clinton Pratt, master photographer, arrived in Aurora in 1853. He had come to the United States from England in the early 1800s first settling in Boston. He soon took off to make his future in the new West. He traveled down the Fox River and became one of the very early settlers of Aurora. Grandson Verneur, who would later become a world inventor and patent holder of the microfilm machine, recalled that D.C. was a large man who could "use his head as well as his big hands . . . was a cabinet maker, photographer and artist." D.C. was also an inventor. He made the first foot-powered lathe in Illinois so that he could make comfortable applewood chairs for his family and friends in Aurora. Verneur still had his in the 1960s!

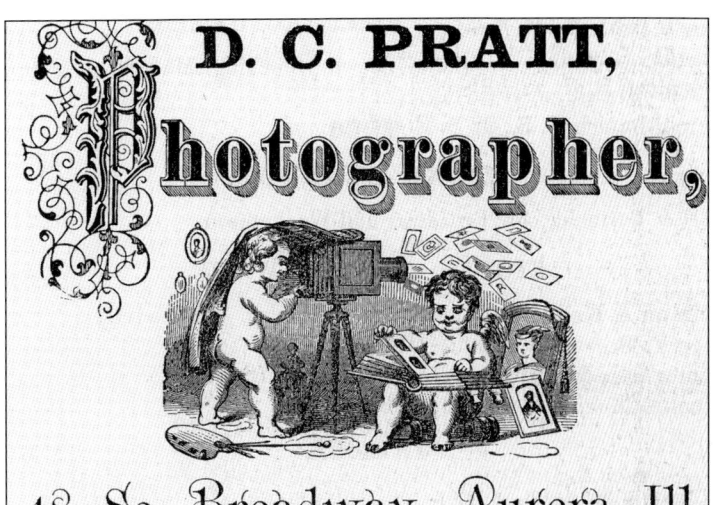

D. C. PRATT, Photographer,

48 So. Broadway, Aurora, Ill.

Lambertype and Chromotype Photographs in Permanent Pigments.

Patented in England, France and America and adopted by all first-class Artists in Europe ; and now American Photographers are securing Licenses and Instructions as fast as possible.

☞ *We have secured the Exclusive Right for this city.*

The Chromotypes, Permanent, Impermeable, and Enameled, are made from life in Card, Cabinet, Promenade, and larger sizes, and are admitted to be essentially different from and far superior to Photographs made with Salts of Silver.

The Lambertypes, also "Permanent, Impermeable and Enameled," are enlargements or copies from Daguerreotypes, Photographs, &c., &c., from the very smallest to life-size, and are better in color and finer in finish than heretofore produced by other processes.

We invite all interested to call and examine these Pictures, and learn what is meant by "Lambertype and Chromotype Photographs in Permanent Pigments."   Respectfully,

D. C. PRATT.

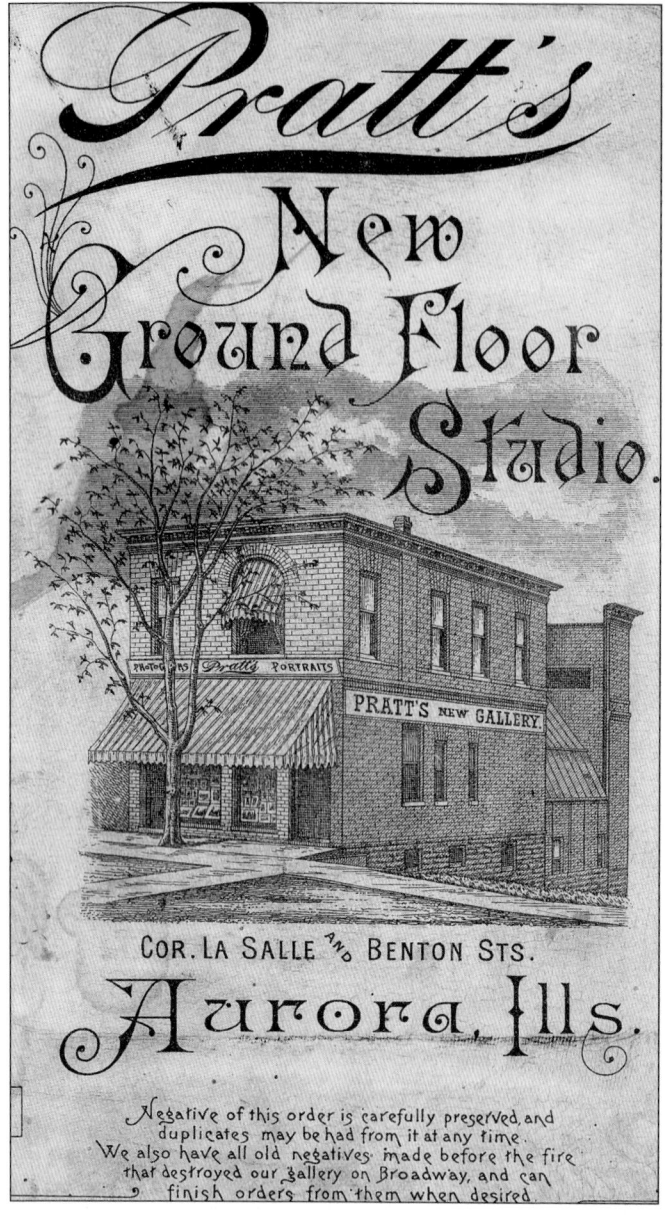

In order to make photographs, Pratt developed his glass "negative" and then took P.O.P. (printing out paper) to make "proofs" for the customer. This was accomplished by placing the paper in a print frame over the negative and exposing it in the sunlight for 10-20 minutes. The result was a red-colored print for the customer to choose or reject. Pratt's studio skylight, both here on Broadway and in his newer studio in the 1870s at LaSalle and Benton, had a northern exposure for maximum lighting. Once the client selected his "views" they were mounted onto cardboard cards to preserve the print. These cards carried, as free advertising, the name and address of the photographer so that, should additional prints be desired, one would know where to go to get copies. These cards, both large and small, are classic examples of early advertising. The most famous of Pratt's illustrated 4 inch by 6 1/2 inch cards shows his studio on the back of the mounting cardboard in the 1890s.

By the 1870s, D.C. Pratt had thousands of views of Aurora and people from all over the Midwest, for he had quite a reputation regionally. This photograph is a typical high-quality image made in his spacious studio. By 1875, he had 22,000 images on file.

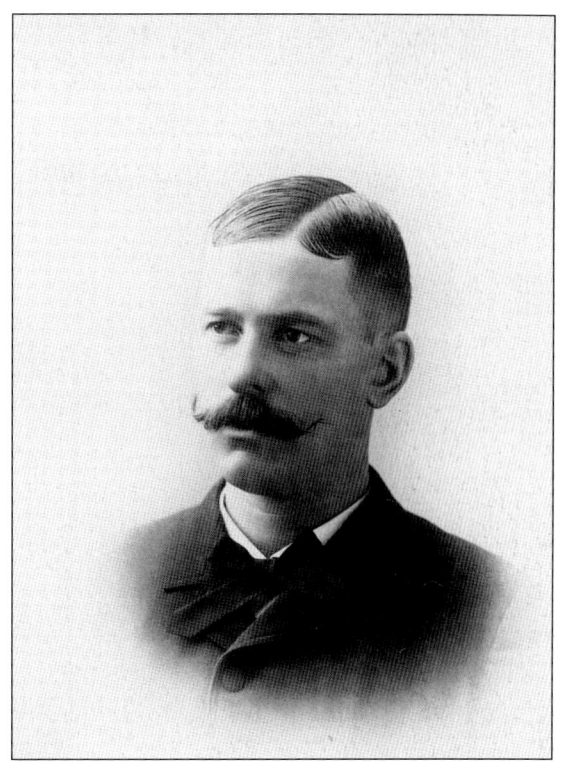

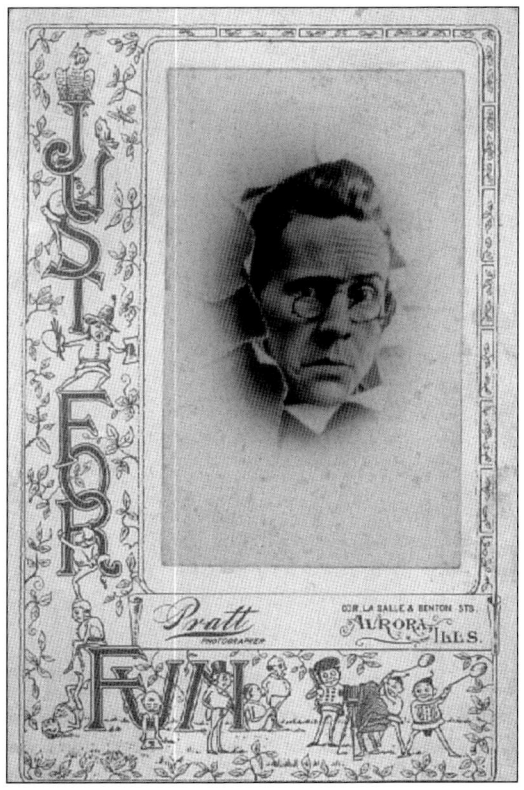

In the 1890s Dewitt Clinton Pratt was joined in the business by his son, Edmund Clinton Pratt, in his new LaSalle and Benton Street studio. D.C. gave his son half interest at age 21. Edmund was described as being mild mannered, more of an artist than a portrait photographer, but possessing a terrific, quick temper. Much later, Verneur Pratt was offered the same deal at age 21, but he refused to join in the trade of his father and grandfather. Edmund's artistic side is very evident in the unusual self-portrait with impish little photography fairies along the border.

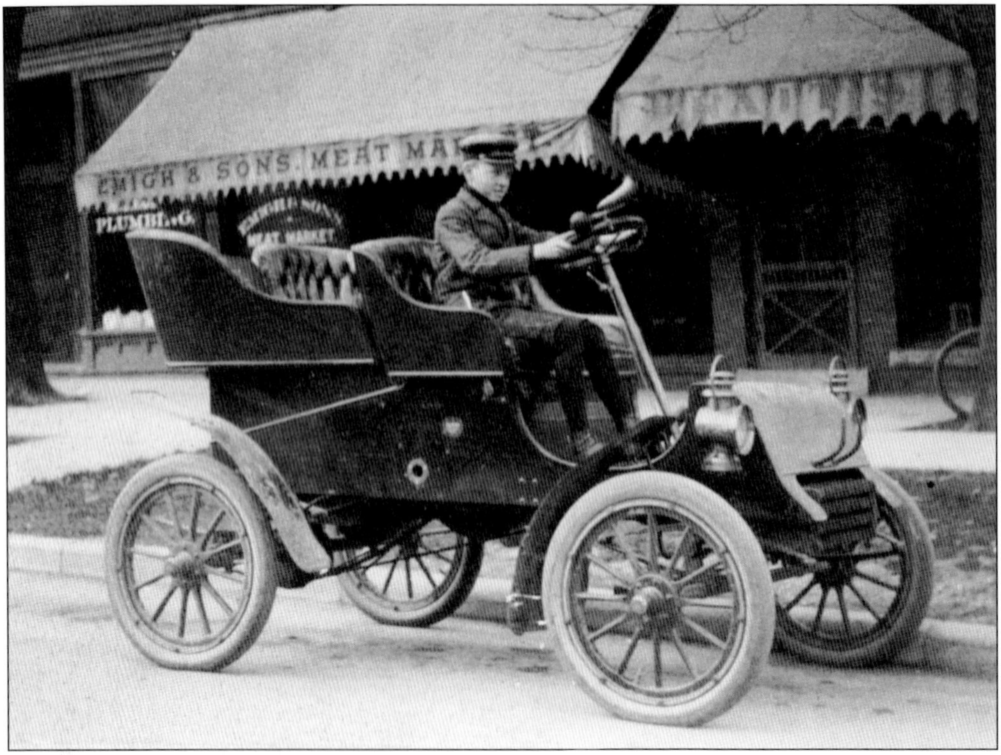

As E.C.'s business flourished for a short time, he moved his family from 176 Fox Street to the famous three-storied Hawley mansion. Soon they were back to simpler quarters. Edmund Clinton Pratt's second love was a wish to own a circus. He bought Jenkill's Pony Hippodrome and hit the road with it for a year. Eventually he sold the circus but did buy a merry-go-round. He also liked the new-fangled cars being produced by Henry Ford. In 1903 he drove to Detroit and returned with Ford car number 505. He claimed it was Aurora's second or third car. Aurorans crowded around this horse-less carriage that could only go 15 mph, but it was troublesome to keep running even though it "satisfied some secret part of E.C.'s complex nature." At the age of ten, Verneur was even permitted to drive the awesome machine!

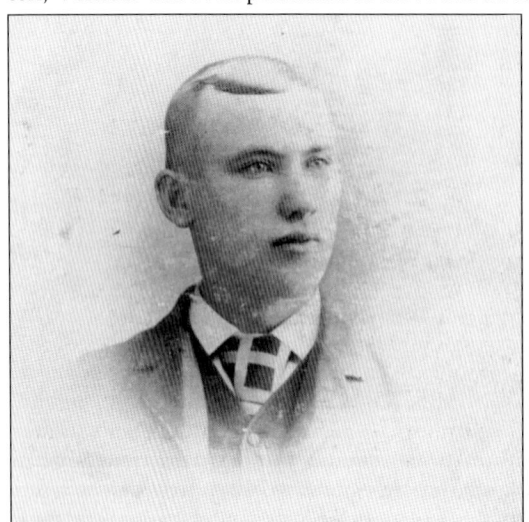

Ira A. Hough & Co. have their "Star Gallery" at 110 Main Street and also on Fox Street and Broadway (1870s). In the 1850s he was located on Fox Street. A handsome young Auroran with a spectacular checkered cravat is pictured. Hough began his business in the four-storied Mercantile Building that was home to many photographers.

An equally impressive image-maker was V.H. Snook who began his practice in Aurora in 1886 with a studio at 46 Fox Street. In 1894 he was joined in business by H.J. Perry and they were listed as being "on the Island." The child in the portrait is Albert Ray Meeks. He is nine months old here and was a very willing subject of the camera lens.

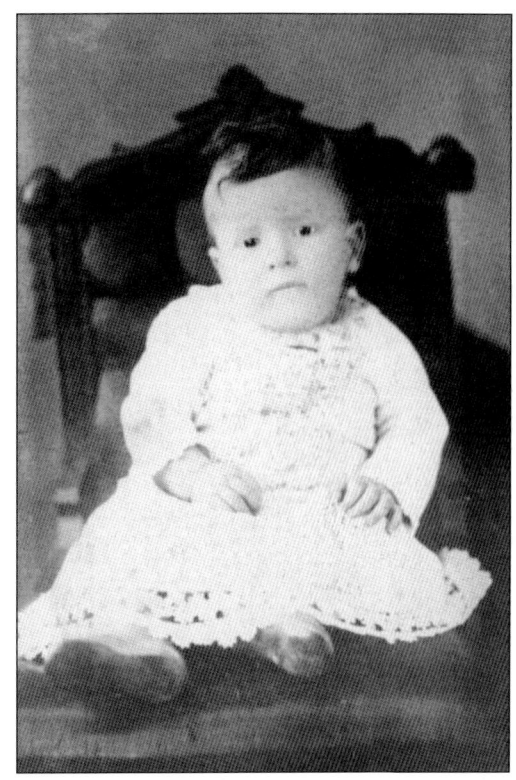

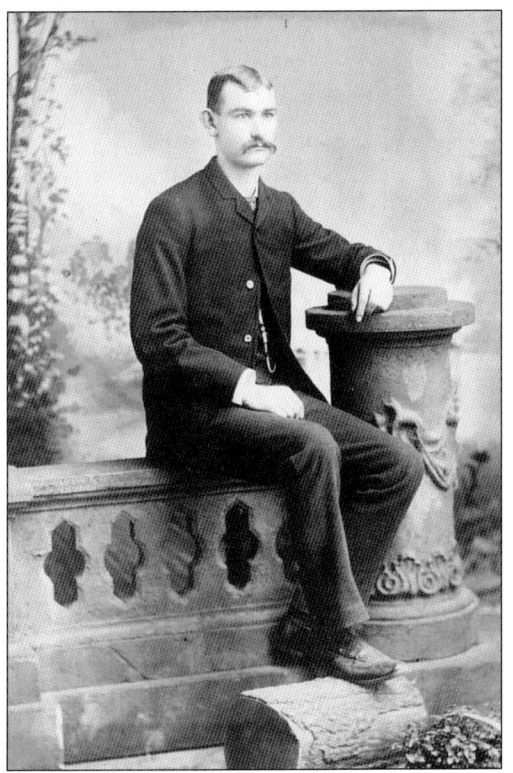

The fake stone wall, log, and backdrop are most impressive in this portrait taken in the late 1880s by Snook. Every businessman or laborer who could afford it wore a vest with a chain and pocket watch, perhaps an Aurora watch. Pocket watches were what all real men used until Valentino popularized wristwatches in the next century.

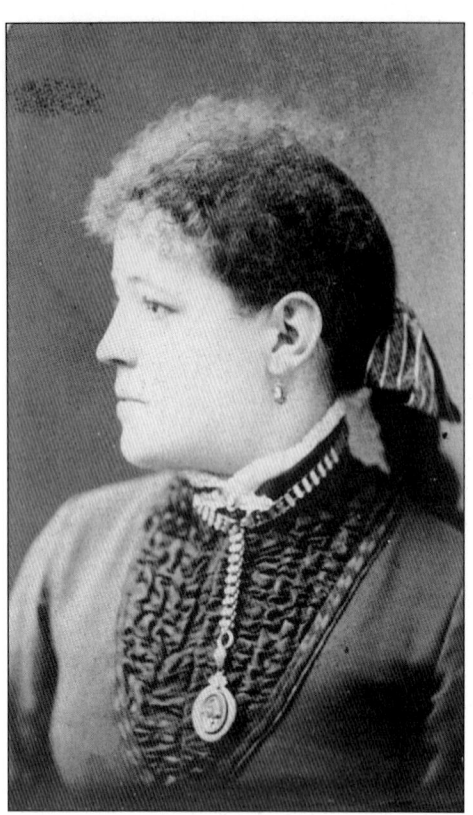

Another early Aurora photographer was Casimir Arcouet who settled in Aurora in 1874 and had a studio at 18 Fox Street. By 1894 he had moved his shop to 91 Fox Street where he remained in business until sometime between 1900 and 1904. The portrait of the lady with the necklace and locket was made while he was at his shop at 18 Fox.

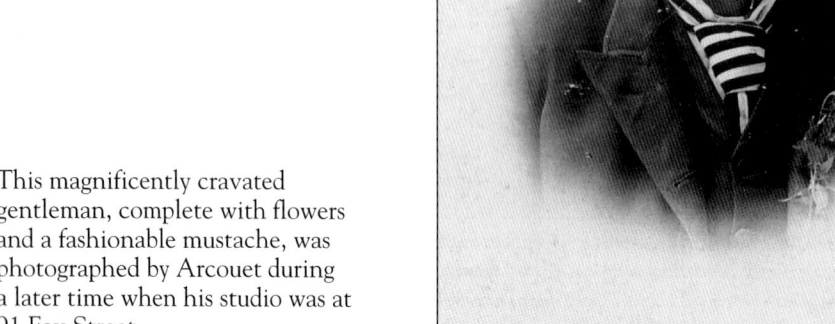

This magnificently cravated gentleman, complete with flowers and a fashionable mustache, was photographed by Arcouet during a later time when his studio was at 91 Fox Street.

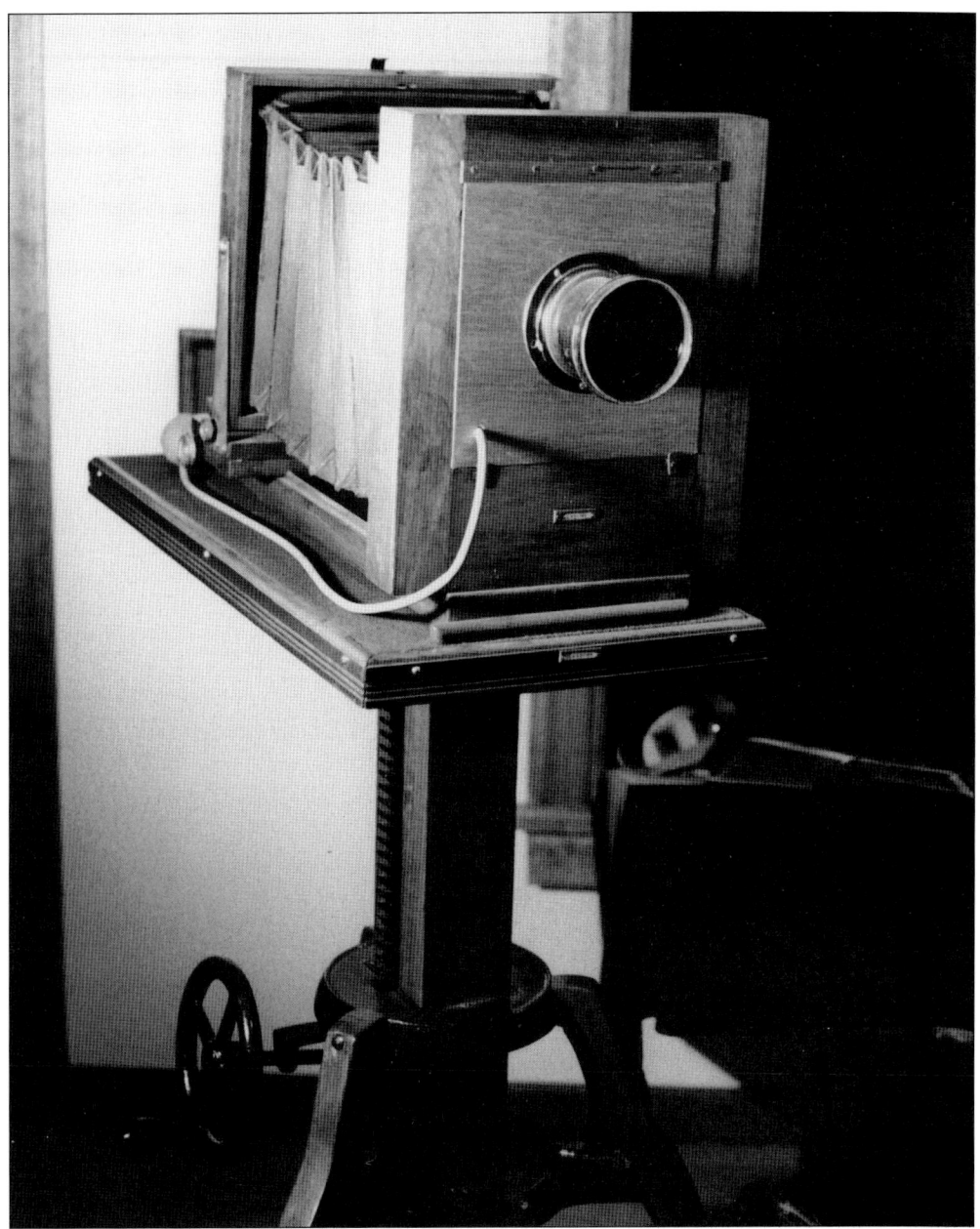

Typical view cameras that these photographers used were bulky monsters, non-portable for the most part. The cloth bellows were in the rear of the camera lens and could be adjusted along a track to focus the image in reverse, or as seen on a plate at the rear of the camera. When the photographer was under a cloth drape to shut out surrounding light, he could clearly see the image on the plate. The photographer put a "negative" plate/frame into the camera and removed a protecting shield thus exposing the film for what seemed like minutes. He capped the lens and removed the plate to develop the image in various etching and fixative chemicals. Some cameras had lenses that enabled the photographer to shoot and cut apart four small pictures from one "negative." Notice the crank on the side of the support that allowed the photographer to adjust the height of his camera.

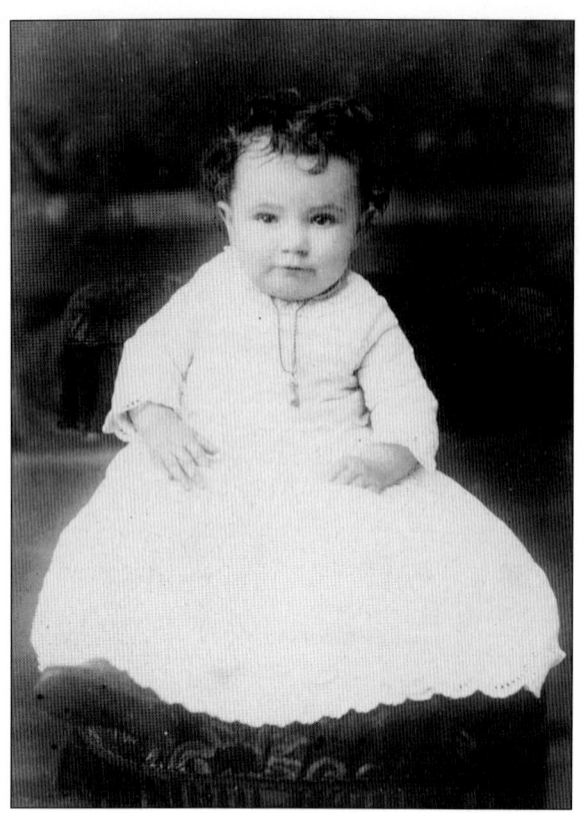

This splendid view of a baby was photographed by Gus Darfler, who had a studio at 148 Main Street around 1890. In 1894 a Jas. C. DeLamatter was photographing at this address until, in 1899, the name of the studio changed to the People's Gallery. After only a few years, the name disappeared and there were no more listings at this address for this photographer.

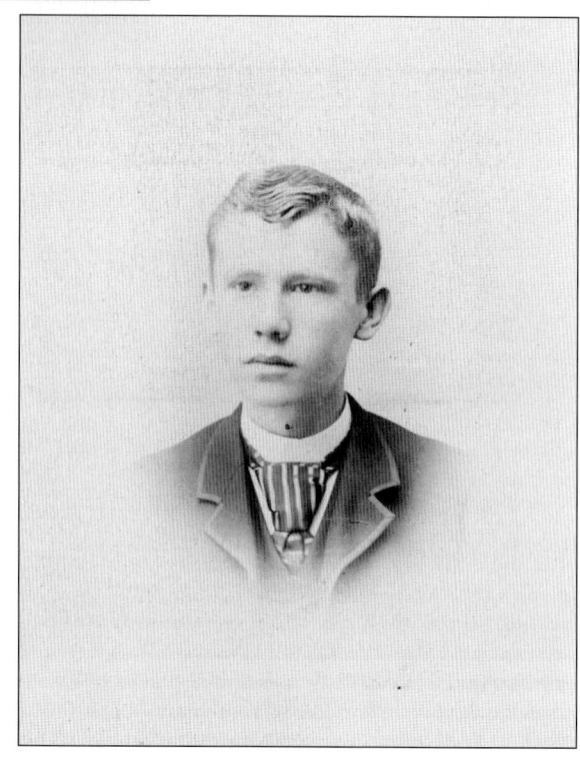

J.F. Reiff was one of about a dozen other early Aurora photographers. His business was at 43 S. River in 1886, but he moved to Downer in 1894 only to disappear from city directories by 1895.

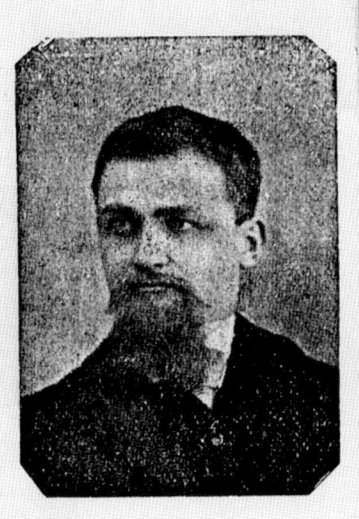

JOE FREILINGER,

66 N. BROADWAY

Watchmaker and Jeweler

PHOTOGRAPHER AND PHOTO-
ENGRAVER IN HALF-TONE......

Everything First-Class and at the Lowest Prices.

Joe Freilinger appeared on the scene in 1899 at 66 N. Broadway. He probably specialized in making small carded pictures called carte de visites, which sold for one to two dollars a dozen. Such cards were the bread and butter trade of many studios. There is no record of him in the city directories after 1904.

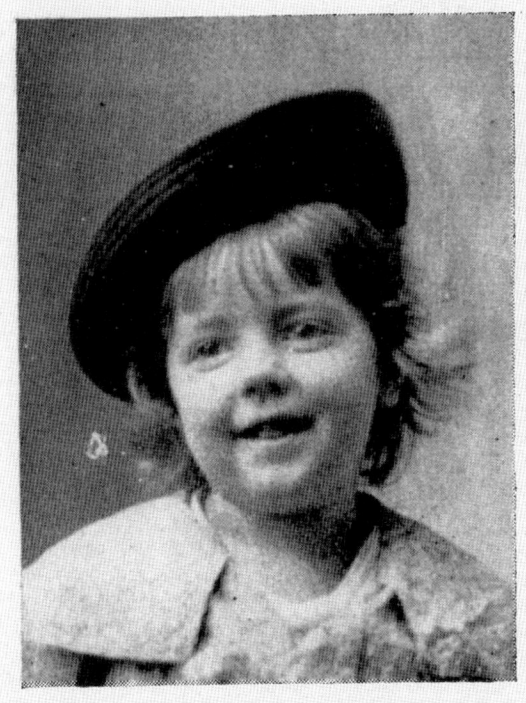

WAREHAM

Photog Rapher

Picture Frames and Mouldings, Medallions, Photo Buttons and Jewelry.

N. W. Phone 633
Chicago 2902
Mercantile Block
AURORA, - ILL.

In the early 20th century, photographers began to place ads with photographs in local papers and city directories. Wareham, an Aurora photographer whose studio was in the Mercantile Block, not only did photographic work, but also dealt in jewelry and photograph accessories.

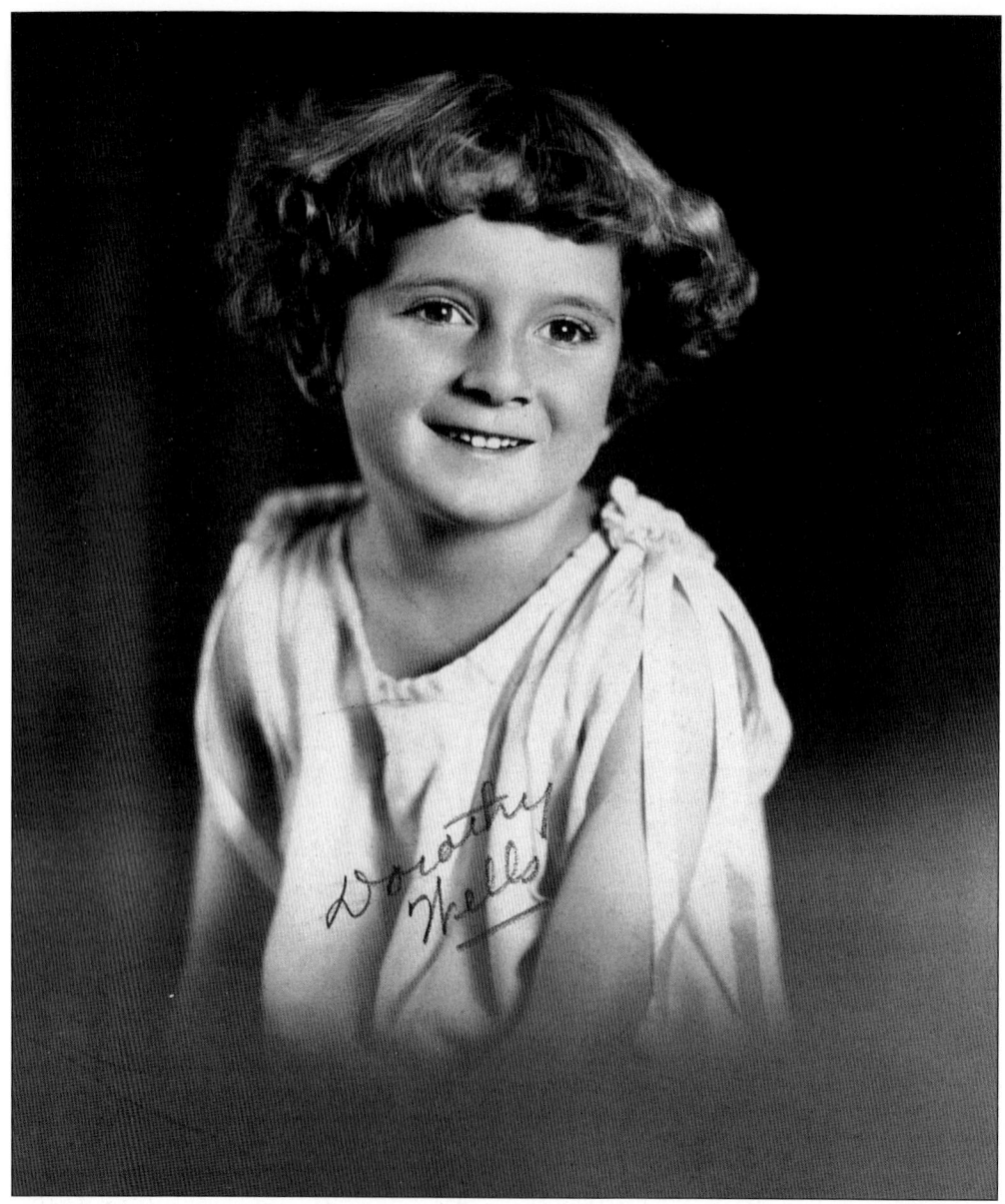

This final view, taken at the end of the period studied, offers a classic view of a young girl. It was photographed at the studio at 109 Main by Murray & Earl. By the end of the 1910s and into the next decade, the complex nature of photography changed and the people themselves became the principal image-makers. They photographed day-to-day events more often and with greater honest candor, if not as skillfully, as the image-makers of the past century.

Additional photographers who served as Aurora's image-makers before WW I were William Giles, Melander and Henderson, Mark H. Yager, W.H. Clark, D.Y. Andre, G.F. Gale, Roy Olson, Miss Leah H. Arcouet (daughter of Casimir), J.W. Krosse, Jordan J. Stonecipher, Andrew Swan, Henry Atkins, E.E. Godfrey, R.G. McReynolds, J.C. Vertergaard, W.W. Van Osdel, T.F. Horne, G.D. Heaton, C.A. Eckstrom, E.M. Cornell, Jensen, and Olaf Mortenson.

Eight
Those Who Served at Home and Abroad

America never seems to suffer from lack of patriotism by its citizens once Congress declares war. Even during WW I, many people, including President Wilson, were afraid of joining the group of countries called the Allies. The fear was that ethnic Americans who had kin in the "enemy's" country, the Central Power, would split the Nation and turn Americans against each other.

Not all those who served their country were soldiers, but those who served in other ways also faced imminent danger from death by violent actions of people and nature. The firemen and policemen in Aurora were at risk, particularly during the later days of the century when they had to protect an expanded wall-to-wall building structure downtown, dozens of factories susceptible to explosions and fire, and an ever-expanding residential area. Keeping crime at bay in Aurora's diverse neighborhoods also proved a challenge.

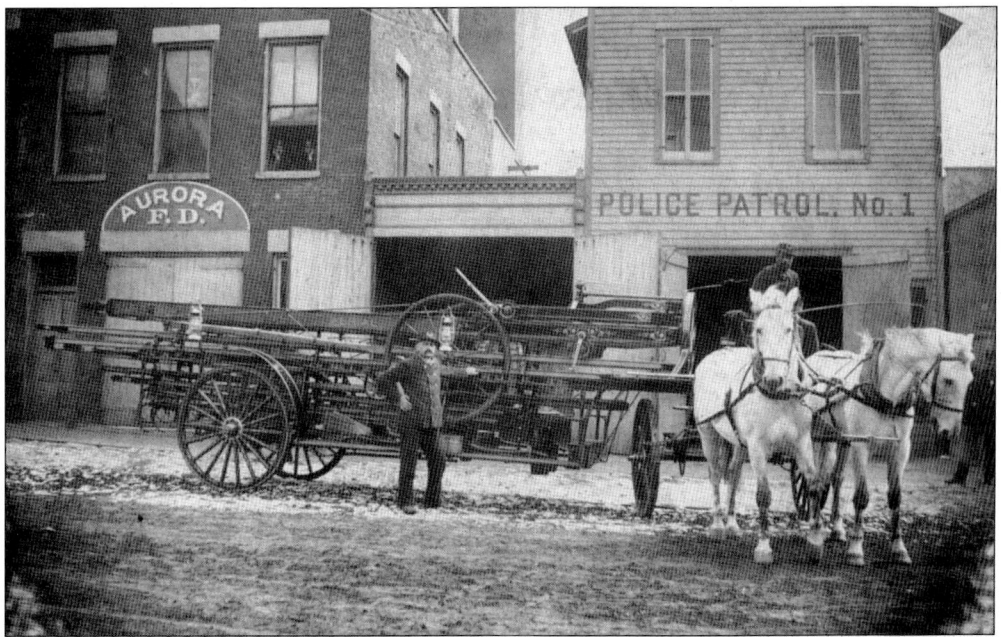

This aerial hook and ladder truck was purchased from a Michigan manufacturer in 1892 and used in Aurora until 1896. In the background is Aurora's first fire station (1856). Neither the firefighter nor the driver are identified.

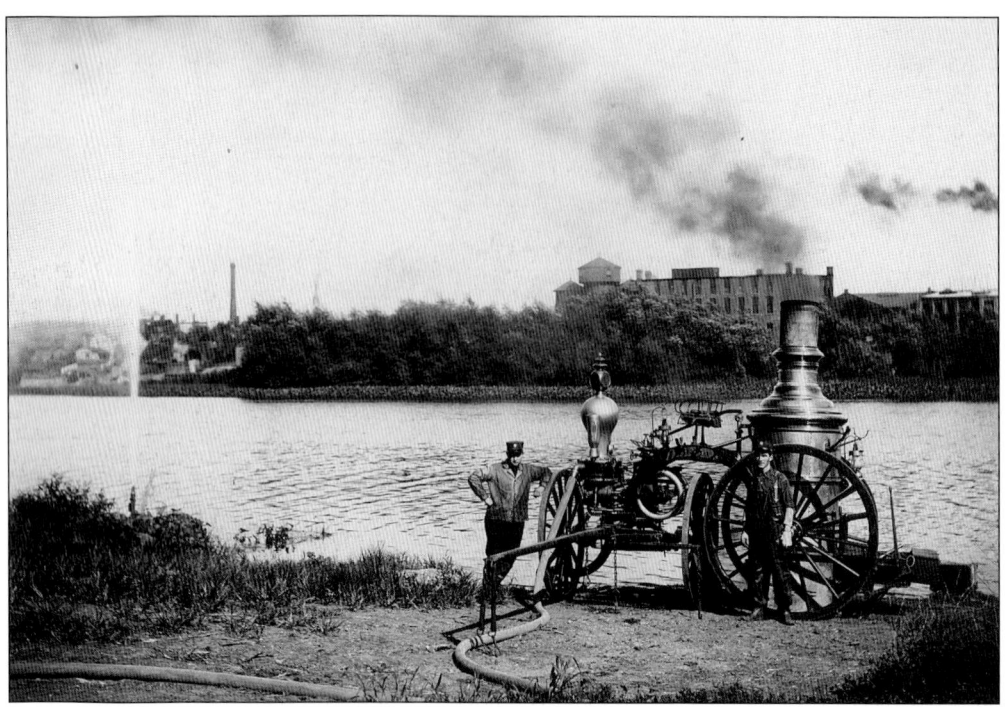

This is an early view showing Aurora's Excelsior Steamer, bought in 1875 at the west bank of the river, fighting a fire. To the left is fireman George Lowe and to the right is fireman Joseph Eye. This view was taken about 1910.

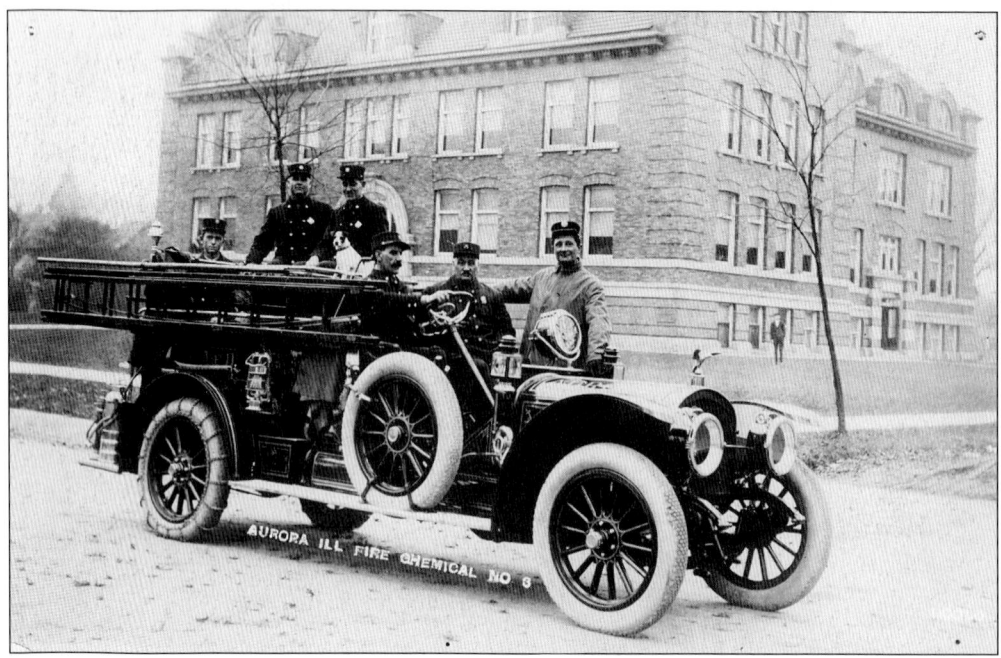

By 1914, hook and ladder trucks had come a long way from two-horse-drawn units. This is a Rambler fire truck complete with new chains for winter use parked in front of West Aurora High School.

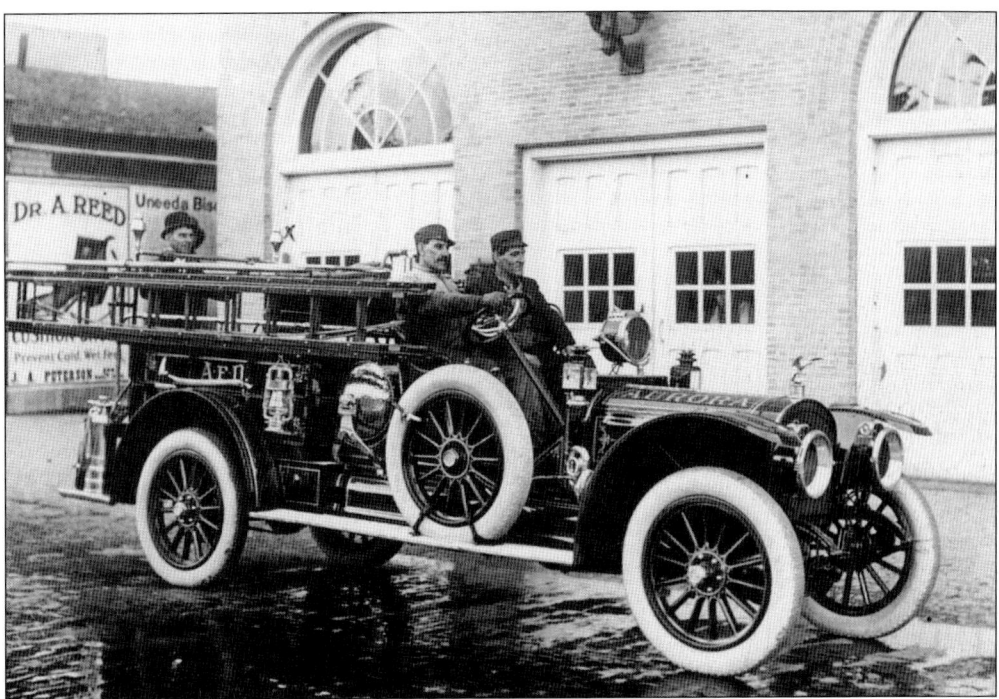

The factory hands that manufactured the Rambler fire truck in Kenosha take a spin before delivering it to Aurora (1911).

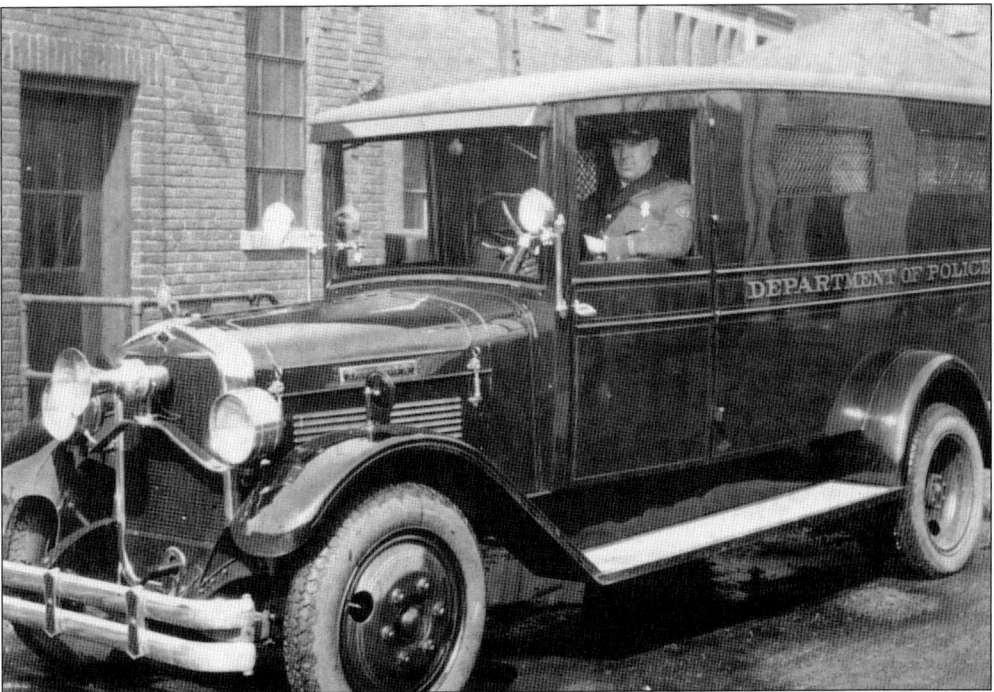

This is not the same paddy wagon that Lottie described in her 1887 essay about Aurora, but a new souped-up 1929 version with more than two-horsepower under the hood. Frank Schuster is at the wheel.

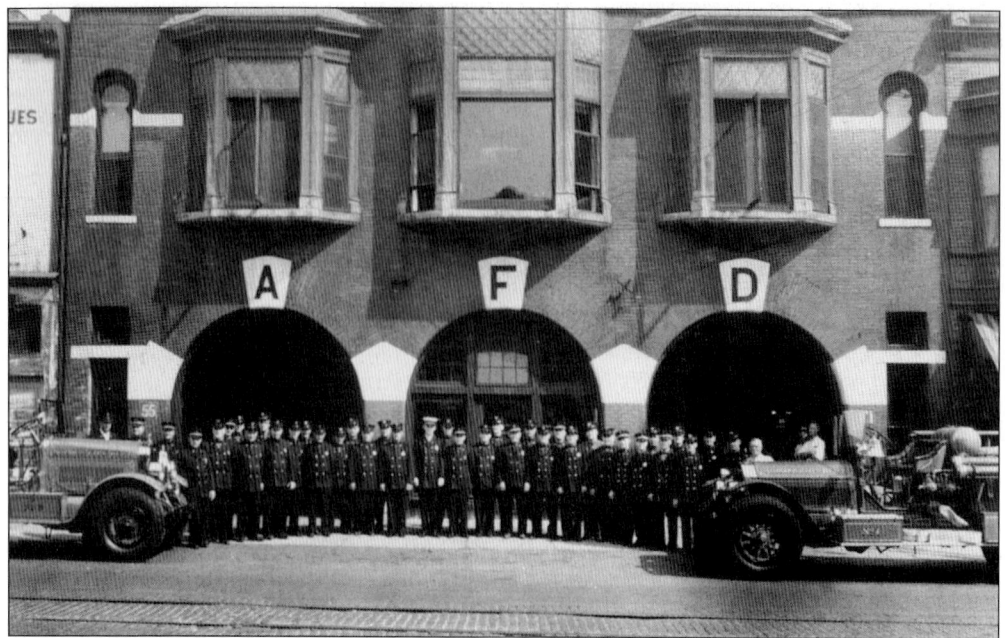

The North Broadway station was still an imposing building in 1937. On either side of the two-exit openings for fire trucks, and at the edge of the entranceway, iron corners protected the building from the wheels of horse-drawn carriages. Today, this 1894 building is the Regional Fire Museum.

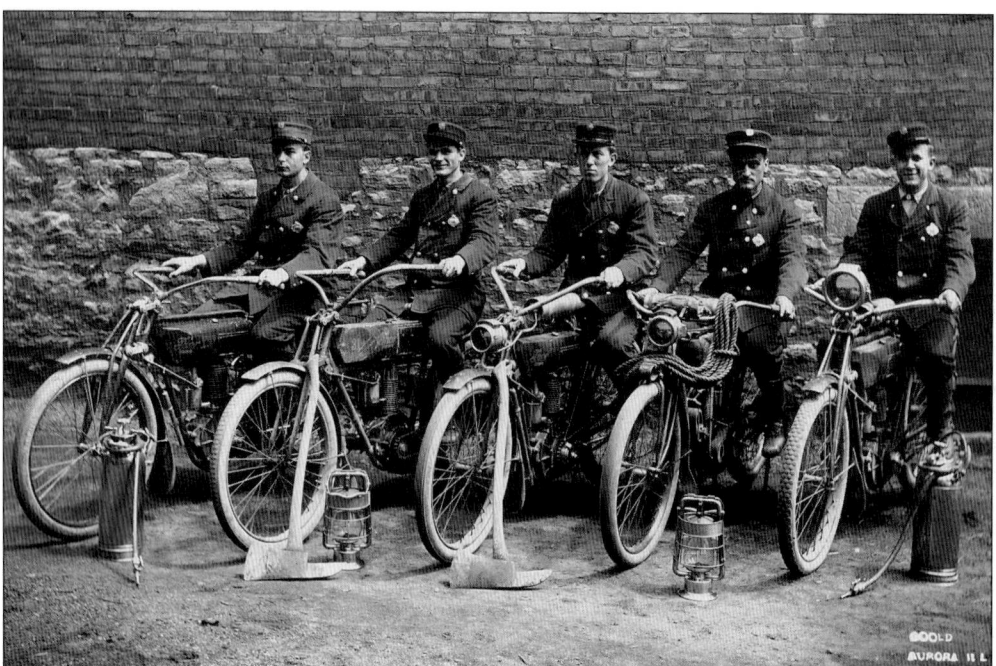

In 1914, the Thor Company of Aurora was making new-fangled motorcycles, and the Aurora fire department had five of them, complete with axes, lanterns, and fire extinguishers. This 1914 photograph features from left to right: "fire warriors" William Froelich, Joseph Eye, John Petersohn, Jessie Bird, and Ed Bettcher.

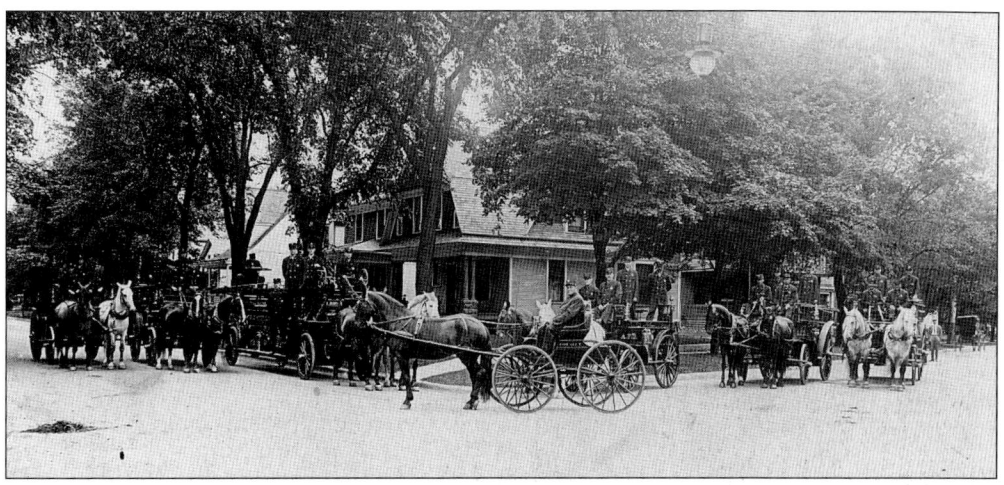

This most spectacular panoramic photograph shows all the Aurora Fire Department's equipment, still pulled by horses, on one of Aurora's tree-lined streets. Only a few years later, horses would be replaced with engines.

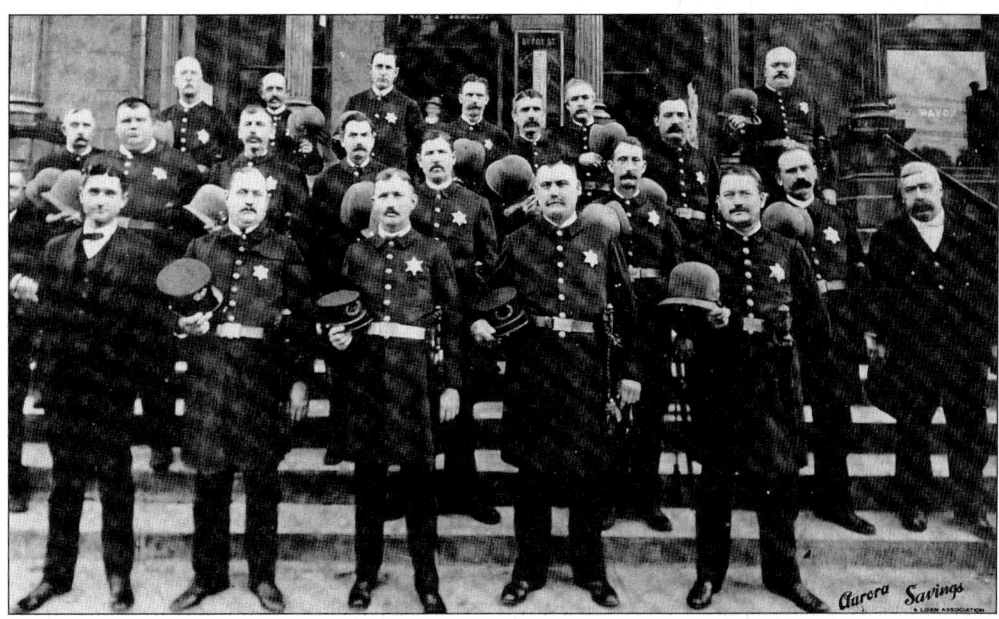

After the mills and factories paid their workers on Saturday night, Aurora's many downtown bars (the exact number varied during the late 1800s from a low of 28 to a high of 40) and neighborhoods served as sites for impromptu brawls and out-and-out bloody fights. Most policemen in this photograph have a mustache and all are carrying billy clubs (1911).

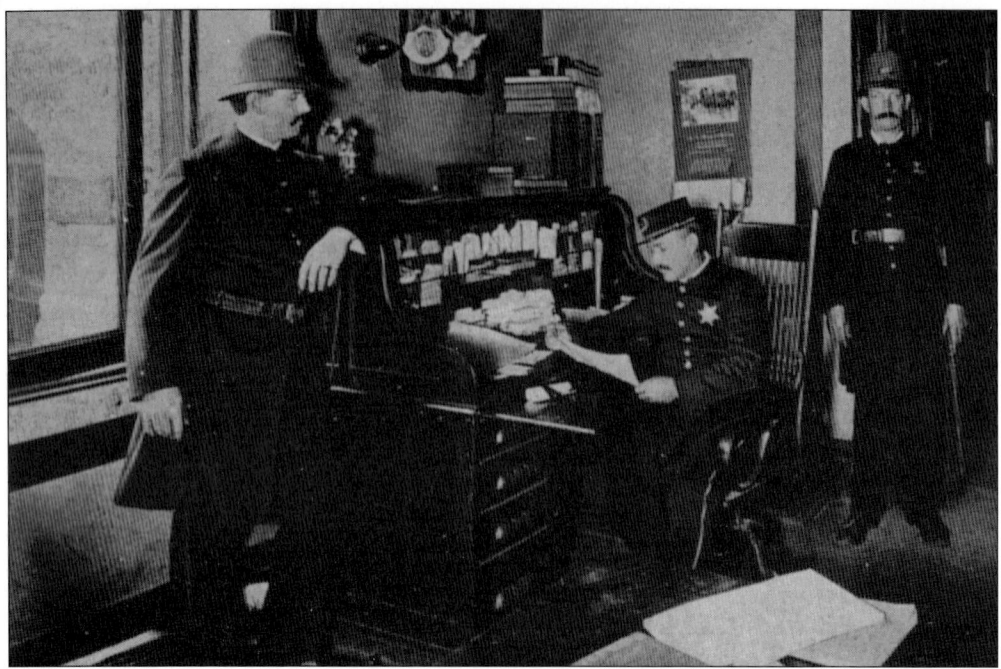
Meanwhile, life back at the station was pretty tranquil according to this pre-1905 photograph showing a desk-bound, paper-pushing officer and two patrolmen checking in or out. The policeman standing to the right is John August Anderson.

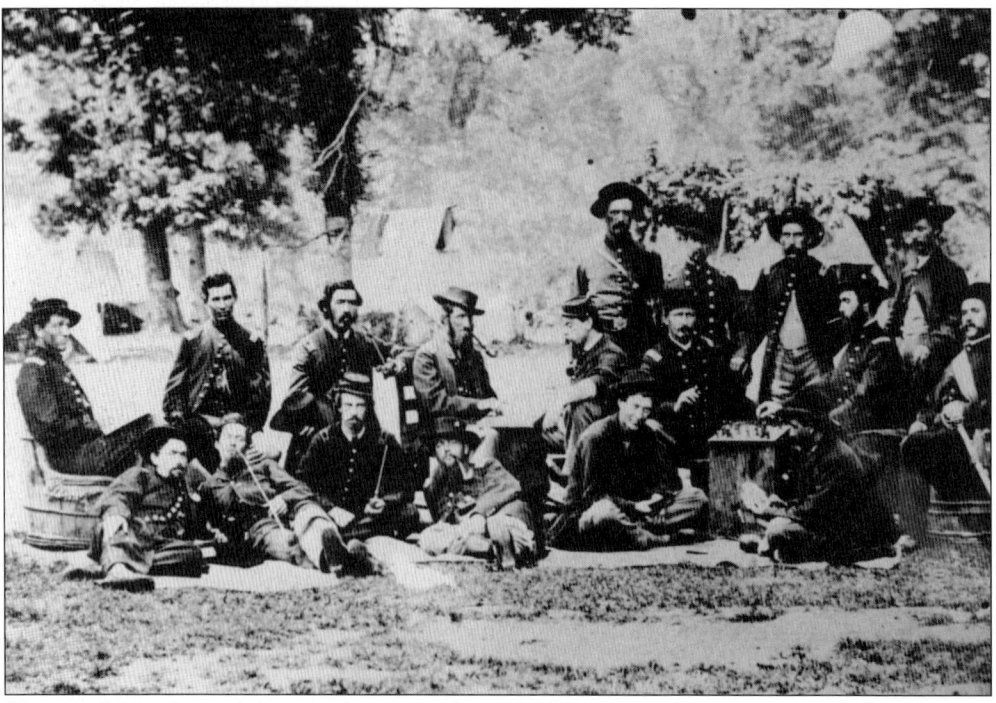
The Civil War drained Aurora's homes and surrounding areas of young men. Some sources say that ten thousand area men left for war from Aurora. This encampment photograph, c. 1864, is of the officers of the Illinois 36th.

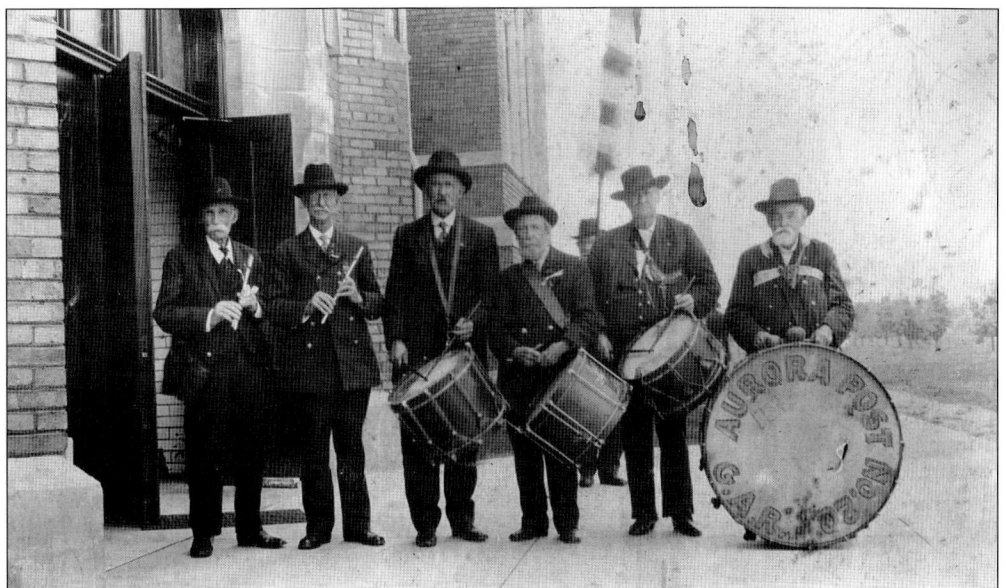

This picture captures aging Aurora Civil War Veterans who were members of the Grand Army of the Republic, Post 20. They may have just taken part in a downtown parade.

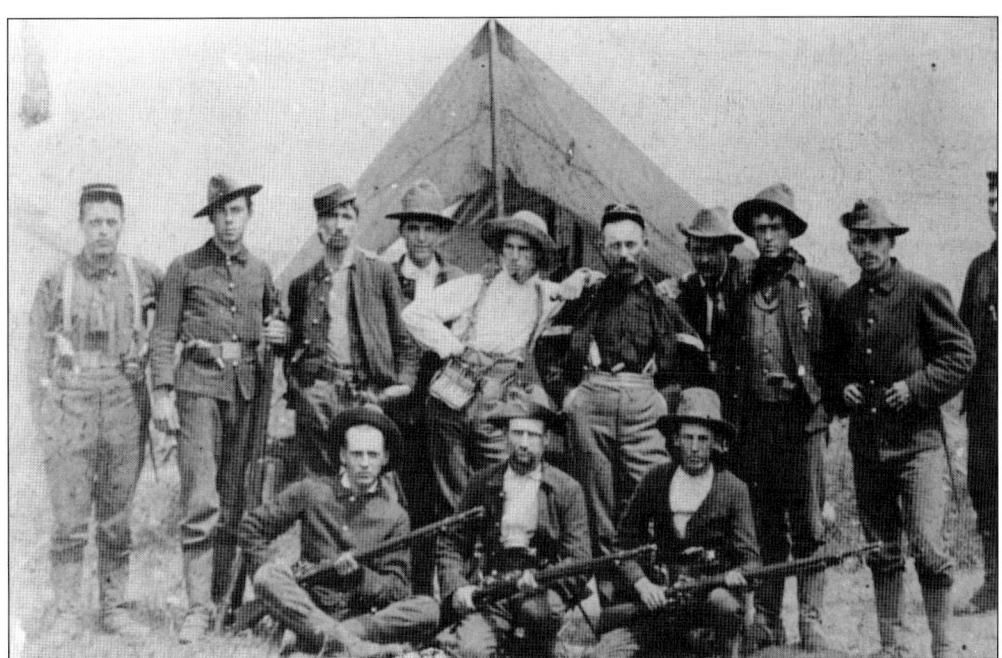

Aurora's National Guardsmen were used to keep order during the violence in Chicago because of the American Railway Union strike in 1894. Shown here from left to right are as follows: (front row) Andrew Smith, Chas. Spatchey, and Geo. Fanbel; (back row) Wm. Roberts, Geo. Goney, Ray White, Roy Lawson, Louis Zimmer, Wm. Snyder, Lieut. Fred Weiss, Archie Sylvester, Cooley Bradshaw, and Capt. L. Sidell.

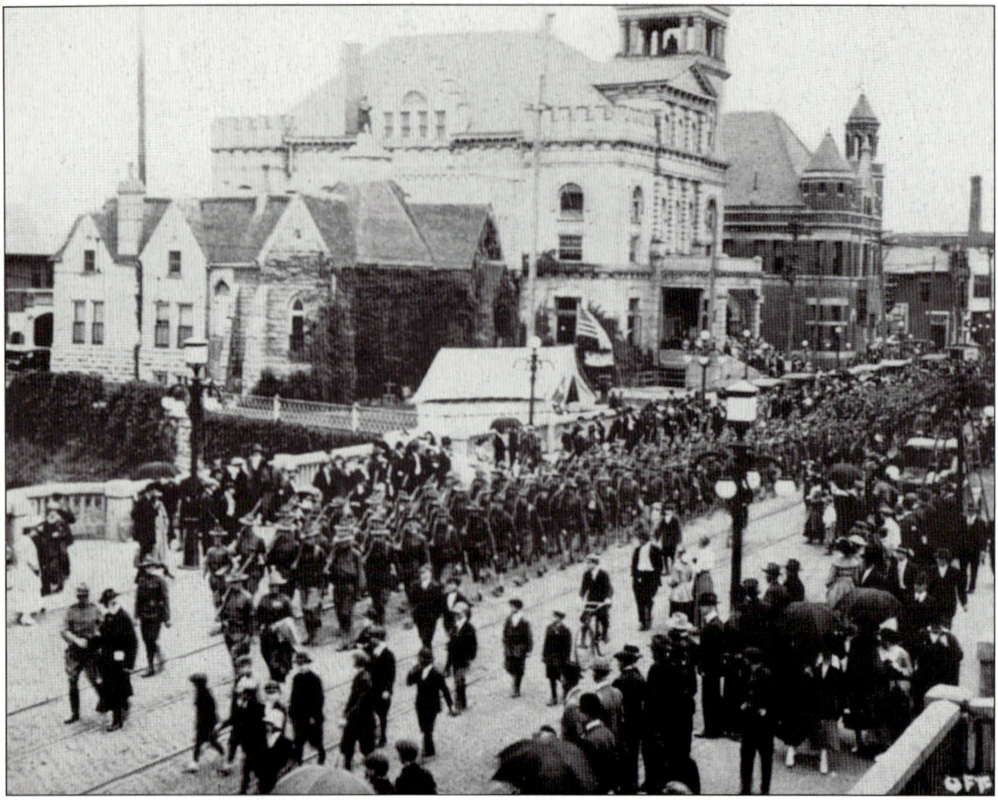

D Company of the Illinois 3rd Army was organized in Aurora in 1884 by E.J. Sill. The company served in the Spanish-American War under Capt. John L. Graves and consisted of about one hundred men. Here they are marching out of the Aurora Regimental Armory in 1917.

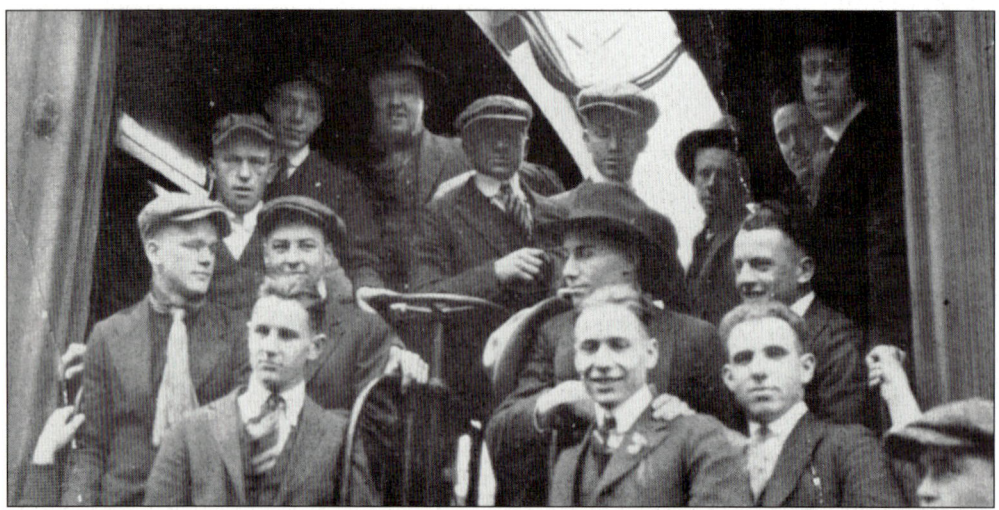
Both Aurora high schools gave up men to WW I. This is a group of West High students as they left Aurora on April 30, 1917, as enlisted men in the U.S. Army. Pictured are: G. Johnson, L. Conway, B. Conway, G. Tebell, B. Wright, J. Paul, G. Herrick, L. Whitford, E. Geipel, H. Hickey, W. Felke, H. Kramer, B. Carlson, F. Kirby, W. Lloyd, and L. Bussey.

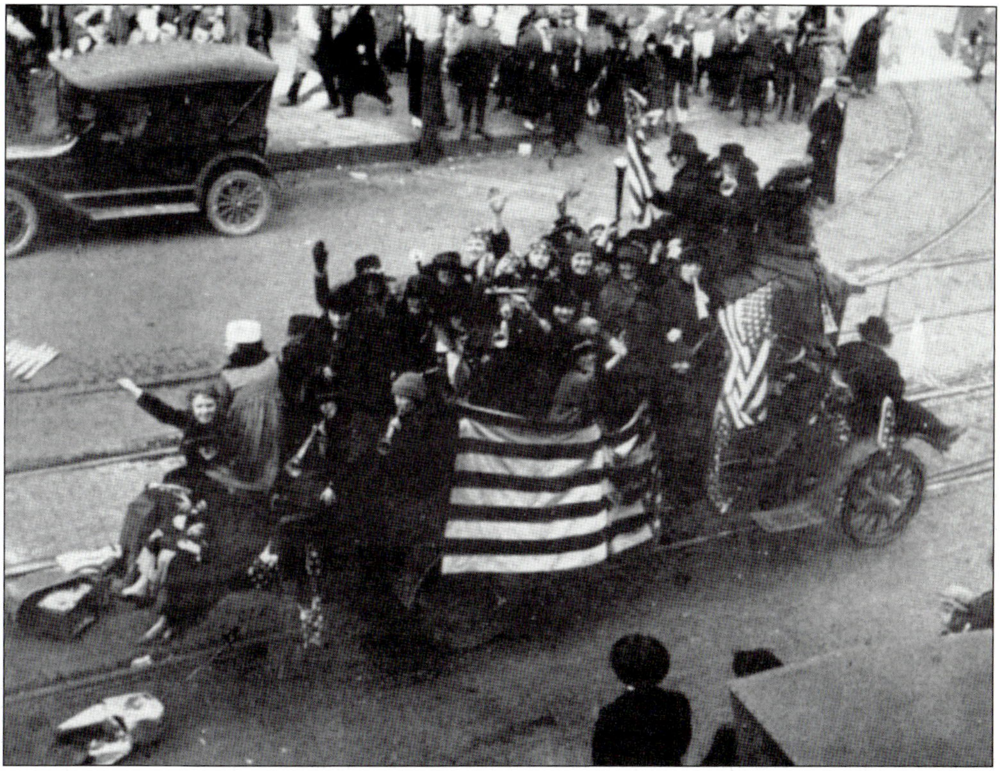

Wartime tearful goodbyes and glorious endings are all causes for public celebration. This is a dramatic shot of a truck in a long stream of trucks loaded with Aurora boys and girls parading on Armistice Day.

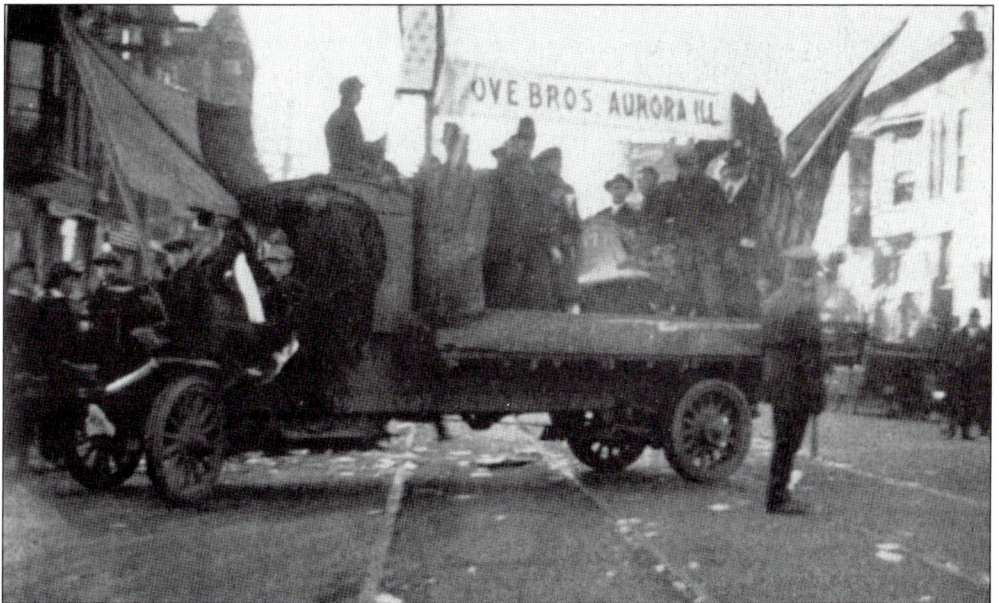

Love Brothers Foundry made a bell, mounted it to a truck, and drove the clanging "Liberty Bell" through the crowded streets of Aurora to spread the news of the signing of the Armistice.

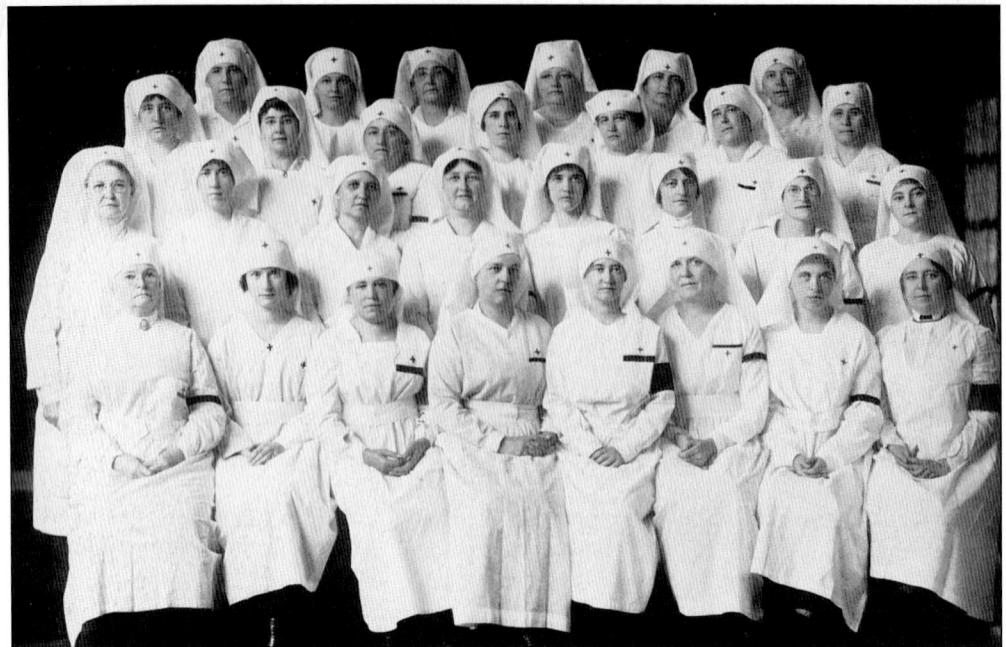

The workers on the Home Front helped give us victory in WW I. Groups such as those affiliated with the Red Cross did essential supportive war work. The Aurora Chapter of the Red Cross was organized in May 1917. These Aurorans were all Red Cross Surgical Dressing Supervisors.

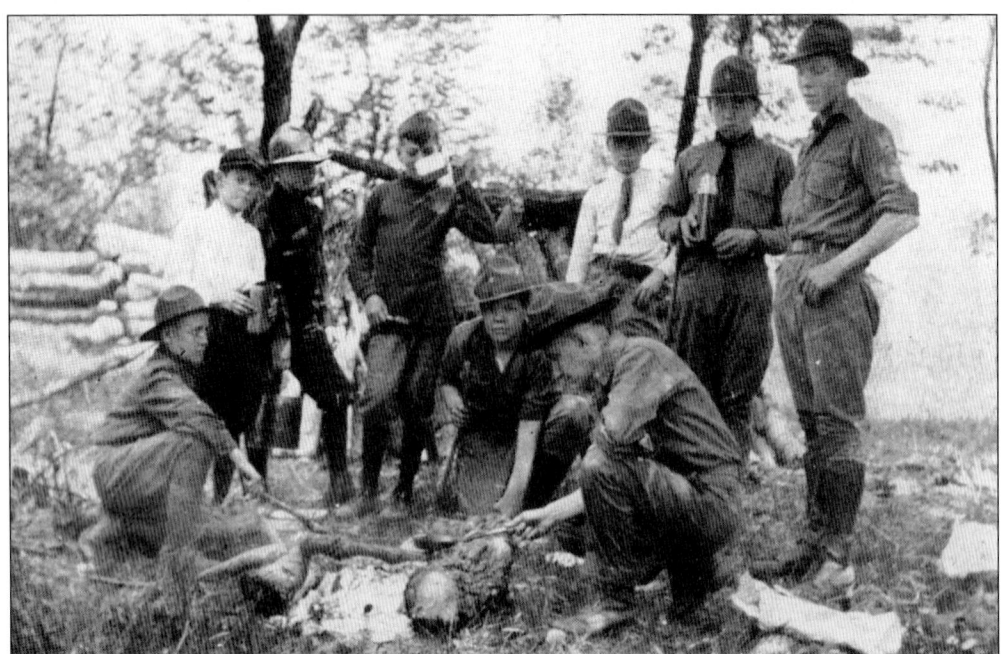

Boy Scouts in Aurora brought in $267,490 for the war by selling in four Liberty Loan Campaigns. They sold $60,000 worth of 1918 war savings stamps, located 300,000 square feet of black walnut for the War Department, collected barrels of fruit pits and nut shells for gas masks, planted Liberty gardens, and distributed 250,000 pieces of literature.

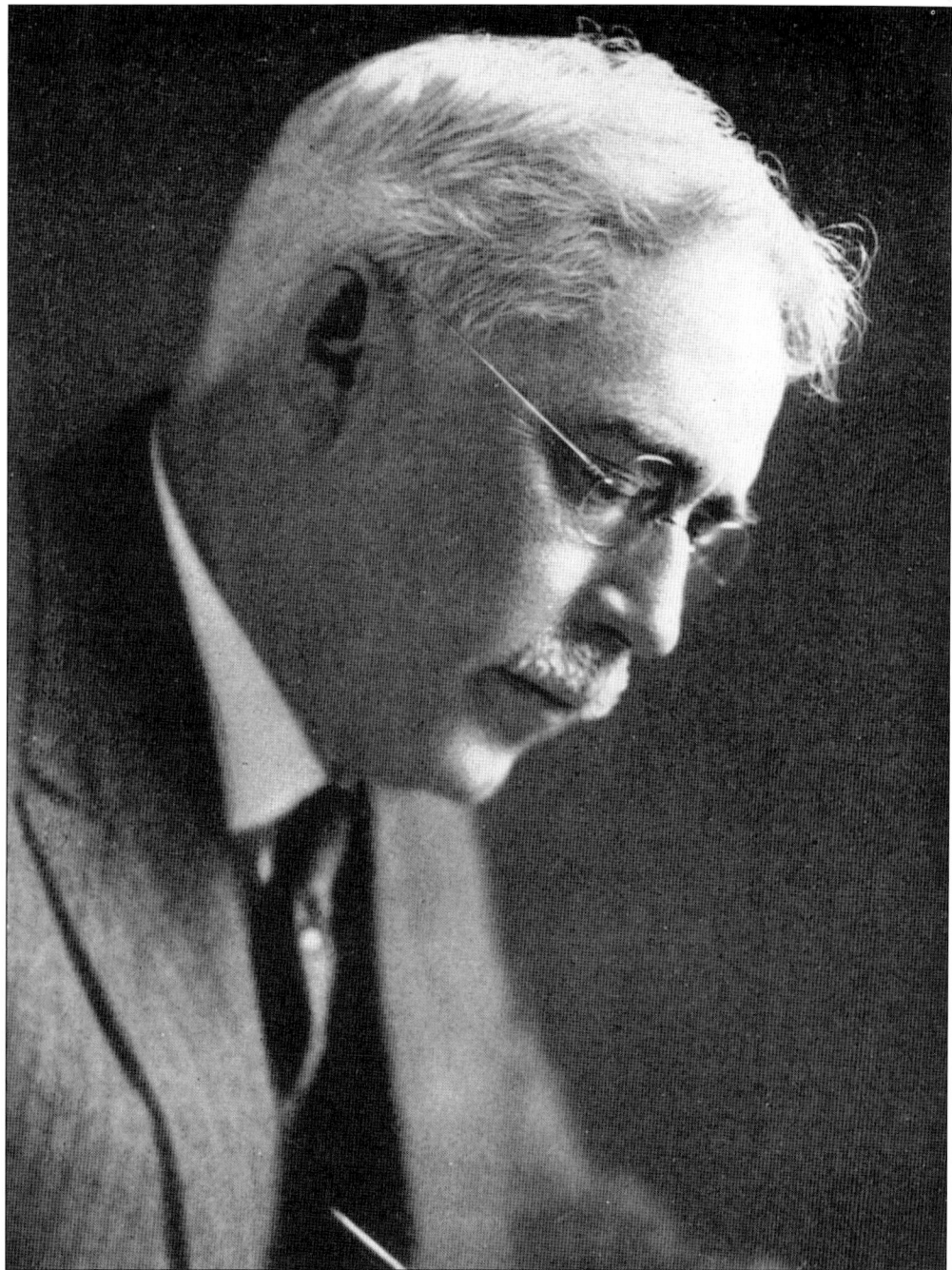

The greatest WW I "warrior at home" was Frank A. Vanderlip, a former Aurora man who came up with the idea of the War Saving Stamps and Thrift Stamps. These stamps were available not only at the post office but also in stores, schools, and factories nationwide. Millions of extra dollars became available for war use by hitting a market untapped by Liberty Bond sales. In Aurora alone, Saving Stamps sales brought in $388,540 in 1917–1918, and Thrift Stamps topped $456,796. One hundred seventeen people in Aurora purchased the maximum number of stamps allowed ($1,000) to any one individual.

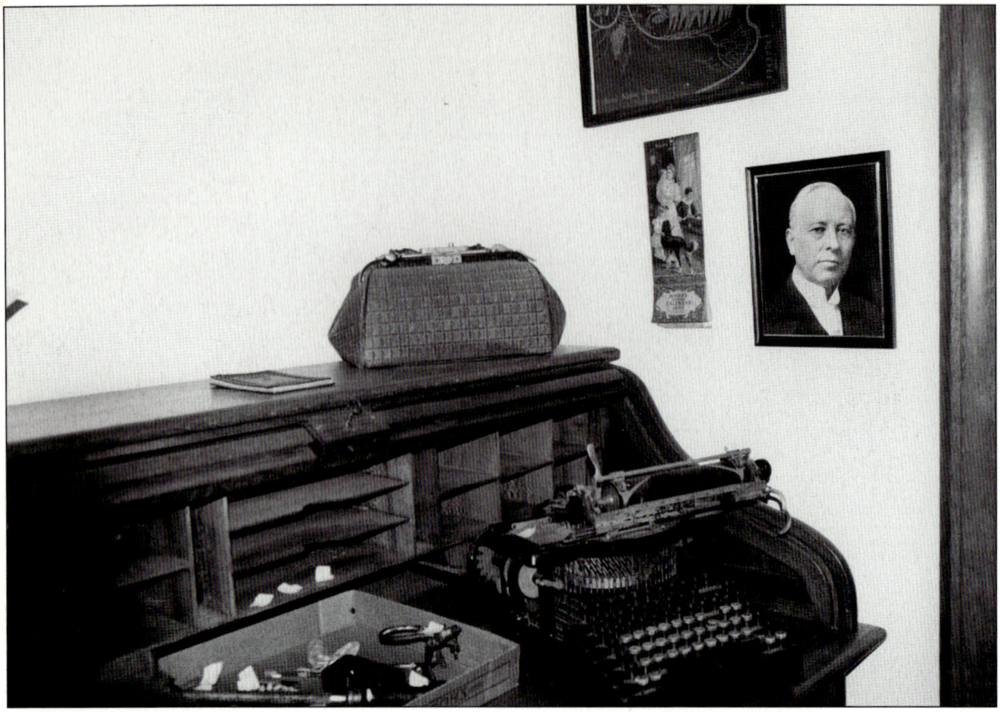

Bernard J. Cigrand, born in 1866, wrote to a Chicago newspaper pointing out that the country needed a special day to honor the flag. Later, working from his roll top desk, he wrote letter after letter for many years in support of the idea. A photograph of Cigrand is on the wall.

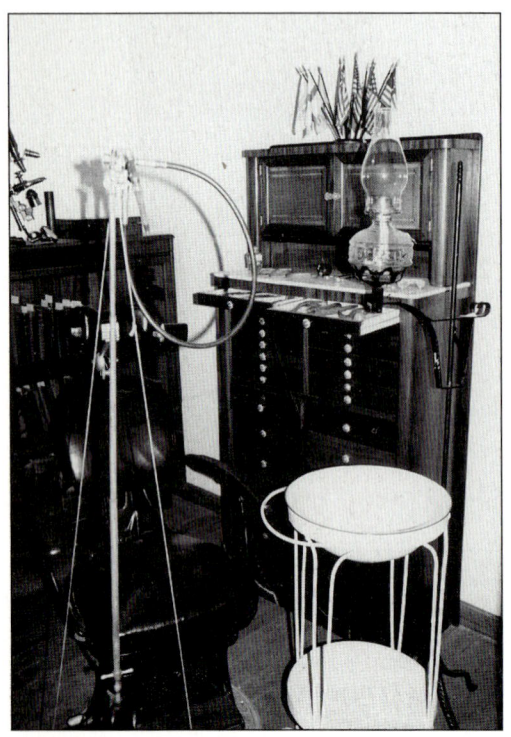

When Cigrand was 50, Woodrow Wilson issued a proclamation calling for a nationwide observance of a Flag Day on June 14. In 1949, Pres. Harry Truman made it a permanent, official observance day. When Cigrand was not following his love of the grand old flag, he was practicing dentistry in Aurora, and pictured are his tools.